The Thought Reader Craze

REDPATH'S LYCEUM.

J. R. BROWN, THE MIND-READER,

will give a public reception in HORTICULTURAL HALL, on MONDAY EVENING, Jan. 11, and WEDNESDAY EVENING, Jan. 13, at which he will exhibit the almost

SUPERHUMAN POWER

which he alone possesses of

READING THE MIND

of every one with whom he comes in contact. Blindfolded, he will find any article wherever concealed in the hall; point out any person thought of by the Committee; tell the birth-place and name of any one selected by the audience; locate real or imaginary pains; and submit to any test that scientific men may propose. Every opportunity will be given to discover the source of his power.

The Professors of Harvard College are hereby invited to make as rigid an examination of his pretensions as were made by the Faculty of Yale and Michigan University.

Tickets for sale at Russell's, 126 Tremont street. 50 cents each. 3t ja 8

The Thought Reader Craze

Victorian Science at the Enchanted Boundary

BARRY H. WILEY

McFarland & Company, Inc., Publishers
Jefferson, North Carolina, and London

Frontispiece: Boston *Evening Transcript*, January 9, 1875

LIBRARY OF CONGRESS CATALOGUING-IN-PUBLICATION DATA

Wiley, Barry H., 1936–
    The thought reader craze : Victorian science at the enchanted boundary / Barry H. Wiley.
      p.   cm.
    Includes bibliographical references and index.

    ISBN 978-0-7864-6470-8
    softcover : acid free paper ∞

    1. Telepathy. 2. Extrasensory perception. I. Title.
BF1171.W485   2012
133.8'209034—dc23   2012035341

BRITISH LIBRARY CATALOGUING DATA ARE AVAILABLE

© 2012 Barry H. Wiley. All rights reserved

No part of this book may be reproduced or transmitted in any form or by any means, electronic or mechanical, including photocopying or recording, or by any information storage and retrieval system, without permission in writing from the publisher.

On the cover: J. Randall Brown, Thought Reading (courtesy collection of William V. Rauscher); *Boston Evening Transcript*, January 9, 1875

Manufactured in the United States of America

McFarland & Company, Inc., Publishers
  Box 611, Jefferson, North Carolina 28640
    www.mcfarlandpub.com

Contents

Acknowledgments ix
Prologue 1

1. Introduction ... and Mrs. Hayden 9
2. The Borderland 17
3. Crookes and D.D. Home 24
4. The First Thought Reader 38
5. The Crookes Galvanometer Tests 47
6. Muscle Reading? 58
7. W.I. Bishop and W.F. Barrett 63
8. The Greatest Rascal 75
9. Proof! The Creery Sisters 82
10. Truth! Barrett and Bishop 85
11. J.R. Brown and His Telegraph Test 92
12. Stuart C. Cumberland, Thought Reader 98
13. Thought Reading Extraordinary: Blackburn and Smith 110
14. W.I. Bishop and "THE SECRET" 122
15. The Thought Reader Craze 131
16. "The Willingness to Deceive" 139
17. The Conjuror and the Physicist (Devant and Lodge) 144
18. The Blackburn Revelations 152
19. Truth ... or Hunger 165

Epilogue 167
An Afterthought 168

Table of Contents

Appendices:
A. Impossible or Supernormal?   171
B. Origins of Second Sight   173
C. The Date of the Coin Is...?   177
D. Coding of a Random Drawing   180
E. Techniques of Thought Reading (Contact Mindreading)   182
F. A Thought Reader's Novel   185
G. The Crookes-Fay Galvanometer Test, February 19, 1875   187
H. SPR Leaflet by Alice Johnson   200

Notes   203
Bibliography   217
Index   227

The Enchanted Boundary

"And so they set forth toward the region which they had vowed to conquer, a band of gallant knights, all bedight in massy armor and bravely bearing lances and swords, all seated on steeds which were both swift and sure. But as soon as the first had crossed the border of that region his weapons became like rotten wood, the joints of his armor began to gape widely, and his proud steed, altered to a sorry jade which stumbled at every pebble in the way. And thus fared it with every knight as he crossed, for lo, it was an enchanted boundary."

Walter Franklin Prince, Ph.D.
1930

"Think mindreading contrary to common sense. Wise provision of the Bon Dieu that we cannot read each other's mind. 'Twould stop civilization and everybody would take to the woods. In 50 or a hundred thousand centuries when mankind would have become perfect by evolution, then perhaps this sense would be developed with perfect safety to the state."

Thomas A. Edison
Diary Entry: July 16, 1885

Acknowledgments

No one can write of historical happenings without drawing heavily on the generous insights, thoughts, patience and resources of others. My experience in writing this book is no different.

First, those who have passed on: Mostyn Gilbert, ranking historian of early psychical research, and a very good friend besides; John Mulholland, magician and historian; Milbourne Christopher, magician, historian, collector, author; Dr. Michael Coleman, whose knowledge and library of psychical research were unsurpassed, as was his generosity; Dr. Eric J. Dingwall, renowned psychical investigator and the last person alive to have personally known Annie Eva Fay (as well as the Blonde Witch of Boston, Margery); H. Adrian Smith, who granted unconditional access to his truly amazing library; Sydney Piddington, one of the great mentalists and showmen of 20th century show business, a man of demonstrated courage whose second sight act with his wife has never been exposed, who provided insights into second sight; legendary occult performer Ormond McGill, who granted permission to quote at length from any of his works.

Then, Mary Warnement, William D. Hacker Head of Reader Services, and Ann Kardos and Marika Cifor, Interlibrary Loan Interns, Boston Athenaeum, for their tireless support, endless patience, and kind good humor; Shona Milton, Historical Centre Officer, Brighton History Centre, Brighton, UK; Gwen Ryan, Tonbridge Library, Tonbridge, Kent, UK; Anne Davenport, for her extensive knowledge of St. George's Hall and David Devant; Peter Meadows, Curator of the SPR Archive at the Cambridge University Library, who provided permission to quote the Alice Johnson SPR leaflet in full—which added special value to the book; Tom Ruffles, who had the Blackburn *John Bull* articles when no one else in the world seemed to; Trevor Hamilton, for the Myers letter where the term "telepathy" was first used and other very special research insights, and lunch in Harvard Square; Leslie Price, founder of the online journal of psychical history, *PsyPioneer*, for his steady support

Acknowledgments

and for sending me on to Trevor and Tom with my questions; Peter Lane, for his knowledge, generosity and hospitality, and permission to reproduce images from his marvelous collection, whose limits I haven't yet encountered; Jeff Evason, who with his beautiful wife, Tessa, makes up the best two-person mental act in the business today, for his thoughtful insights to 19th century second sight; Adam J. Perkins, Curator of Scientific Manuscripts, Cambridge University Library, for his help with the Darwin-Galton letter; Ed Hill, for his quick sharing of new finds, even that third Harry Houdini–Jack London photo; Byron Walker, who opened his bottomless library; Joe and Cindy Atmore, historians of mentalism, for their early editorial insights, and willingness to read early drafts of short stories and novels; Ray Goulet, master collector and source of endless information, for much steady support over the years; Bruce Abrams, New York County Clerk's Archives, who located the W. Irving Bishop affidavit; George P. Hansen, for his research into the "trickster" mentality; the Rev. William V. Rauscher, for his continued support and permission to reproduce images from his collection; Dr. Edwin A. Dawes, the premier conjuring arts historian of our day, for his permission to reproduce images from his collection; the late Warren Schoonmaker, who, as *C. L. Boardé*, wrote three of the definitive books on modern mentalism, and who left the copyrights to his unpublished books to Sal Franchino and me; George Daily, for generously allowing me to copy his AEF/Houdini correspondence and permission to publish his Bishop Assassination poster; Stephen Minch, Publisher of Hermetic Press, Seattle, for insightful discussions over lunch at The Ram; Tim Wiley, for patiently digging out Montague and Bishop; the staffs of the British Library, London; the Lamont Library and the Houghton Library, Harvard University; the McManus-Young Collection at the Library of Congress; the Carl W. Jones Collection at the Firestone Library of Princeton University; the University Library of Stanford University; and the Rare Book Room of the Public Library, Boston, for their kind patience and professional support.

Special appreciation to Jennifer K. Nieves, Registrar/Archivist, Dittrick Medical History Center of Case Western Reserve University, for permission to quote from Darwin letter 8258; and Peter X. Accardo of the Harvard Theatre Collection, Houghton Library, Harvard University, for permission to publish two images of Washington Irving Bishop from their holdings; the Harry Ransom Research Center for the Humanities, University of Texas at Austin, for permission to publish images of J. Randall Brown and Washington Irving Bishop from their collections;

Any factual or interpretive errors are all mine.

Prologue

Great Britain

On a warm Friday afternoon in London at about 5 P.M., May 23, 1884, having been given only twenty-four hours notice, thirty men and women gathered at the editorial offices of the *Pall Mall Gazette* (*PMG*) on Northcumberland Street. London. They came at the invitation of the *Gazette's* editor, William Thomas Stead. Under Stead's relentless innovative drive, styled The New Journalism, beginning in 1883, the *PMG* was fast becoming one of the most influential newspapers in England and the British Empire.[1]

The group of thirty came to experience, and perhaps interpret, the alleged extra-normal mental faculties of handsome, dark-eyed, 27-year-old Stuart Charles Francis Cumberland.

They did not come principally to be entertained, but, at Stead's direction, to be challenged to consider the implications of Cumberland's demonstrated capabilities. Apparently, Stuart Cumberland's talents could possibly redefine the limits of the mind of man, limits that Charles Darwin had suggested in his recently published work, *Descent of Man*,[2] were under constant modification and change — but not always easily characterized changes. Darwin first used the word "evolution" in print in *Descent of Man*, Vol. 1, page 2.

In the fifth edition of *Origin of Species* (1869), at the suggestion of philosopher Herbert Spencer, Darwin had first used the Spencerian expression "survival of the fittest." He used that phrase only twice in the 864 pages of *Descent of Man* — but that four-word expression had become the popular shorthand description for all of Darwin's evolutionary writing. Thought reading could obviously give its possessor a decided competitive advantage over other members of the constantly evolving species *Homo sapiens*. Was Stuart Cumberland, along with the American thought reader Washington Irving Bishop, concrete evidence for Darwin's theory? Was he evidence for the "fittest" human?

The thirty invited individuals represented the full spectrum of Victorian intellectual, scientific and artistic culture. The American, London, continental and provincial presses were also represented. Three invitees had sent regrets: conjuror John Nevil Maskelyne; Henri Labouchère,[3] radical Member of Parliament and publisher of the journal *Truth*[4]; and John Tyndall, professor of physics at the Royal Institution.

The remarkable attributes and implications of thought reading had begun to attract English scientific attention when the American performer Washington Irving Bishop, introduced thought reading to Great Britain with his first public performances in London in 1880. There was immediate extraordinary press and public response to Bishop's remarkable demonstrations. At the time of the *PMG* meeting, W. Irving Bishop was touring the Continent.

Skeptical and guarded articles regarding Bishop's and Cumberland's performances, with possible explanations for the observed phenomena, had been appearing in the major British scientific and medical journals since 1881.

Even with Bishop's chaotic style of performing, most writers were still dubious that thought reading was anything other than some form of Dr. William B. Carpenter's theory of unconscious cerebration or unconscious muscular action, an insight that Michael Faraday had first suggested in 1853[5] to explain table tipping and turning phenomena in spirit séances.

But not all scientific investigators accepted that position.

Stuart Cumberland had been asked to demonstrate his unique talents at the *PMG* offices because he seemed more open to investigation. Bishop, in any case, was not available and with his often erratic behavior, highly unreliable.

Though also invited, Edmund Gurney,[6] the honorary secretary of the recently formed Society for Psychical Research[7] (hereafter SPR), had refused to attend. Gurney dismissed Cumberland's thought reading performances as scientifically meaningless because he was a professional public performer, and it appeared that Cumberland required physical contact with his subjects. Gurney, in his extensive investigations of telepathy, considered thought transference only *without* physical contact as worthy of consideration.

Among those present at the *PMG* offices were zoologist (and exposer in 1876 of the notorious spirit medium Dr. Henry Slade) Edwin Ray Lankester; Dr. Horatio Donkin (co-exposer of Slade); Ernest Hart, editor of the *British Medical Journal*; Andrew Carnegie, American businessman; Colonel Henry Steele Olcott, occultist and theosophist; Edmund Grosse, writer and essayist; scientific journalist Grant Allen; and writer-playwright Oscar Wilde, who at the time, needing the money, was writing all the unsigned book reviews for the *PMG*. Olcott was the only committed believer in the occult in the group but was only a passive observer, declining to participate in any of the demonstrations.

Stuart Cumberland could apparently detect in some subtle manner the unspoken thoughts and intentions of strangers, whether low born or royal. Sometimes Cumberland detected the hidden thoughts in mere seconds, sometimes in minutes — but sometimes, not at all.

Since June 1880, Cumberland had been publicly demonstrating that he could read the serial number of a bank-note sealed in an opaque envelope, a number held in the mind of only one person present; that he could detect and reproduce a "crime" imagined and acted on while he was out of the room and, though securely blindfolded upon his return, identify the victim, the weapon and the criminal within only a few minutes; and, the most difficult effect for any thought reader, that he could accurately reproduce an arbitrary design drawn in secret, even to writing in Arabic and Russian though understanding nothing of either of those languages.

It appeared that Cumberland could discern these unspoken thoughts whether he actually touched the subject, as Gurney had complained, or was connected to the subject by only a handkerchief or by a length of copper wire — or, in a few remarkable instances, by simply holding his hand within a few inches of the subject. On several occasions, Cumberland performed his wonders even with a third neutral person separating the thought reader and the subject, holding the hand or wrists of the thought reader and the subject, with the neutral person having no knowledge of the test at stake.

Thus, it appeared that Carpenter's theory of unconscious cerebration might not readily explain all the thought reading phenomena of Cumberland — or of Bishop — or of the feats of the originator of thought reading, the American J. Randall Brown.

Stuart Cumberland had only just returned from performing triumphs in Paris and Vienna — much wealthier than when he had left — to happily discover himself the object of serious philosophical argument in the pages of the *Pall Mall Gazette*. The *PMG* remarked:

> Mr. Stuart Cumberland, the "thought reader," has been the sensation in Paris for the last few weeks, and the papers have been full of him and his wonderful works. His success is the more remarkable, because the Parisians started with strong prepossessions against him, being anxious to show their superiority to the English, who (as M. Francisque Sarcey marked) are the easiest people to gull in the world.[8]

But where had Stuart C. Cumberland come from — and how had he discovered his strange talents?

And were he and the other thought readers actually redefining the limits of man?

America

> The Society for Psychical Research will be grateful for any good evidence bearing on such phenomena as thought-reading, clairvoyance, presentiments, and dreams, noted at the time of occurrence, and afterwards confirmed; unexplained disturbances in places supposed to be haunted; apparitions at the moment of death or otherwise; and of such other abnormal events as may seem to fall under somewhat the same categories.
>
> Advertisement, *New York Nation*, August 28, 1884

Almost simultaneously with the expectant gathering in the London offices of the *Pall Mall Gazette*, on the other side of the Atlantic, Simon Newcomb, Professor of Astronomy and Mathematics at Johns Hopkins University, was unimpressed, even mildly disgusted with the SPR advertisement that he found in some of the New York City newspapers. Responding to the appearance of the SPR advertisements in the journal *Science*, the renowned scientist wrote, "It would be difficult for the Society to put forth anything better fitted than this advertisement to lower the estimation in which their work is held by common-sense people."[9]

Newcomb then did a sample calculation based on general assumptions to demonstrate how often an event of interest to the SPR should occur in America. Assuming that at least eight points of agreement would be necessary between the dream or vision and the actual circumstances of the death of the friend or relative to be relevant, Newcomb calculated that there would be an event of interest to the SPR in America, *based solely on coincidence and not on any psychical factors*, of one per day, every day of the year.

He bluntly dismissed a basic and frequently stated tenet in psychical research.[10] "The idea seemingly entertained by psychists—that the residuum, after they have eliminated all cases in which the natural causes could be found, must be genuine—has no logical foundation." The lack of a natural explanation for an event does not necessarily equate to a psychic occurrence—all it means is that there was a noise or knock or other incident for which there was no chance for observation and explanation.

He then turned to telepathy, the study of which had become a central focus of the SPR investigations—and the object of the *PMG* meeting in London:

> The general question at issue is whether there is any such process as what the psychists very happily denominate "Telepathy," which may be defined as *feeling at a distance* without the intervention of any physical agent. And just here we have the real point at issue between them and those people "of the earth, earthy," who think their work is all nonsense.

The issue came down to one question, in Newcomb's opinion: "is it possible that mind can affect mind otherwise than by some physical connection between the nervous systems with which the two minds are associated? That there is a natural tendency to believe in the possibility of the so-called Telepathy is, no doubt, well-known to all who have considered the subject." Telepathy, in Newcomb's opinion, could only be proven by finding that the percipient was affected by an agent "when the latter was not within sight or hearing or knowledge of the former."

In seeking a scientific basis for the demonstration of thought reading, Newcomb said, "A feature of these coincidences which ought not to have escaped the notice of the Society is, that they have no feature in common by which they can be traced to the action of a general cause, and not even tend to show that there are particular persons who possess the faculty of being influenced by Telepathy."

And finally the scientist concluded, "The only case that looks at all strong in favor of Telepathy is that in which one person is made to draw figures similar to those thought of by another in his neighborhood"—so long as the agent with the original figures was out of sight and hearing of the percipient, and no clues were given to the percipient of the kind or type of figures being considered. To inform the percipient of the type of telepathic information being considered, e.g., a playing card, a name, a location, or a random figure, would render the experiment, in Newcomb's opinion, scientifically useless.

A renowned scientist, polymath and autodidact who spoke five languages, Simon Newcomb had already received the Gold Medal of the Royal Astronomical Society in 1874. When offered the directorship of Harvard College Observatory in 1875, Newcomb declined as he felt more drawn to the mathematical aspects of astronomy than to the observational. He was elected a foreign member of the Royal Society in 1877.[11] He received honorary degrees and awards from the most prestigious universities and global scientific organizations throughout the rest of his active life.

But there was a phenomenon that drew Newcomb's close attention. Beginning on a stage in Atlanta, Georgia, January 21, 1884, a fifteen-year-old girl, Lula (later Lulu) Hurst, demonstrated she could apparently set aside the laws of physics at will. She called it the Power, or the Wonder, while she in turn came to be called the Georgia Wonder, the Magnetic Girl.[12] The appearance of a young girl on stage was rare enough in itself, but Hurst appeared to exhibit a power which seemed to drain the strength from grown men, even including a Sumo wrestler in New York City, enabling her, without apparent effort, to toss the men about the stage to the glee and delight of always exuberant audiences who filled theatres throughout the Eastern and Mid-Western states who enjoyed guying the often prominent subjects of the young girl's power. No one had ever seen anything like Lulu Hurst before. Hurst never revealed how or where she had come on the techniques she used, adding new stunts to her routine as her performing experiences added to her self-confidence. Even though most of her early competitors, all young girls, came from the same area of Georgia, all of them based their acts on having first seen Hurst.

About two years later, Hurst abruptly ceased performing in Knoxville, Tennessee, and walked away, rejecting the pleas of her family and her manager (later her husband) to continue her lucrative career — which left the field open to her growing number of competitors.

When later asked by reporters how much money Lulu's Power had made, William E. Hurst, her father, refused to say, but then responded, "Lula certainly lifted that mortgage off our home while she was lifting around editors, senators, governors and congressmen." Her career income was estimated at $70,000, most of which was saved; thus she retired at the age of seventeen the modern equivalent of a millionaire.

Twelve years later, writing in her autobiography,[13] Lulu Hurst observed:

> In viewing and thinking about the phenomenon connected with the Power, which they saw and read most wonderful accounts about ... they came to my tests with a pall of mystery draped over their minds, and their thoughts and faculties shackled with a *blind expectancy and anticipation that some weird, occult wonderful force was to take possession of them, and cause them to do my bidding!* In other words, to put it plainly, their blind delusive expectation of what was to happen, took such complete possession of their minds as to render them obedient, though unconscious, in doing to perfection what they expected would take place [emphasis in the original].

She commented further:

> Then also I got to be an excellent judge of human nature. I could discern the temperaments, idiosyncrasies, delusions and superstitions of a man almost as soon as he came on the stage. I could tell the skeptics from the rank believers at a glance.

Newcomb described,[14] shortly after the meeting of the American Association for the Advancement of Science, in Philadelphia, September 1884, "a long wished-for opportunity to witness and investigate what, from the descriptions, was a wonder as great as anything recorded in the history of psychic research or spiritualism. A tall and well-built young woman named Lulu Hurst, also known as the 'Georgia magnetic girl,' gave exhibitions in the eastern cities which equaled or exceeded the greatest feats of the Spiritualists." And he noted with relish, "There was no darkening of the rooms, no putting of hands under tables, no fear that spirits would refuse to act because of the presence of some skeptic, no trickery of any sort."

When Hurst arrived in Washington, her manager sent invitations to prominent scientists, including Newcomb, to attend a private exhibition prior to Hurst's scheduled public performances. But due to Newcomb's schedule, he could not attend. However, some who had attended the Hurst exhibition were so struck by her performance that a second exhibition was scheduled for the laboratory of Alexander Graham Bell.

Newcomb had reviewed the report from the first performance. It was said that after Lulu had scarcely touched a rod with her fingertips, that same rod had then jerked around so that a man holding the rod as tightly as he could was thrown to the floor. Another man took hold of the rod and when the girl touched the ends of the rod with her fingers, the rod began to whirl around on its central axis with so much force that the skin was nearly taken off the man's hands. A straw hat was laid on the table, crown up. Hurst extended her hands over it and the hat was lifted up. The hat was nearly torn to pieces by those attempting to stop its levitation. There was more. The wonders were truly impressive. "We must remember," Newcomb said, "that this was not the account of mere wonder-seekers, but of trained scientific men."

Then Newcomb wrote, "So much for the story. Now for the reality."[15]

The reality was much different. When asked about the whirling rod, Hurst didn't know what Newcomb was talking about. She had never seen such a feat. That impressive performance was solely in the imagination of the observing scientist. Newcomb saw that the straw hat levitation was done by Hurst catching the inner edge of the brim in the fold of the ball of her extended hand. The other wonders were also quickly disposed of through the use of scales to prove that she did apply force even though the observers had claimed she could not have. To Hurst's credit, in Newcomb's eyes, she stopped the demonstration, acknowledging that she could go no further, even when her parents pleaded with her to continue.

"The assumption," Newcomb wrote, "that because Miss Lulu begins by touching the articles deftly with her fingers, she never takes them with a firm grip, is one which the spectator takes upon himself without any effort on the performer's part to cause that illusion."

Graciously taking her leave of Professor Newcomb and the others, Lulu Hurst went on to appear to packed theatres in Washington with the newspaper reports praising her wonders without restraint, as would the papers in New York, Boston, and elsewhere.

The American Society for Psychical Research was founded following the AAAS meeting in Philadelphia in 1884. Newcomb accepted the position as the first president of the new society, a decision which one scientist, John

Wesley Powell, termed "ridiculous to the highest degree." To prepare for his new duties, Newcomb diligently reviewed the publications of the parent society in London, but was unimpressed with what he found. "I could not feel any assurance that the [English] Society, with all its diligence, had done more than add to the mass of mistakes, misapprehensions of facts, exaggerations, illusions, tricks and coincidences, of which human experiences are full." He urged the SPR to tighten its conditions for investigating mind-to-mind thought transference and gave suggestions for how to do it.[16] The search for confirmation of telepathy as a fact of human nature continued.

Albert Einstein would later consider Newcomb's scientific work to be "of monumental importance to astronomy" noting that Newcomb himself was "the last of the great masters" of classical astronomy.[17]

1

Introduction ... and Mrs. Hayden

> When the call for scientific investigation is responded to, the method by which it is carried on is usually unscientific, although associated with scientific principles and conducted by scientific men. Nearly always the scientific men are disposed to believe some new mental condition has been demonstrated, and they hunger for the honour of defining its characteristics and marking out the limits of its influence.
> — Frederick Wickes, *Thought Reading Explained*, 1907

The Thought Reader Craze ran from about 1870 to just before the First World War. It was, in its simplest, most direct form, a dedicated effort on the part of many prominent scientists, philosophers, psychologists and other highly intelligent men and women to confirm through exhaustive investigation that mind to mind communication without customary sensory input was a *fact* of normal human experience. Occurring parallel to and occasionally interacting with this effort was the growth of mind reading as a form of professional entertainment, with performers like Stuart Cumberland and others sometimes seen as supporting the scientific search. The public interest in thought reading was sustained and strengthened over the years through the public pronouncements of the scientists and their societies as well as the astonishing performances of the thought readers — each using the other for his own purpose — along with the rapidly changing industrial culture that seemed to be working its own kind of magic.

With the background provided by the rise of modern Spiritualism, which began in Hydesville, New York, in 1848, there was another implicit question on the table: Could mind to mind communication between the living and the dead be put to scientific investigation and validation?

And the ultimate background question: Would the proof of telepathy serve, as well, as a major step toward proof of human survival after death? Confirmation of the transmission, mind-to-mind, of information without the customary sensory input would argue that the mind of a disembodied spirit could communicate with the mind of a living person.

But there were equally prominent scientists, like Simon Newcomb, who said that the whole Thought Reader Craze and the attendant claims of the Spiritualists were all simply nonsense, an innocent imposture in some cases, a malicious predatory con in many others.

Who then was right? Or, in fact, could the scientific "hunger" described by Frederick Wickes overwhelm more rational considerations?

The solid rock of the Newtonian universe, at once so logical and reassuring, had began to develop small cracks in the early nineteenth century as further scientific investigations suggested that observed phenomena were more complex than what had been explained by Newton and his crisp equations. Victorian science was beginning to be characterized by a growing belief that almost anything could be possible — a kind of philosophical Wild West. Even the word "scientist" to mean someone experienced in the scientific method of disciplined experimentation was first coined by the English polymath William Whewell, at the suggestion of the poet Samuel Taylor Coleridge, only in 1833. (Whewell also later provided the term "physicist" along with suggesting "anode," "cathode," and "ion" to Michael Faraday as convenient descriptive electrical terms.)

Even then, a scientist was not necessarily someone whose entire living came from the practice of science. Along with the natural philosophers drawing most of their financial support from various public universities, many scientists were largely independent, oftentimes wealthy gentlemen with a curiosity about the world surrounding them coupled with the talent, the time and the money to indulge their interests.

Nineteenth century scientific understanding would be advanced over a broad frontier by such talented amateurs. A prime example was Sir William Huggins (1824–1910), who at the age of thirty sold the family brewing business and, though lacking any university training, with the able assistance of his devoted and highly intelligent wife, Margret, constructed an observatory to explore the mysteries of astronomy. Building on the work of Robert Bunsen and Gustav Kirchoff, who, by building the first spectrometer in 1859, had demonstrated that all pure substances exhibited a characteristic spectrum, Huggins designed and built a spectrometer in his observatory — and founded the field of stellar spectroscopy. He was the first to demonstrate that the elements of the stars were the same as those found in the sun and on the earth. He was also the first to differentiate between nebulae and galaxies. Craters on the moon and on Mars have been named for him, as was the asteroid #2635 Huggins. However, even with his own unveiling of many of the mysteries of the universe, William Huggins remained a skeptic regarding psychical occurrences throughout his life, even when he experienced phenomena that he acknowledged he could not explain.

1. Introduction ... and Mrs. Hayden

A materialistic view of the universe was spreading among the universities, directly conflicting with traditional Victorian theological teachings. Most significantly was the publication, on November 24, 1859, of Charles Darwin's polemical work *On the Origin of Species by Means of Natural Selection*,[1] which not only supported a materialistic philosophy but proposed a simple mechanism by which the known world had come into existence. Darwin's arguments began to shake the very rock on which Isaac Newton had stood, the biblical view of creation. Darwin's proposition was not only that the physical world had *not* been created in a single act of an omnipotent supernatural power or being, but that the world was still changing daily in a manner not wholly understood.

The suggestion was further expanded so that ideas were changing, not only about the physical world, but about human beings. Darwin's further challenge, that the development of humankind had come about by means other than supernatural intervention, was published in 1871 under the title *Descent of Man and Selection in Relation to Sex*.[2] In the same year, the term 'psychic' was first proposed by Serjeant-at-Law, Edward William Cox, as a word to describe apparent human abilities or talents outside of the normally experienced five senses.

Other challenges to the Victorian perception of man and his universe had appeared even earlier. Table turning, an odd phenomenon that had proliferated from Europe, had become a widespread mania in Britain, infecting all classes. Families and other groups gathered around tables, touched their fingers to the table-top, and watched as the table began to rotate and move, apparently without the intervention of those sitting around it. Michael Faraday and other scientists dismissed the table turnings as simply the unconscious muscular action by the group gathered around the table, but that declaration did not convince the table turners, and the turnings, rappings and mania continued. Another suggestion to offset the more scientific explanation was that the table turnings were manifestations of disembodied spirits.

Spiritualism first arrived in England in October 1852 — four years after its first appearance on the evening of March 31, 1848, at Hydesville, New York — in the person of Mrs. Maria B. Hayden.[3] Hayden was the wife of W. R. Hayden, a successful and well connected Boston journalist and editor. The Haydens were ardent abolitionists, as were many Spiritualists of the time.

The Haydens had crossed the Atlantic as a result of the strong encouragement of George W. Stone,[4] an American lecturer who had in only three years established a strong reputation in Great Britain for his demonstrations of Electro-Biology, a technique of suggestion that used small copper-zinc discs to induce a mesmeric trance. During their stay in London, Stone acted as the Hayden business manager. Upon their arrival in London on October

20, 1852, Stone began to place appropriate advertisements in the *Times* and other journals with the initial séances to be held at his residence at 26 Upper Seymour, Portman Square. A few weeks later, the Haydens moved to their own quarters at 22 Queen Anne Street, Cavendish Square.

Only a few days after Mrs. Hayden opened at Stone's boarding house with her séances of table rappings and spirit messages for a guinea a head (five guineas for ten), the assault on the American seeress and her "powers" began. Though initially described politely in the London press as "a woman of some education," Mrs. Hayden swiftly became an object of relentless ridicule and caustic jibes.

Hayden's first attackers were Henry Morley and W. H. Wills, who wrote "The Ghost of the Cock Lane Ghost," which appeared in Charles Dickens' weekly journal, *Household Words,* November 20, 1852. In the article, the writers described their experiences in detail, from being met by G. W. Stone at the door, to séances in which the American medium produced messages for the two men from non-existent relatives or from still living friends.

The answers to questions came via the inquirer tapping on an alphabet which was printed on a piece of cardboard, along with the digits 1 to 0. When the right letter was touched, the spirits would rap on the table. The letter was recorded and the process repeated. Quickly detecting Hayden's technique of observing the movement of the quill pen used to touch the alphabet, Morley and Wills were able to lead the spirits to give absurd answers. In their subsequent article, the men openly encouraged unbridled criticism of the odd American woman with her strange declarations about talking to the dead, and, in their view, her even more absurd, even pathetic tricks.[5]

After all, wags asked, why would disembodied spirits come all the way back from eternity only to converse by beating on tables — and then only to communicate trivialities devoid of insight or wisdom, and nothing at all of the *outré tombe*.

The humor paper *Punch, or the London Charivari* contributed its opinion on the subject of spirits:

> White sheeted ghosts have grown mere fables,
> Instead of groaning, ghosts rap tables.
> The grisly ghosts of old have vanished;
> The ancient bogies are all banished.
> How much more credible and pleasant
> Than the old spirits are the present.

Even with the public criticism, the Hayden séances, held either in the well-lit but scantily furnished drawing room at the Queen Anne Street house around a shabby Pembroke table, or in the homes of fashionable clients and prominent scientists like mathematician Augustus de Morgan, naturalist

> **SPIRITUAL PHENOMENA or MANIFESTA-TIONS** —Mrs. W. R. HAYDEN will continue her SEANCES, at 22, Queen Anne street, Cavendish-square, for a short time previous to her departure from London, where those who desire to witness or test the truth of these beautiful manifestations can have an opportunity from 12 to 3 and 4 to 6.

Maria B. Hayden advertisement, Saturday, *London Times*, April 16, 1853.

Thomas Henry Huxley, and socialist Robert Dale Owen, created a growing interest in spirit phenomena — along with a growing uneasiness. Even with the various methods publicly proposed by observers for explaining the results that Hayden obtained from "her spirits," there were still many well known participants for whom such minimal methods simply could not account for what they had observed. Science seemed unable to constrain the public interest.

T.R. Huxley, writing in the *Pall Mall Gazette* some thirty-seven years later on January 1, 1889, in an article called "Spiritualism Unmasked," commented on his mediumistic experiences. He summarily dismissed all the mediums he had encountered as only "utter impostors" with nothing to recommend them — with the exception of Mrs. Maria B. Hayden. Huxley had steadfastly refused to meet any medium unless it was at the home of someone whom Huxley trusted. Consequently, all the Hayden séances he attended were held at his brother George's house. Huxley considered the American "a pleasant, intelligent and well-mannered woman." The raps were loud and abundant; "and the company declared they came from all parts of the room; indeed, there were some who maintained their persistence in the house for days afterwards." Huxley further noted that the suggestion that "the quiet woman who sat easily talking at the head of the table could be all the while making these wonderful noises seemed at first to be outrageous." Huxley admired Mrs. Hayden not for the authenticity of her craft, but for the ingenuity of her practice.[6]

The séances generally followed a regular routine. After the room had been searched to their satisfaction by the querents, everyone took their place at the table. The medium then seated herself at one end of the table. There often would be several moments of silence, sometimes extending to almost an hour, at which point a few sharp raps would seem to come from the center of the table. "They are coming," Mrs. Hayden would quietly announce. "Who is to speak to them?" she would ask of the spirits, as she moved her thrust-out forefinger slowly around the circle. The table would rap when Hayden's finger was pointing at one of the clients. The cardboard printed with the alphabet would be slid across the table to the designated client. "Ask your question of the spirits," Hayden would direct. The person would ask a question; then, using a pencil, quill pen or just a finger, the person would move from one letter to the next until the spirit would rap. That letter would be recorded; then the client would start again with the message being assembled one letter at a time. When the message was completed and affirmed by the client as accurate, Hayden would again move her finger around the table to allow the spirits to select the next person to whom a message would be given. The messages would almost always contain some information that the querents were certain the medium could not have known.

Even considering the many proposed "exposures" of Hayden, Augustus de Morgan requested a séance at his home. In a letter written July 1853 and later repeated in a preface to a book written by his wife in 1863, the mathematician described the Hayden séance:

> Mrs. Hayden, the well known American medium, came to my house alone [underlines in the original]. The sitting began immediately after her arrival. Eight or nine persons were present, of all ages, and all degrees of belief and unbelief in the whole thing being imposture. The raps began in the usual way. They were to my ears clean, clear, faint sounds such as would be said to ring, had they lasted. I never had the good luck to hear those exploits of Latin muscles, and small kicking done on the leg of a table by machinery, which have been proposed as the causes of these raps.
>
> Mrs. Hayden was seated some distance from the table, and her feet were watched by their believers until faith in pedalism slowly evaporated.
>
> The séance lasted three hours.
>
> On being asked to put a question to the first spirit, I begged that I be allowed to put my question mentally—that is, without speaking it, or writing it, or pointing it out to myself on an alphabet—and that Mrs. Hayden might hold both arms extended while the answer was in progress. Both demands were instantly granted by a couple of raps. I put the question and desired the answer might be in one word, which I assigned; all mentally. I then took the printed alphabet [card], put a book upright before it, and bending my eyes upon it, proceeded to point to the letters in the usual way. The correct word, chess, was given, with a rap at each letter. I had now a reasonable certainty of the following alternatives: either some thought-reading of a character wholly inexplicable, or such superhuman acuteness on the part of Mrs. Hayden that she could detect the letter I wanted by my bearing, though she (seated six feet from the book behind which hid my alphabet) could see neither my hand nor my eye, nor at what rate I was going through the letters. I was fated to be driven out of the second alternative before the sitting was done.

The mathematician continued with his detailed description of the complete séance, during which he did not detect any fakery.

A friend of de Morgan, who was sure the whole Hayden affair was a crude imposture, went to Queen Anne Street to see the medium alone for himself. He did not give her his name. No individuals except Mrs. Hayden and himself were in the room. Mrs. Hayden's husband, often present at séances, had left at the visitor's request. De Morgan's friend had insisted on taking his alphabet card behind a large folding screen. He asked his questions of the spirits by the alphabet and a pencil, as well as receiving his answers the same way. "My friend," wrote de Morgan, "told me he was 'awe-struck' and had nearly forgotten his precautions."

De Morgan and his wife, Sophie, long after Maria Hayden had returned to America, decided that indeed they had witnessed non-human activity, whether spirits, as Sophie came to believe, or something else, as de Morgan himself accepted. The intellectual ambiguity of the de Morgans would be repeated with other equally diligent observers.

Mrs. Hayden continued her work on Queen Anne Street for almost a year, after acquiring, according to critics, the substantial sum of two to three hundred pounds from the sprits, she returned with her husband to America on Monday, October 10, 1853, where in the years ahead she studied medicine, becoming in 1865 one of the few licensed female physicians in America.

Shortly after the Haydens departure, a reporter who had visited Mrs. Hayden wrote in the London *British Banner*, October 12, 1853: "Ought not a Medium to constitute an appendage to every Police-office in the Metropolis, and indeed throughout the Land? Why should not Mrs. Hayden be taken into the service of the Government? She is worth more than all the 6,000 Blues united."

A second American medium, Mrs. Roberts, with her husband, "Dr." Roberts, arrived in England April 1853, to immediately advertise her séances on the front page of the *London Times* for April 16, 1853, at 1a Devonshire Street, Portland Place, or "at the home of any respectable person." She promised "Spiritual Manifestations and Communications from departed friends, which so much gratify serious enlightened minds, exemplified daily." (Later in 1853, according to W. R. Hayden, the *London Times* refused to insert such advertisements any longer.)

Mrs. Roberts' routine differed somewhat from Mrs. Hayden's in that it was basically table-turning, a phenomenon which was still popular throughout Europe, and automatic writing; but even then she was subjected to the same attacks that Mrs. Hayden had experienced earlier. Roberts returned to America after only a few months. She never penetrated the British upper social levels as had Hayden, nor ever attracted the interest or the endorsement of a noted scientist.

Still publicly ridiculing spirit communications, Charles Dickens observed in a letter to a friend, Mrs. Fanny Trollope, in 1855, "I have not the least belief in the awful unseen being available for evening parties at so much per night. Although I shall be ready to receive enlightenment from any source, I must say I have very little hope of it from the spirits who express themselves through mediums; as I have never yet observed them to talk anything but nonsense."[7]

The number of professional public mediums in Great Britain grew much more slowly than in America primarily because of the preference in England for home circles rather than patronizing a professional. Table tilting and turning at home circles continued throughout Great Britain with the wealthy fashionable classes well represented.

It would be this gradual penetration of the intellectual and moneyed classes that further distinguished European spiritualism from the American movement, which was basically rooted in rural and working families and the newly developing middle class.

Not until the arrival from America of the twenty-two-year-old Scottish-born medium Daniel Dunglas Home,[8] in March 1855, and then his return from the Continent with a wealthy Russian wife and a son in the autumn of 1859, did interest in modern Spiritualism take full root in Great Britain. It then began to draw the close attention of the nobility along with prominent literary and scientific men.

Home, it seemed, could work truly strange wonders — and not at a guinea a head. Levitations, elongating his body, handling red-hot coals straight from the hearth, and materializations were only a portion of his séance phenomena. It was clear that Home was in a far different class than Mrs. Hayden or Mrs. Roberts. Though he would accept the hospitality of his generally wealthy host or hostess for extended periods, Home never openly charged for his séances. He gave the séances whenever he "felt the power"— which was generally when skeptics were not present.

Professor John Tyndall, writing in the *Pall Mall Gazette* of May 17, 1868, described scientist Michael Faraday's attitude toward Home and Spiritualism: "Faraday regarded the necessity even of discussing such phenomena as are ascribed to Mr. Home as a discredit, to use no stronger term, to the education of this age."

But the spirits were not to be denied.

2

The Borderland

> "We have actually touched the borderland where Matter and Force seem to merge into one another, the shadowy realm between Known and Unknown, which for me has always had peculiar temptations."
> — William Crookes, F.R.S., 1879

No scientist of the nineteenth century committed more in professional reputation and personal finances, or endured more harsh ridicule and criticism in order to investigate the claims of spiritualists and psychical research, than William Crookes in the years 1869–75. Even after terminating his research efforts into the psychic questions, Crookes would still sometimes encounter public reproach from other scientists who recalled his intense support for the existence of a new force, the Psychic Force — along with his dalliance in dark rooms with such attractive young female spirit mediums as Florence Cook, Rosina Showers, and the American, Annie Eva Fay. But Crookes always staunchly defended his position, acquiring the reputation in some quarters as being "a litigious and quarrelsome fellow," as Crookes himself suggested in an 1862 letter to a member of the Council of the Pharmaceutical Society.

Born in 1832, the eldest son of the twenty-one children from two marriages of the prominent and well-connected London tailor Joseph Crookes, William Crookes was later described by a friend, the physicist Sir Oliver Lodge, as "a scientific amateur who forced his way to the front by sheer ability and brilliance of discovery."[1]

With the comfortable wealth of his father, Crookes could have lived the empty life of the dilettante, drifting as the years passed from one idle interest to another, as did many elder sons of wealthy fathers in the Victorian period. But as Fournier d'Albe accurately pointed out in his biography of Crookes, "What saved Crookes from this fate was his consciousness of mastery. He felt fit to be in the front rank, he asserted his right to be there, he established a good title to his place, and maintained it against all competitors to the end of his life."[2] Thus William Crookes never put his hard won reputation at risk without careful consideration of the investment required against the likely return. The seductive lure of the Unknown, appealing to his almost unquenchable need for scientific, even public recognition, however, would sometimes conceal the true depth of that risk.

Crookes published his first scientific paper, "On the Selenocyanides," in 1851 at the age of nineteen while still an assistant to Professor August Wilhelm Hofmann at the Royal College of Chemistry. The college itself had only been founded in 1845. Only ten years later, using the new art of spectroscopy and his personally designed and constructed spectrometer, Crookes, in a brilliant laboratory observation while investigating a sample of the residue from a sulphuric acid factory, discovered the radiant green spectral line of a new element, which he came to call thallium.

The creation of the Periodic Table by Dmitri Mendeleev in 1869 created a major controversy when he stated that the chart could predict the characteristics of unknown elements, but it was not until November, 1875, when a French scientist, Lecoq de Boisbaudran, discovered an element predicted by the Russian's chart, which the Frenchman called Gallium, that the full value of Mendeleev's work was recognized. But until then, discovering an element was a random affair in which a scientist needed to be acutely aware of the unusual, however small, in his work — a talent with which Crookes was richly endowed.

Writing to C. Greville Williams on March 5, 1861, Crookes asked, "Have you ever noticed a green spectrum line as far from $N\alpha$ on the one side as $Li\alpha$ is on the other? If not, I have got a new element."[3] In its pure form, thallium is a highly toxic soft bluish-white metal that oxidizes quickly in air and can be cut by a knife. Compounds of the element can also be dangerously toxic. In a parallel event, characteristic of some later discoveries in Crookes' career, thallium had been almost simultaneously discovered by the Belgian chemist Claude-August Lamy. As Lamy was the first to produce an ingot of the metallic thallium, he claimed priority in discovery; however, Crookes, in the pages of the *Chemical News*, a journal of which he was publisher and editor, and in other scientific outlets, fought back to protect his own claim of priority. In the end, both scientists received gold medals for their joint discovery from the London International Exhibition of 1862, while final priority was granted Crookes as he was the first to determine the chemical properties and describe the metallic nature of the element. In a characteristic example of his meticulous standard of laboratory work, Crookes' determined the atomic weight of the new element as 203.642, well below the currently accepted measurement of 204.37.[4] His laboratory procedures in the thallium measurements were lauded at the time as virtually the standard to which other scientists should aspire.

2. The Borderland

But, as Crookes learned, discovering a new element did not generate new funds; in fact the effect was the opposite. It would require a subsequent annual expenditure of £100–£200 through the years in order to sustain his claim to primacy of discovery, which supported his continuing analyses of multiple thallium compounds.

On January 16, 1863, Crookes received a letter from Professor Alex W. Williamson asking Crookes' permission for Williamson to offer his name in nomination for membership in the august Royal Society.[5] The Crookes Certificate of Proposal in support of his nomination was signed by eighteen scientists including John Herschel, Michael Faraday and John Tyndall, three of the most prominent names in Victorian science. Of fifty names put forth for consideration that year, William Crookes was one of only fifteen selected for the honor of Fellow of the Royal Society. Thus at the age of only thirty-one, he was able to put the much coveted initials, F.R.S., behind his name.

William Crookes, ca. 1874.

Even so, after several frustrating disappointments, 1864 was the last year in which Crookes attempted to gain an academic appointment at one of the public colleges. From that time on, all of the Crookes funds had to come from the income generated by his journal, the *Chemical News*, and his establishing a solid reputation as a freelance technical consultant and analytical chemist. Gaining a contract to perform chemical assays of copper from a copper factory was a breakthrough; at 10 shillings per assay, it would provide over £200 annually, enough to provide for his growing family.

To further enhance his position as scientific editor and publisher, on January 1, 1864, Crookes launched the *Quarterly Journal of Science*, which would allow Crookes to become involved in a still wider scope of scientific activity — and, always, to enhance his income, and to add to his list of useful contacts.

But in the weekly journal *The Athenaeum* of March 28, 1870, p. 552, under the columnar heading of *Science Gossip* was disclosed:

> Dr. Donkin, of Durham University, is preparing a history of the British Diatomaceæ.
> Lion-breeding is very successful at the Dublin Zoological Gardens. The Society was the first to rear lion cubs in Europe; and six have been recently born, of which five are doing well.
> Mr. Crookes, editor of the *Chemical News*, is engaged in an investigation on spiritualism, but, it is said, with far from satisfactory results.
> The municipal authorities throughout France have this year sent in official reports with regard to hydrophobia, which will shortly be published.

This was *not* how Crookes had planned to announce his decision to subject the claims of Spiritualism to the rigors of scientific scrutiny — not as simply one of the items in one of the gossip columns of a popular weekly magazine, and most assuredly not with a premature judgment regarding his results.

But there it was.

In July, Crookes responded publicly for the first time in the pages of his *Quarterly Journal of Science*:

> Some weeks ago the fact that I was engaged in investigating Spiritualism, so-called, was announced in a contemporary; and in consequence of the many communications that I have since received, I think it desirable to say a little concerning the investigation which I have commenced. Views or opinions I cannot be said to possess on a subject which I do not pretend to understand. I consider it the duty of scientific men who have learnt exact modes of working, to examine phenomena which attract the attention of the public, in order to confirm their genuineness, or to explain, if possible, the delusions of the honest and to expose the tricks of the deceivers. But I think it is a pity that any public announcement of a man's investigation would be made until he has shown himself willing to speak out.[6]

Crookes, however, by 1870 had already reached a firm opinion upon Spiritualism, something he chose not to reveal publicly. Which strongly suggests that his interest in scientifically investigating the claimed wonders of the spirits was not driven by scientific objectivity, but rather by his need to confirm a position he had already taken. By the time of the *Athenaeum* announcement, William Crookes was already a Spiritualist.

The event that had changed William Crookes' considered opinion of life itself occurred on September 22, 1867, when his youngest brother, Phillip, only just turned twenty-one, died of yellow fever as part of a cable-laying expedition to Havana, Cuba. So angry was Crookes at what he saw as gross negligence on the part of the leaders of the expedition that he printed and circulated an open letter to the directors of the India Rubber, Gutta Percha,

2. The Borderland 21

and Telegraph Works Company, demanding, "in the name of justice and humanity," that severe disciplinary action be taken against F.C. Webb, who had commanded the Cuba and Florida Cable Expedition. At the time of Phillip's death, seven other crew members had already died of yellow fever, while five more would die of the disease before the ship reached New York. The end result, however, was a libel action brought by Webb against Crookes, which Crookes lost.

For part of 1868, Crookes suffered from illness that suspended his scientific research, Meanwhile he also had to devote his resources to defending his *Chemical News* from plagiarism in America, and from the challenge of his English competitor, *The Laboratory*.

It was through the astronomer William Huggins, F.R.S., in a letter dated November 10, 1870, that Crookes received an invitation to become a member of the Government Eclipse Expedition. This voyage was to be made by two groups, one traveling to Sicily, and in parallel, one to Spain and Algiers to observe the total eclipse of the sun of December 22, 1870. The principal objective of the expedition was to study the corona, or white halo, surrounding the sun.

The Huggins letter, however, had been primarily focused on Spiritualism, as were many others exchanged between the two scientists in those months.

The friendship with Huggins had come about through their joint growing interest in Spiritualism, an interest Crookes also had come to share with Cromwell Fleetwood Varley, the leading expert on electricity in Great Britain, the engineering hero of the laying of the second Atlantic cable in 1866, and already a firm believer. It had been Varley who had first suggested that Crookes attempt to contact his dead brother through mediums. By the time of the eclipse expedition in December, Crookes had become convinced that he had communicated with Phillip, and that many of the claims of Spiritualism appeared to be genuine.

In the Crookes diary from the eclipse expedition,[7] it is clear that he had become not just a believer, but an advocate of the claims of the spirits. On December 6, after a lunch of bread and cheese on the deck of the ship *Urgent*,[8] he was joined by John Tyndall, a leading physicist and doyen of the Royal Institution. Another of the scientists on board, Benjamin Coleman, had earlier that day raised the subject of Spiritualism to Tyndall, and Tyndall asked, as Crookes later recorded, whether "he was going on."

Responding to Tyndall, Crookes recalled his own strong response in his diary: "Yes, and as he [Tyndall] seemed evidently wanting to talk on the subject, I spoke as strongly as I could, telling him of many of the phenomena I had seen, but confining myself to the physical movements only. He was at first inclined to ridicule and explain away, but Huggins then came up, and the combination was too strong for him."

John Tyndall had written a paper,[9] "Science and the 'Spirits,'" in 1864, describing his experience at a séance, in which all forms of spiritual manifestation, thought reading, sensitivity to magnets, and table rapping utterly failed whenever he looked closer. Tyndall noted, "The present promoters of spiritual phenomena divide themselves into two classes, one of which needs no demonstration, while the other is beyond the reach of proof." His tone in the paper, though polite, had been gently mocking. His position through the years had not changed.[10]

Their vigorous conversation on the poop deck of the *Urgent* continued with Tyndall finally declaring he was very willing to attend several séances and to meet the most famous medium of all, Daniel Dunglas Home. Crookes was elated, writing in his diary that night that "to have got Tyndall into such a mode of thinking is a great triumph."

Other passengers came to join them, and the spirits remained the topic through the afternoon and into dinner, with several passengers contributing ghost stories from their personal experiences. Crookes happily wrote that the "whole thing reminded me strongly of a Xmas number of *All the Year Round*" (Charles Dickens' popular weekly journal famous for its ghost stories at Christmastime). Clearly then, Crookes was not telling the public the whole truth when he wrote in his response to the item in the *Athenaeum* gossip column:

> But I cannot, at present, hazard even the most vague hypothesis as to the cause of the phenomena. Hitherto I have seen nothing to convince me of the truth of the "spiritual" theory. In such an inquiry the intellect demands that the spiritual proof must be absolutely incapable of being explained away; it must be so striking and convincingly true that we cannot, dare not deny it.
>
> Faraday says[11] "Before we proceed to consider any question involving physical principles, we should set out with clear ideas of the naturally possible and impossible." But this appears like reasoning in a circle: we are to investigate nothing till we know it to be *possible*, whilst we cannot say what is *impossible*, outside pure mathematics, till we know everything.

Crookes assured the public that he would move ahead, noting that Faraday had also said: "Nothing is too wonderful to be true, if it be consistent with the laws of nature; and in such things as these, experiment is the best test of such consistency."

A year later, in his *Quarterly Journal of Science*, July 1, 1871, Crookes would publish his first report on his investigation of the claims of Spiritualism. Called "Experimental Investigation of a New Force," the report would provoke a firestorm of outcry — from Spiritualists as well as the scientific community.

Crookes' expressed commitment to subjecting the spirits to cold, calculating measurements offended some of the Spiritualists. One Spiritualist, G.

2. The Borderland

Damiani, whose long letter had been published earlier in the *London Human Nature*, appeared prominently in the *Banner of Light*, December 24, 1870. The writer dismissed Crookes out of hand:

> Unlike his colleagues, he [Crookes] appears to have given more than one half-hour of his "valuable time" to the observation of the Phenomena of Spiritualism, and his soberness of language and decency of demeanor show how a *philosopher* can talk nonsense without forgetting himself. A thousand pities that so cool-headed and keen observer as Mr. Crookes has hitherto shown himself to be in his special department of science, should have thought it expedient to go investigating Spiritualism with brass pendulums in his pocket, and glass shades under his arm; and because the invisibles refuse compliance with his modest request to make clock springs and cog wheels of themselves, he arrives at the logical conclusion that they have no brains and are no entities at all.... Another fatal error of Mr. Crookes is his belief that attending half-a-dozen séances, or, for that matter, a dozen, confers upon him the right of pronouncing judgment.

The Spiritualists were split among several philosophical and religious groups, divisions that were reflected in the journals and newspapers that had appeared to discuss and report on the doings of mediums and spirits. Of the group, the two most prominent were *The Spiritualist* (1869–1882), published and edited by William Henry Harrison, and *The Medium & Daybreak* (1870–1895) by James Burns. They also reflected the opposite poles of the Spiritualist vision.

Harrison had been an engineer for several years with the Electric Telegraph Co., where he encountered Cromwell Fleetwood Varley, and through Varley, became an ardent convinced Spiritualist. He wrote articles on scientific topics for several London newspapers, including the *Daily Telegraph*, but having encountered a wall of suspicion and prejudice in the public press regarding Spiritualism, he founded *The Spiritualist*, with its sub-title of *A Record of the Progress of the Science and Ethics of Spiritualism*. He was relentless in exposing fraud, though, like many others, he was conned by the better mediums such as Florence Cook. When he learned of Crookes' announcement, Harrison immediately sent a letter offering support and full cooperation in any way.

In contrast, James Burns was a successful publisher and printer of journals, tracts and pamphlets of numerous suitably "progressive" subjects, not just Spiritualism. A radical and enthusiastic self-promoter, Burns kept his journal non–Christian and decidedly plain spoken. He had nothing but contempt for the scientific approach to spiritual matters as embodied by the Crookes announcement. The weekly *Medium & Daybreak* achieved the highest circulation of any of the Spiritualist publications.

Embarking on his investigations, Crookes then faced hostile criticism inside the Spiritualist community and from the outside scientific world.

3

Crookes and D. D. Home

> Could all the paraphernalia of Mr. Crookes' workshop reveal to him the presence of a spirit?
> No.
> Nay — let us say even his maid-servant or his little dog?
> No.
> The cause is psychological; not "material" as the chemist understands matter.
> — James Burns, editor, *The Medium and Daybreak*, September 30, 1870

Though he had sat with a few mediums earlier, William Crookes' more disciplined involvement in Spiritualism began in earnest the summer of 1869 with his growing involvement with various mediums through family and close friends — and with his meeting the principal medium of the nineteenth century, Daniel Dunglas Home. Home had arrived in London from St. Petersburg, in early July 1869, with a letter of introduction to Crookes from Alexander von Boutlerow, professor of chemistry at St. Petersburg University and Home's future brother-in-law. Home first contacted Crookes on July 22, 1869.[1] The medium would subsequently become a regular visitor to the Crookes home at 20 Mornington Road, London, N.W., and a family friend. (Later mediums under investigation, as Florence Cook, would live at the Crookes residence for a week at a time.)

Published in July 1869, and certainly read by Crookes, were the unedited diaries of young Lord Adare. Appearing under the title *Experiences in Spiritualism with D. D. Home,* their publication had been arranged privately by Lord Adare's father, Lord Dunraven. The episodes, numbered consecutively 1–58, which often carried erotic homosexual overtones, demonstrated how thoroughly Home had come to dominate and control the mind of Adare. Together most days of the week, the two men often slept in the same room and sometimes in the same bed. The events and powers so casually attributed to Home by Adare are astonishing. Given the intimate relations of the two

3. Crookes and D.D. Home

men, attempting to consider any natural explanations for the events, other than hallucination or hypnotic suggestion, would be fruitless.

The surrounding English culture, however was also changing. Along with the changing scientific perceptions of the universe, interest in the mysterious spread progressively across all social levels. Louis Blanc, a celebrated French journalist and historian, wrote at length of his impressions of England 1861–1870, recounting the growing love of the marvelous and the almost eager acceptance of superstition during that time, a craving for marvels that led directly to a "cult of the ridiculous." He recalled that one could count by the thousand fortune-tellers of both sexes, sorcerers, readers of cards, rural and urban astrologers, and prophets, with a commensurate clientele to match.[2] For a man like Daniel Dunglas Home, the fields of those years had been particularly fertile.

At the time of his first meeting William Crookes, Home was, at 36, one year younger than the scientist, with clear blue eyes, thick reddish-brown hair and a luxuriant mustache. According to Alexandre Dumas, who met the medium in 1858, Home was "guileless as a child, of average height, slenderly built, frail and highly strung." The writer further commented that his hands, "white and ladylike," were "beautifully kept and covered with rings." Home's appearance twelve years later had not changed appreciably, except for his advancing tubercular condition, a state that would finally kill him in 1886.

Home had been the most controversial medium in the world of the spirits since 1855[3] and the most celebrated. Crowned heads of Europe, including Tsar Alexander II, Queen Sophia of Holland, Napoleon III and Empress Eugenie of France, along with members of the titled aristocracy and commanders of industry, eagerly sat in the darkened rooms to experience Home's regularly produced wonders, which ensured that others of lesser social stature would even more eagerly join them. The medium never accepted payment for any séance, thus evading any potential charge of criminal fraud while adding implied credibility to his performances. He would, however, readily accept the prolonged hospitality of the wealthy which was frequently offered, and such gifts as the affluent and titled might "insist" he accept, often in the form of elaborate jewelry.

With virtually all of his séances given in private homes, generally under the auspices of a socially well-placed host and hostess, all guests sitting around the séance table would feel strong social pressure to forgo directly challenging Home, or to interfere in any way with the conduct of the séance, as both cases would be an affront to the hospitality of the evening. Thus protected, Home was left free to manipulate the event as he chose — even to cancel the séance outright with the plea that he "didn't feel the power," if he felt a skeptic was observing him too closely. A blank séance was always a subtle though strong assertion of implied genuineness — much as a juggler might intentionally miss on one stunt in order to set the stage for the next feat of apparently greater difficulty.

Home's ostensible medial talents ranged over virtually every kind of psychical phenomena known, with new powers appearing as the months went by: spirit voices, trance mediumship, raps ("percussive sounds," as William Crookes would call them later), as well as physical phenomena not matched by other mediums such as levitations, both in the dark and in half-light. He exhibited the ability to alter the weights of objects, to make musical instruments play without being touched, to handle red-hot coals without harm. It seemed there was no end to it all. Home would also be quick to denounce as a fraud any medium who claimed any powers which Home did not exhibit — or who appeared to be arousing of interest among his titled clients.

Home would further enhance his reputation by describing to loyal followers his remarkable experiences in other generally fictional séances. His supporters would then, with some embellishment, recite them to still others oftentimes with their claiming to have been sitters themselves in the imagined séances.[4]

With his remarkable physical phenomena, D.D. Home appeared to be the perfect tool for Crookes' scientific evaluation of psychical phenomena. The scientist wanted to publicly focus only on physical phenomena as only they were conducive to unambiguous measurements. If something moved, then how far? From where to where? Could anything or anyone have touched it? While much of the dark room séance experience could be, and frequently was, attributed to hysteria, hallucination and suggestion, physical events could be measured, and those measurements presented to an orthodox scientific audience for objective evaluation — and, perhaps, duplication by other scientists in other laboratories, a basic requirement for confirming any new scientific discovery.

And there was one other element that appeared to separate D.D. Home from most other mediums: light. Though he would engage generally in dark room séances, many of Home's most celebrated séances were claimed to have been presented in partial darkness or, on a few occasions, in full light. But "light" as Home and his followers would describe would often amount to only one or two candles, perhaps augmented by the glow from a fireplace or by light coming through a window. Home would adjust the lighting to accommodate the evening's events — with no objections from the sitters.

Characteristically, Home himself would write later in 1877 after his retirement:

> "Light!" was the dying cry of Goethe. "Light" should be the demand of every Spiritualist; it is the single test necessary, and it is the test which can and must be given. By no other tests are scientific inquirers to be con-

vinced. Where there is darkness there is the possibility of imposture, and the certainty of suspicion.[5]

Virtually all of Home's recorded séances were given late in the evening, generally after a full dinner, when the sitters would be fatigued and consequently less observant. Home, like all successful mediums, relied on dulling the sitters' clarity of observation to help facilitate any manipulations necessary.

The medium's apparent willingness to accommodate the test conditions of investigators, the Spiritualists vehemently argued, provided only further proof of Daniel Home's *bone fides*— and he, as they were quick to assert, did it all without charging a cent in fees. And, the believers further insisted, D. D. Home had never been publicly exposed — which was certainly true, as Home never gave public séances.

So, it was to Daniel Dunglas Home that William Crookes turned for his initial rigorous scientific examination of the spirit world.

To increase the probability of experiencing phenomena, Crookes' approach to testing mediums had quickly evolved into putting the sensitives at their ease, guaranteeing that they knew there would be no surprises or tricks played on them — even having them for dinner, the dining room being later converted into a séance room. Home quickly became the comfortable Dan to his host and hostess, Willie and Ellen.

When Home arrived at 20 Mornington Road for the first of the planned investigations, the evening of May 31, 1871, the medium knew what awaited him, and most certainly, he was well prepared to deliver the wonders sought by the scientist.

Crookes made his first public report in the *Quarterly Journal of Science* (*QJS*):

> Among the remarkable phenomena which occur under Mr. Home's influence, the most striking, as well as the most easily tested with scientific accuracy, are — (1) the alteration in the weight of bodies, and (2) the playing of tunes upon musical instruments (generally an accordion for convenience of portability) without direct human intervention, under conditions rendering contact or connection with the keys impossible. Not until I had witnessed these facts some half-dozen times, and scrutinized them with all of the critical acumen I possess, did I become convinced of their objective reality.[6]

Crookes further described the experimental conditions for his readers: the meetings took place in the evening (9:15), in a large room lighted by gas. The scientist then described the accordion, emphasizing that he had just purchased the instrument at Wheatstone's shop on Conduit Street, and that Home had never seen it before. Crookes and Charles H. Gimingham, his laboratory assistant, had built a cage of two wooden hoops wrapped with 50 yards of insulated copper wire to enclose the accordion leaving open meshes of only 2 inches by 1 inch high, too small to allow a hand to be thrust through. It was constructed to fit under the Crookes dining room table but too high to enable a hand to be easily put down into the center of the cage, and equally to prevent a foot being pushed underneath it. The wires ran to two Groves batteries in another room, so that the mesh could be electrified if necessary to determine if that had any effect on the phenomenon.

Crookes includes in his write-up additional multiple details of the experimental setup, such as the temperature of the room (68°–70° F), the weight of the dining room table (140 pounds), and so on, to suggest a "scientific" thoroughness, possibly to ward off later criticism, though many of the recorded observations were irrelevant. It could, however, be fairly argued that he included such data as he could not be sure what elements might prove germane to the subsequent understanding of the experiment.

In his public report, Crookes does not name the other observers present that evening, but they were astronomer William Huggins, Serjeant-at-Law Edward W. Cox, Crookes' brother, Walter, and Charles Gimingham. Crookes' report gives the impression that only scientific observers were present, and only male observers at that. Crookes does not mention the four women who were also present, and most importantly, he does not mention that instructions were given the group either through Home's altered spirit voice, or through spirit raps on the dining table around which they all sat—instructions that were never challenged.[7]

Consequently, instead of the well-prepared scientist, William Crookes, officiating at a set of carefully planned scientific experiments, as his public report strongly implied, it was Daniel Home via the spirit presence who largely directed the proceedings.

The rapped spirit messages were spelled out, one letter at a time, by someone pointing at a printed alphabet card and the spirit rapping when the correct letter was touched — the same tedious communication technique used by the spirits of Mrs. Maria B. Hayden nineteen years earlier. Home often would not wait for the entire message to be spelled out. After two or three letters were identified, he would declare the meaning of the message to which the spirits would happily rap their agreement.

The presence of the spirits was not mentioned at all in the *QJS* article, as that would have detracted from Crookes' scientific staging, reducing his investigative account to just one more séance report. The presence of the spirits and the women in the sittings with Home were not revealed until 1889, when Crookes published *Notes of Séances with D. D. Home*.[8]

In the *QJS* article, Crookes continued to explain his experimental setting:

3. Crookes and D.D. Home

Before Mr. Home entered the room, the apparatus had been arranged in position, and he had not even the object of some parts of it explained before sitting down. It may, perhaps, be worthwhile to add, for the purpose of anticipating some critical remarks that are likely to be made, that in the afternoon I called for Mr. Home at his apartments, and when there he suggested that, as he had to change his dress, perhaps I should not object to continue our conversation in his bedroom. I am, therefore, enabled to say positively, that no machinery, apparatus, or contrivance of any sort was secreted about his person.

Crookes does not inform the *QJS* reader of Home's prior history with the accordion manifestation. The medium first presented the accordion effect in England in the summer of 1855 at a séance held in Ealing at the home of wealthy solicitor John S. Rymers, with whose family Home was staying. The Rymers were ardent Spiritualists.

Present at the séance were Robert and Elizabeth Barrett Browning. Described by a friend as "great upon mysticism," Elizabeth had been particularly eager for an invitation. She found Home to be of an unreliable nature,

D.D. Home at the Crookes accordion. *Quarterly Journal of Science*, Vol. 8, July 1, 1871.

"weak as a reed and more vulgar." Though disliking the man, Elizabeth firmly believed Home's phenomena to be "above Nature." Writing in a letter to her sister, Henrietta, a few weeks later, she said: "To me it was wonderful and conclusive; and I believe that the medium present was no more *responsible* [emphasis in the original] for the things said and done, then I myself was."[9]

Robert, however, found Home personally and the medium's display to be disgusting, later writing: "On the whole I think the whole performance most clumsy, and unworthy anybody setting up for a 'medium.'" Browning then commented on "Mr. H's loose clothes & sack-like *paletot* & and inordinate sleeves ... which should convey some half a dozen strings & no more, to his breast [to manipulate the false hands which Browning thought he saw exhibited during the séance] just as he did, and easily. There are probably fifty more ingenious methods at the service of every 'presdigitateur.'" At one point of Robert's description of the séance, he noted: "Then Mr. Home took an accordion with one hand, held it below the table, and sounds were produced and several tunes played — on it, I suppose, — but how it is difficult to imagine — (there was light in the room for this experiment)."[10]

Thus, by the time of the Crookes investigation, Home had been performing the accordion feat for over fifteen years under various conditions, but always within the medium's control. Browning's grudging of "on it, I suppose" raises the question of whether the sounds and tunes actually came from the accordion itself, or from something nearby simulating an accordion sound. The tunes played by the spirits over the years were usually two: "Home Sweet Home" and "The Last Rose of Summer," both one-octave songs, though at one séance the accordion played the familiar song "Ye Banks and Braes," at the request of Edward Cox.

Crookes continued his public report in *QJS*:

> Mr. Home took the accordion between the thumb and middle finger of one hand at the opposite end to the keys. The cage was then pushed under the table as far as Home's arm would permit, at which point some sounds were heard and "finally some notes were played in succession...." Mr. Home still holding the accordion in the usual manner (one hand at the top) in the cage, his feet being held by those next to him, and his other hand resting on the table, we heard distinct and separate notes sounded in succession, and then a simple air was played (Home Sweet Home).

Observers looked under the table to report that Home's hand had not moved from the top of the instrument, and that the bellows of the accordion were inflating and deflating.

Crookes then had Gimingham connect the batteries, but the electrical current did not appear to have any impact on the accordion's movements or the sounds.

Finally, Crookes wrote with Home still holding the accordion at the top with the keys on the bottom against the floor,

> [The accordion] then commenced to play, at first, chords and runs, and afterwards a well-known sweet and plaintive melody, which it executed perfectly in a very beautiful manner. Whilst this tune was being played, I grasped Mr. Home's arm, below the elbow, and gently slid my hand down it until I touched the top of the accordion. He was not moving a muscle. His other hand was on the table, visible to all, and his feet were under the feet of those next to him.

The notes published in 1889 for this séance revealed that, incredibly, Crookes had been reading to the observers from Lord Dunraven's introduction to Lord Adare's recently published book on Adare's experiences with Home at the same time that Home was replacing his hand in the cage. The tune played, "Home Sweet Home," ceased the moment that Crookes touched Home's hand. When one of the women extolled the beauty of the playing, the spirits rapped out, "Minus one note, broken. Accident." The company sat silently for a few moments until the spirits spoke again, "We are unable to do more."

At which point, the scientific experiment was concluded.

In Crookes' considered opinion the accordion manifestation had been completed with "striking results"—and had been a genuine display of Home's supernormal powers—but not of the spirits. Attributing these results, and others, to the spirits would have required proofs beyond the established experimental boundaries. A "Psychic Force" could be legitimately postulated, assuming no fraud, under the experimental conditions described. However, given Home's performing experience with accordions over the previous fifteen years, the experiment would have been more remarkable if nothing had happened.

Crookes then turned to the board and balance spring apparatus. As Crookes explained in his *QJS* report, he had previously witnessed Home's altering the weight of objects without contact on several occasions. The scientist described his experimental set-up:

> In another part of the room an apparatus was fitted up for experimenting on the alteration in the weight of a body. It consisted of a mahogany board, 36 inches long by 9½ inches wide and 1 inch thick. At each end a strip of mahogany 1½ inches wide was screwed on, forming feet. One end of the board rested on a firm table, whilst the other end was supported by a spring balance hanging from a substantial tripod stand. The balance was fitted with a self-registering index, in such a manner that it would record the maximum weight indicated by the pointer. The apparatus was adjusted so that the mahogany board was horizontal, its foot resting flat on the support. In this position its weight was 3 lbs., as marked by the pointer of the

balance. Having met with such striking results in the experiments with the accordion in the cage we turned to the balance apparatus already described. Mr. Home placed the tips of his fingers lightly on the extreme end of the mahogany board which was resting on the support, whilst Dr. Huggins, and myself sat, one on each side of it, watching for any effect which might be produced. Almost immediately the pointer of the balance was seen to descend. After a few seconds it rose again. This movement was repeated several times, as if by successive waves of the Psychic Force. The end of the board was observed to oscillate slowly up and down during the experiment.

Mr. Home now of his own accord took a small hand-bell and a little card match-box, which happened to be near, and placed one under each hand, to satisfy us, as he said, that he was not producing the downward pressure. The very slow oscillation of the spring balance became more marked, and Dr. Huggins, watching the index, said he saw it descend to 6½ lbs. The normal weight of the board as so suspended being 3 lbs., the additional downward pull was therefore 3½ lbs. On looking immediately afterwards at the automatic register, we saw that the index had at one time descended as low as 9 lbs., showing a maximum pull of 6 lbs. upon a board whose normal weight was 3 lbs.

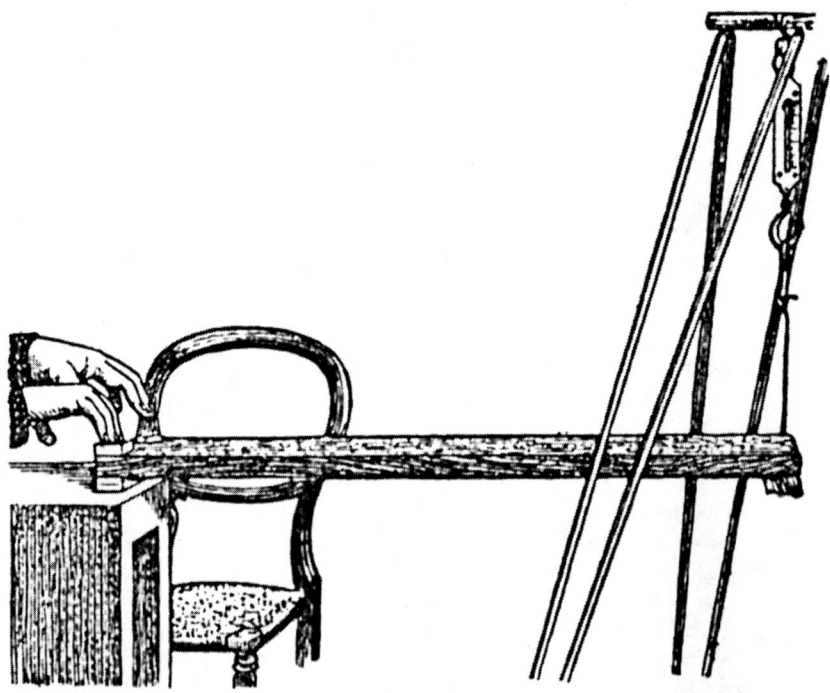

D.D. Home's fingers on the Crookes Spring Balance Apparatus, *Quarterly Journal of Science*, Vol. 8, July 1, 1871.

3. Crookes and D. D. Home

Determined to see if any weight placed at the point where Home's fingers had been could move the index, Crookes climbed onto the table and stood with one foot on the end of the board. Huggins, watching the index, reported that Crookes' 140 lbs. pressed down on the board at the fulcrum caused the index to descend only 1½ lbs. or 2 lbs as the scientist jerked up and down.

Crookes felt that the results of the balance test were even more striking "if possible" than the results for the accordion. The following day he wrote up his report, and sent copies to Cox and Huggins for their comments.

Cox, responding to Crookes on June 8, 1871, felt the two experiments had proven the presence of a "force proceeding from the nerve-system capable of imparting motion and weight to solid bodies within the sphere of its influence." He further noted that the force "was exhibited in tremulous pulsations and not in the form of steady continuous pressure, the indicator rising and falling incessantly throughout the experiment."

Cox added in conclusion: "I venture to suggest that the force be termed the *Psychic Force*; the persons in whom it is manifested in extraordinary powers *Psychics*; and the science relating to it *Psychism*, as being a branch of *Psychology*."

William Huggins, however, writing on June 9, 1871, was much more reserved. While confirming that Crookes' description of the two experiments was correct, he also stated, "I wish it to be understood that I express no opinion as to the cause of the phenomena which took place."

The scientific and public response to Crookes' article in the *QJS* was, for the most part, disbelief, while within the Spiritualist community there was qualified joy. The scientist had proven the existence of physical phenomena under apparently rigorous conditions in the presence of scientific witnesses, which the Spiritualists celebrated; but he had attributed the power behind the manifestations not to the spirits but to something called a Psychic Force, which Crookes had suggested was a natural human capability. The Spiritualists got the endorsement they wanted, but had to give up their spirits in order to embrace it!

Writing again in the *QJS*, October 1, 1871, on "Some Further Experiments on Psychic Force," Crookes responded to the wave of criticism and even ridicule while detailing further similar experiments with Home. Criticism appeared even from America, in the *Journal of the Franklin Institute,* where Coleman Sellers questioned, among other things, the mahogany board and asked, "Did Mr. Crookes make this board himself, or did Mr. Home furnish it as one of his pieces of apparatus?"

In response, Crookes wrote with some asperity in the October *QJS* article:

> But is it seriously expected that I should answer such a question as "Did Mr. Home furnish the board?" Will not my critics give me credit for the

possession of some amount of common sense? And can they not imagine that obvious precautions, which occur to them as soon as they sit down to pick holes in my experiments, are not unlikely to have also occurred to me in the course of prolonged and patient investigation?

The answer to this as to all other like objections, Prove it to be an error by showing where the error lies, or, if a trick, by showing how the trick is performed. Try the experiment fully and fairly. If then fraud be found, expose it; if it be a truth, proclaim it. This is the only scientific procedure, and this it is that I propose steadily to pursue.

So, if it all is a trick, then how did D.D. Home do it? He was never caught *during* a séance using fraud. The literature discussing Home's potential tricks and techniques is large and is primarily marked, not by demonstrations to verify the proposed method, but with speculations and plausibility statements. In the same manner, through the years most of the exposures of spirit mediums by magicians (including Houdini), and later by thought readers, were often of the same mode. Spiritual manifestations, such as those demonstrated on the stage of the Egyptian Hall by Maskelyne and Cooke, could not have survived even the most casual inspection by serious investigators, the very people that the magicians were ridiculing. Only the much later demonstrations in 1887 by the young magician S.J. Davey, to be discussed later, were actually done under legitimate séance conditions and were confirmed by the séance sitters to be genuine spiritual manifestations — after which Davey revealed his methods.

Serjeant Cox, writing later in the 1874 edition of *Mechanism of Man*, Vol. 2, p. 355, recalled in a footnote:

> Maskelyne and Cooke were invited to exhibit at a private house, and informed the enquirer that he must send a wagon and horses for two tons of machinery necessary for their *spiritual* performances [emphasis original]. [The magician] Dr. Lynn was publicly offered £1,000, if he would produce the same phenomena as [mediums] Hearne and Williams, under the same conditions, in a private room, and he declined the offer, though professing to reveal the mystery of their manifestations.

Few conjurors of the time knew magic trickery as well as barrister Angelo Lewis, who, under the name Professor Hoffmann, wrote the foundational books of late nineteenth century conjuring: *Modern Magic* (1876), *More Magic* (1889) and *Later Magic* (1904). These books are still in the libraries and on the reading lists of present day magicians, with first editions in good condition bringing serious money at auctions.

Lewis wrote in 1889:

> The item to which I attach most importance is Mr. Crookes' experiment of the board and spring-balance. Had the apparatus been devised and con-

structed by Home himself the experiment would have had very little value, but as described (and putting aside the hypotheses of untruthfulness or hallucination of Mr. Crookes) it seems to me to be distinctly outside the range of trick and, therefore, to be good evidence, so far as we can trust personal testimony at all, of Home's possession of some special power of producing motion, without contact, in inanimate objects. This does not, of course, involve the admission of his Spiritualistic hypothesis. Possibly a series of sufficiently delicate tests would show that the operative force (whatever it may be) is common to all persons in a greater or less degree.[11]

But then the inner ambition of all magicians, even of the rankest amateur, is to fool other magicians. Consequently the confident assurance by one magician that an observed effect cannot be a trick cannot always be accepted as confirmation — only as evidence that the specific magician couldn't detect the method. After all, knowing card tricks and stage illusions does not mean the conjuror understands the techniques of the medium. For example, the prominent American illusionist Harry Kellar, while appearing in Calcutta in 1882, admitted he had been baffled by the mediumistic effects and levitation of the English medium William Eglinton.[12] Eglinton was exposed as a fraud several years later.

The only valid confirmation of fraud, one way or the other, is through an actual demonstration by the critic under identical test conditions, which was the point made by Alfred Russel Wallace in challenging Dr. William B. Carpenter's cynical criticisms of the Crookes 1875 galvanometer tests with the American medium Annie Eva Fay, to be discussed later.

"I venture to think," wrote Wallace:

> that ... all men of science will agree with me that Dr. Carpenter is bound to *prove by direct experiment* [emphasis original] that Mr. Crookes and his coadjutors were the victims of imposture on the particular occasion referred to; or if he fails to do this, that he should in common fairness publicly withdraw the injurious accusations he has made against Mr. Crookes and all who are engaged in similar investigations. If this is not done it is equivalent to deciding that no *possible* proof of such phenomena is admissible — a position which is not that of Dr. Carpenter, or, as far as I am aware, of the scientific world generally.[13]

To which Carpenter promptly responded:

> The fundamental difference between Mr. Wallace and myself as to the validity of testimony in regard to the "occult" comes out so strongly in this case that we have really no common ground for a discussion which I cannot consider it profitable to continue.[14]

Carpenter simply walked away from the debate, arrogantly dismissing the honest point made by Wallace.

But just looking at the board and the accordion tests, how might they have been done? Note that Home never allowed Crookes to sit next to him, and Crookes was often preoccupied in writing notes of the séance. Frank Podmore, after noting Crookes' confident assertion that Home could not have hidden any gimmicks or tools on him as Crookes had watched the medium get dressed, wrote in 1910:

> But what was there to prevent Home's slipping into the pocket of his overcoat a small music box, a loop of black thread, and a hook with a sharp end? No further "apparatus" would be required.[15]

While Podmore was probably correct regarding Home's overcoat, the sounds heard in the séance were those of an accordion, not of a music box. So, how then? The usual explanation[16] has been that Home had a one-octave harmonica in his mouth, concealed by his heavy mustache, with which he could play the usual two songs and approximate others, while providing accordion-sounding noises. However, no such one-octave harmonicas are in the Home collection[17] of the Society for Psychical Research.

In the balance test, as Podmore suggested, Home could have used a black thread to pull down the board when the scientists weren't looking, then just let it fall to the floor unobserved. Given Home's overriding control of the proceedings via the spirits, that could have been possible, but unlikely. I asked a world-renowned professional mentalist how he would have done it, in Home's situation. His answer was one word: "resin." With resin on his fingertips, Home could have *lifted* the board a fraction of an inch, causing the pulsations observed by Cox, and with proper synchronized timing, the pulsations could become larger, pushing the index from 3 lbs. to some larger number. The apparent weight increases were always momentary, never sustained; consequently Home only had to nudge the index to convince the scientists that a new force was being displayed.

The thinking of Crookes, Cox and Huggins was narrowly focused only on how much *downward* pressure Home would have had to exert in order to create the movements recorded by the index of the spring balance. In the October *QJS* article, Crookes calculated such movements would have required a downward pressure of 74.5 lbs, which would have been impossible under the conditions in the séance room.

Throughout the period of the Thought Reader Craze, approximately 1870–1909, in their search for confirmation of the preternatural or supernatural, or of the presence of disembodied spirits, scientists would accept *any* departure from the normal as evidence of some non-normal occurrence. Crookes' conclusion on the balance experiment would have been the same if the index had depressed to only 3½ lbs. rather than 6 lbs. That the index of the spring balance changed *at all*, under the apparent test conditions, was all he was looking for. He would build his theory from whatever he observed. That mind-set would continue, not just for Crookes, but for other scientists using non-scientific methods in their search for new forces and for evidence of thought transference. Frederic Wickes' insightful observation in 1907 held true: When the call for scientific investigation was responded to, the method by which it was carried on was usually unscientific, although associated with scientific principles and conducted by scientific men.

Home's knowledge of sitter and séance control, along with his innate grasp of the techniques of showmanship, made him more than a match for any scientists who had crossed the enchanted boundary. He knew exactly what Crookes and others were yearning to confirm, and so built credibility with his apparent openness and support for their search by suggesting experimental changes, apparently tightening the conditions to ensure sound data. Scientific affirmation only served to open yet more useful doors to wealthy patrons.

In the end, perhaps Home's greatest problem may have been keeping from laughing at the "rigorous scientific precautions" presented so earnestly to him.

4

The First Thought Reader

> "...a new revelation to physiologists as well as to the scientific world in general."
> — George M. Beard, M.D., 1877

In England, with the retirement of D. D. Home in 1872 because of medical problems, William Crookes continued his psychical investigation into the phenomena of Florence Cook, Annie Eva Fay, and other mediums, an investigation which would continue through 1875.

Meanwhile in America, a new phenomenon was being observed under not quite scientific conditions — in the amazing demonstrations by twenty-two-year-old John Randall Brown, in a Chicago drinking establishment on Monday morning, August 5, 1873. (Though Jacob is suggested in some sources as his birth name, Brown used John predominately throughout his career.)

Brown was born near St. Louis, Missouri, October 28, 1851. His father, William Brown, was an engineer who worked in a machine shop but harbored ambitions to own and run his own shop. When J. Randall Brown was about two, his family moved to Muscatine, Iowa.

In public school in Muscatine, Brown discovered that he had an uncanny talent for finding hidden objects with his eyes closed, so long as he held, pressed against his forehead, the hand of the schoolmate who had hidden the object. Without asking any questions, with his eyes closed, or using a blindfold, Brown could invariably find the hidden object in only a minute or two. As a result, he created a local stir, with many speculations about what kind of powers the young student's capability implied. The Spiritualist movement was only three years old when Brown was born and by the time he entered school, the thriving movement had already spread rapidly across America.

On August 2, 1873, J. Randall Brown, accompanied by one of his former teachers, M. R. Kelly, traveled to Chicago to buy equipment for the machine shop business that Brown owned with his brother, Vincent, in Red Oak,

4. The First Thought Reader

Iowa. William Brown had died a few years earlier and the two brothers had taken over the family business.

J. Randall Brown became the first person to publicly perform a one-man thought reading act on Monday morning, August 5, 1873, in a saloon when Kelly urged Brown to demonstrate his strange skills that Kelly had personally witnessed years earlier in the Muscatine school. The implication is that Brown had continued to demonstrate his powers for years after leaving school.

After he had first been taken into a back room while various objects were hidden somewhere in the saloon, Randall Brown, first blindfolded with folded handkerchiefs, was led out into the saloon. Then, using a reporter as his initial subject, Brown swiftly located the hidden objects without questions or promptings. He only held the reporter's left hand pressed against his forehead, and it appeared to the early morning audience that he was dragging the reporter behind him, not waiting for the subject to lead him.

Brown repeated the demonstration with others in the saloon and using other hidden objects, as the drinking at the bar had completely stopped, with some observers standing at the bar wondering if what they were experiencing was due to the beer rather than to Brown.

Astonished by Brown's mysterious powers, the several Chicago newsmen at the tavern enthusiastically wrote up their experiences, referring to J. Randall

"He takes your hand and reads your thoughts." J. Randall Brown Poster, ca. 1874. Courtesy Harry Ransom Center, University of Texas. (The Brown poster image was based on a sketch that first appeared in the July 10, 1874 issue of the New York *Daily Graphic*.)

Brown as the "Red Oak Wonder," or "The Great What-is-it?" In their articles, the reporters urged Brown to give a public demonstration of his enigmatic powers.

As a result of the widespread newspaper publicity, Brown gave the first professional performance of thought reading at the Union Park Congregational Church, 1613 West Washington Boulevard, Chicago, on Saturday evening, August 11. The church had been extensively rebuilt in 1871 following a major fire.

The reconstructed meeting hall, with a seating capacity of 2,000 including balconies, was packed at 50¢ a ticket (the equivalent of $8 a ticket in 2010). Responding to the intense interest, Brown repeated his performance at the same location three days later, on August 14, again to a packed house.

In the midst of a national recession — the Great Financial Panic of 1873 — and after deducting printing and rental costs, Brown had collected the equivalent of three years' average wages[1] for a working man in less than three hours!

J. Randall Brown was no fool, and by January 1874, he had withdrawn from the family machine shop business to become a professional performer.

At the urging of friends, Brown and his remarkable powers were first examined at the Rush Medical College in Chicago; then by Dr. Crocker, professor of mental science, at the University of Michigan. Crocker announced, "Only a hint can be given as to what is the true hypothesis. A few of the cases he (Brown) gives are instances of imageal representations of concrete objects in space ... so that Mr. Brown really sees through the brain and eyes of another." Dr. Crocker's statements were subsequently incorporated into the thought reader's flyers and handbills.

As Brown traveled and performed through the midsection of the country, individual physicians at various towns also examined the young man from Red Oak. The news from each such testing only added to public interest in his celebrated powers of thought reading, whatever the source of those powers might be.

No one seemed to know.

Standing 5' 10" and 150 pounds, Randall Brown was typically described in the newspaper notices and reviews along the lines offered by one correspondent: "A handsome fellow, blue-eyed, brown-haired, medium figure, a tasteful chooser of wearing apparel and an interesting conversationalist — with a mysterious air."

Brown's talents as a showman became readily apparent almost from that first show at the Chicago church. Within a few weeks, he had developed the basic techniques of promotion he would use the rest of his professional career. First, on entering a new town, he would contact prominent citizens and do a private demonstration, with the press invited as witnesses. Brown had quickly discovered that local endorsements of his powers carried greater public weight than anything attested to by outside individuals, regardless of their exalted positions. He would ask the local group to then extend a public invitation to him to demonstrate his powers, to which he would promptly and publicly respond. Though the invitation to perform would be published in less than a third of the situations, what invitations did appear would be quoted in future handbills.

Brown styled himself as a scientific lecturer and investigator, not as a performer or entertainer. This fitted Brown's unemotional, professorial style of performance and also allowed him to present thought reading on Sundays without competition, as Sunday Blue laws in many locales prohibited public entertainments.

J. Randall Brown, Thought Reading. Courtesy collection of William V. Rauscher.

With his act now honed and the details of his routines worked out, Brown was looking for larger markets with greater financial potential. In June 1874, he quit the small town Midwest for New York City. He took rooms at Leland's Sturtevant House, a hotel on Broadway between 24th and 25th streets. It was a centrally located hostelry noted for its style and elegance, and its prominent visitors.

The Red Oak machinist turned promoter had quickly recognized in his Midwest travels that he could not draw the necessary prominent people to his private pre-public demonstrations except at a major hotel that suggested that he, J. Randall Brown, was also of serious importance. Brown first demonstrated his powers in New York City on Friday afternoon, July 3, 1874, in his rooms at Leland's Sturtevant House.

A long article called "Spiritualism Outdone" appeared in the *New York Times*[2] the following day. The unidentified reporter observed: "Mr. Brown is possessed of powers which would have made Anton Mesmer delight to make his acquaintance. He can, certain conditions complied with, read your thoughts however much you may endeavor to conceal them."

Brown explained to the men gathered in the room around him that he needed "a certain amount of machinery," which consisted of letters of the alphabet printed on pieces of pasteboard and "a long piece of brass wire." But he didn't have the wire at the time. While the observers patiently waited, he fastened the letters along the walls of the parlor.

Brown asked that while he was blindfolded, one of the men present take any object and hide it somewhere within the Sturtevant House. Upon the man's return, Brown said, he would find the object by reading the man's mind.

When the man returned, Brown passed his hands several times over the man's arm and across his forehead. Then, taking the man's left hand with his right, Brown led, or rather pulled, the man through the halls of the hotel, through groups of other visitors and hotel tenants, as the other observers trailed behind. The thought reader went into, then back out of, a half-dozen different rooms until finally he stopped in a room. He walked up firmly and stopped before a bureau of drawers. "You will find it there," the thought reader said, indicating one of the drawers. To the utter astonishment of the gathered crowd which now included a number of other hotel guests as well as the original group, the hidden object, a pocket knife, was found in the drawer.

The man involved was astonished as he explained that the course that Brown had taken through the hotel was exactly the same that he had taken in deciding where to hide the knife.

In the next test, another man went into an adjacent room and selected a design on one of the three damask curtains. Blindfolded as before and with the subject's left hand in his right, Brown went immediately to one of the curtains, hesitated over a tassel, then placed his finger on the selected rosette. The subject explained that he had, in fact, first thought of the tassel, but had changed his mind to the rosette.

Lewis Leland, general manager of the Sturtevant House, then asked

J. R. Brown divining thoughts using letters hung on the wall, 1874. Courtesy Collection of William V. Rauscher.

4. The First Thought Reader 43

Brown to name his birthplace. Blindfolded and holding Leland's left hand, Brown passed his free hand over the letters strung along a wall of the room. Within only a few moments, Randall Brown spelled out "Langrove," the village in Vermont where Leland had been born.

A *Times* reporter present asked Brown for the Christian name of his brother who had drowned some months past. Brown spelled out "George," which was correct. Another asked for the name of a town in Turkey where he had been born, which Brown spelled as "Abeib." The subject stated that it was wrong by one letter — then admitted that he had forgotten the letter himself when he had been concentrating on the town.

Other observers then asked for names and places that Brown could not have known, with the thought reader successfully spelling out each challenge.

Explaining that he did not always need to have direct contact, Brown then demonstrated what later came to be called the "double test," in which a disinterested third party who knew nothing of the challenge was placed between the subject and the thought reader.[3] The intermediate neutral person placed one hand against Brown's forehead while the subject held the wrist of the other hand. The three then moved around the room, successfully finding objects or spelling out words. The subject and the third party were changed as all the men present participated. Brown was consistently successful.

Finally, a *Times* reporter called on Lewis Leland to be the third neutral party, then asked Brown if he could alter the style of the challenge. Without hesitation, the thought reader agreed.

As Brown led the three of them toward the door to the room, the thought reader stopped as though unsure. The reporter, believing that the scent had been lost, then concentrated first on one thought-of object, then immediately shifted his mind to another, with Brown quickly leading them to the next object, and then the next. Finally, the reporter made a "violent effort" to focus on the original object, the metallic tag attached to the key in the door lock, which he had allowed to drift from his mind at the beginning of the test. Brown at once led the reporter to it.

The *Times* reporter stated that he was satisfied that Brown was in fact reading his private thoughts as the workings of his mind dictated. Brown, in his view, was the real thing — a genuine mind reader.

In response to a reporter's question, Brown said that he was ignorant of the cause of "his wonderful power," but was certain that Spiritualism had nothing to do with it, and that the thought reader regarded "all professional spiritualists as humbugs."

Then the reporter explained: "In the experiments yesterday, he [Brown] was obliged to lead those making tests around the room by the hand. If provided with a long brass wire, the person testing his power could take hold of one end of the wire and remain in his chair, as the thought reader carried out tasks in the mind of the sitter. Brown stated that he is not infallible, however, in the use of the wire, and prefers to hold the hand."

Even then the reporter commented: "It does not appear that Mr. Brown's gift can be made very useful, although he says that by means of it he has discovered the guilt of several criminals in the West. He says also that he is able to sometimes read the thoughts of others sitting near him, but cannot remember them for any length of time."

J. Randall Brown said, in closing his exhibition, that in the course of time and practice, he hoped to be able to "express the thoughts of others without the use of the alphabet cards."

Given the complexity and high degree of success of the demonstrations, it is remarkable that John Randall Brown had attained such performing skill and self-confidence in less than six months of public performances. How he came to develop the double test as one of his effects is unknown.

One of the men observing Brown's demonstration at the Sturtevant House was Dr. George Miller Beard, a graduate of Yale and a pioneering physiologist. With better reason than anyone else present, Beard was more astounded than the others by what he had just witnessed.

Beard understood from his studies of past scientific investigations and his own experiments that the mind could act on the body to produce unconscious muscular motion in a very limited way, but, he had found, principally only in women and only in some general way.

But in witnessing "Brown's brilliantly successful demonstrations of his skill" Beard acknowledged that it was "a new revelation to physiologists as well as to the scientific world in general."

Brown became a sensation, with appearances at generally full theatres in towns surrounding New York City. The uproar was favorably fueled in the newspapers by the controversy ignited by Beard's public insistence that Brown's thought reading was in fact a physical phenomenon, not a mental one.

Beard adamantly insisted that thoughts could not be "read" by Brown but only uncovered by the performer through his detecting and responding to unconscious physical clues to direction and location.

To refute Beard's statements that physical contact was a necessary condition, Randall Brown responded with demonstrations using the double test, as well as walking sticks or long pieces of wire to separate him from the subject—and, on a few occasions, no contact at all, with his hands close to but not contacting the subject at any time.

Naturally, not all demonstrations were successful, but that only undergirded the public's perceived genuineness of Brown's powers. After all, only a trickster would be successful every time. It was a perception that Dr. Beard continued to dispute.

When Brown appeared in New Haven, Connecticut, October 23, 1874, he was examined by members of the faculty of Yale University. To press their investigation beyond any possibility of trickery, the Yale investigators asked the thought reader to perform eleven experiments in which Brown had first to determine, what the experiment was to be, by reading the mind of the experimenter; and second to execute the experiment while blindfolded. Brown was successful in seven out of the eleven experiments.

The preliminary conclusion of the committee was that there was something in play in Brown's demonstrations beyond normal human sensibilities, something that the Yale professors did not fully understand.

Following the initial experiments, the Yale investigators supervised eight further experiments in which Brown, always blindfolded, held one end of a piece of copper wire, the length of which the experimenters varied from a foot or two to 210 feet, while various professors held the other end in order to put the prevailing theory of unconscious muscular action to a more rigorous test. Six of the eight experiments were completely successful with the failures equally amazing.

In one experiment that was judged a failure by the professors, Brown, holding a copper wire twenty feet long, after struggling for close to fifteen minutes, finally gave up trying to locate and identify the thought-of object. At the time of failure, Brown's hand was on a table next to the object thought of—a ball of twine. The "failure" may have been intentional, given Brown's rapidly growing skill at manipulating the public's perception.

Brown succeeded in apparently detecting thoughts where the subject, Professor Brewer, was at the end of a wire 210 feet long. The wire stretched down to the basement, then back up to the lecture room where Brewer and Brown stood within a few feet of each other. Holding the wire, Brewer thought of a hammer lying on the ledge of a blackboard in the lecture room. Within nine minutes Brown seized the hammer.

In the end, Professor Lyman's response was emphatic. "I would stake my reputation upon the genuineness of the phenomena. The theory of unconscious muscular action is entirely opposed to the facts observed."

In England in February 1875, with the D.D. Home investigation behind him, its results largely ignored by the Royal Society, William Crookes steadfastly resisted implications of perhaps sexual dalliance with young attractive mediums in dark rooms. His public endorsements and even photographs supporting the genuineness of Katie King, the full form spirit materialization of

Florence Cook, had been met with the enthusiastic cheers of the Spiritualist press and believers — but had also drawn down astonishment at what appeared in the photographs to be obvious fakes, and then unbridled scorn from the scientific community. Typically, Crookes refused to be intimidated and continued his investigation into the physical phenomena of the American medium Annie Eva Fay, called "a fascinating little blonde" by magician J. Nevil Maskelyne, and, years later, "the greatest female mystifier" by escape artist Harry Houdini.

Following an initial experiment by the electrician Cromwell Fleetwood Varley with the medium Florence Cook, Crookes designed his Fay investigation around a scientific technique utilizing a mirror-galvanometer. The key in any psychical investigation was to so physically restrain the sensitive that whatever phenomena occurred could not have been created through any efforts or tricks of the medium herself. William Crookes would not tie Annie Eva Fay with ropes, chains, or straps. Crookes would tie her with *electricity*.

# 5

The Crookes Galvanometer Tests

> "Now I am aware of no people, however refined and learned or however savage and ignorant, which does not think that signs are given of future events, and that certain persons can recognize these signs and foretell events before they occur."
> — Cicero, De Divinatione August, 45 B.C.

It was the confinement that, at the same time, was both so critical and so apparently simple. Bind, tie or restrict the spirit medium's movements, so that whatever then happens cannot have been produced by any human means; thus one confirms the medium's claimed demonstration of communication with a spirit world. But over the years clever fraudulent mediums frequently evaded every such attempt until they were in turn finally exposed by an even more clever investigator, or by their own dumb arrogance. Each exposure, however, was a painful embarrassment to the rapidly expanding Spiritualist movement and its advocates, and critically raised the personal risk to the professional reputations of the serious searchers for what seemed to be a priceless chance to pierce the veil into the unknown mysterious world beyond. There had to be a better way to ensure that a truly scientific study of the legitimacy of psychical events could be accomplished.

There had to be...

On a misty and cold Friday evening, February 19, 1875, several men gathered at 20 Mornington Road, N.W., London, the home of the prominent chemist William Crookes, to try once again to determine if the spirit world could be reached through the strange gifts of a young beautiful blonde American woman, Annie Eva Fay. Only twenty-three, Eva, as the men enjoyed calling her, had never been inside a school in her native Ohio, and her awkward scrawl was almost impossible to read, but she possessed a sharp raw intelligence coupled with a ruthless determination to survive—and Annie knew what was probably going to happen, whereas the investigating gentlemen did not. Like other successful mediums, she had learned to read her prospects far better than any man of science and industry.

Also present for the evening were Sir Francis Galton,[1] psychologist; Sir William Huggins,[2] astronomer; Serjeant-at-law Edward W. Cox,[3] barrister and experienced exposer of fraudulent mediums; C.A. Ionides, industrialist (and later client of Auguste Rodin, becoming the first to own a cast of Rodin's ionic work "The Thinker"); and finally William H. Harrison, a former electrical engineer turned editor of the newspaper, *The Spiritualist*. Galton and Huggins, along with Crookes, were fellows of the Royal Society.[4] Huggins and Crookes would later become the society's president, in 1900 and 1913, respectively. All had wide experience in the suspicious workings of spirit mediums. Crookes, in fact, later estimated that in the course of his investigations he had already sat with over a hundred mediums, most of whom had practiced some fraud at some point.

In Victorian England, a proper young woman never ventured into an evening alone. Only whores traveled alone — and Americans. A condition of the evening experiments was that Eva would arrive without her husband, Henry Fay, who, as a result of his earlier visits to Great Britain before meeting Annie, had earned a reputation of being an unscrupulous con man. His presence was uneasily tolerated by believer and unbeliever alike so that they could enjoy and examine the gifts of his beautiful young wife, who was often pitied by the older English ladies for having to live with so unprincipled a man while possessing in her own right such obvious beauty and talents.

At about eight o'clock, as agreed, Crookes and his party heard the hooves and jangling of a hansom cab pulling up outside on Mornington Road. Once the maid had taken her wrap, Annie Eva Fay was welcomed into the warm home by Mrs. Ellen Crookes. Annie was dressed in the latest style, a full-length blue satin gown with rich white lace at her wrists and neck, a gold brooch over her heart.

The medium stood only five feet tall, weighing less than a hundred pounds. Her large luminous blue eyes matched her glistening satin in the candles and gas light, and her straw-gold blonde hair was wrapped around her head with curls falling down over her right shoulder, a current style called "frizzled." Her smile was quick and engaging — and, the men noted, a bit mischievous.

More than 100 years later in 1988, Dr. Eric John Dingwall, then 92, prominent anthropologist and the last person alive to have known Annie personally, would recall for this author that while she was talking to him nothing else could intrude; her smile, eyes and bell-like voice completely enwrapped every particle of his attention. When I asked him regarding her accent, which

5. The Crookes Galvanometer Tests

some reporters had described as English, Dingwall laughed, shaking his head. "Pure Yankee!" he emphatically declared. She was sixty-two when Dingwall had last spoken with her and was still utterly captivating. Her usual expression was a barely suppressed smile, about to break out in an instant. When enthused about a subject, she would lean forward eagerly, clapping her hands, smiling widely — but not on this chilly night.

Gathering in the drawing room, everyone quietly conversed for about a quarter hour, then the gentlemen excused themselves from the ladies to go downstairs to complete the preparation of the library and laboratory — and to set up the electrical apparatus.

Crookes later wrote regarding the evening's events:

> Experience has shown that the best conditions for the production of the most striking phenomena in Mrs. Fay's mediumship are, that she should be isolated from the others present, and in darkness; therefore, in order to get manifestations under test conditions, it was necessary that the medium should be so tied that she could not be freed by herself or by any other power without the knowledge of the observers. Mrs. Fay is usually tied with tapes or string; I proposed to tie her with a current of electricity. The method has the advantage of *absolute certainty* [emphasis original], since if the medium has her hands or body removed from the wires, in a state of trance or otherwise, the galvanometer outside lets the spectators know the moment the circuit is broken. On the other hand, if the wires should be joined together so that the current can still pass, the effect is quite as surely made evident by the galvanometer.[5]

Crookes further assured his readers that the medium had known the names of only two of the men who would be present — which in his view made the events of the evening even more remarkable.

The instrument used that night was identical to that developed and used by Cromwell Fleetwood Varley, F.R.S., to check the continuity of the second telegraphic cable then being laid across the Atlantic. Incorporating a circuit somewhat different from that used by Crookes, i.e., using a series shunt rather than a parallel shunt and different contacts to the medium, Varley had already used the galvanometer to apparently confirm the legitimacy of the medial powers of Florence Cook. And Annie herself had been briefly placed in the Crookes circuit, shown below, on two previous occasions at the Crookes home February 5 and 6, but not in the presence of such a group of experienced and determined observers.

The laboratory and library were separated by a single doorway hung with a curtain, with the library to be used as the dark séance room.

Each member of the committee searched the library, put strips of paper over the fastenings of the window shutters, sealed them with wax, and marked them with their signet rings. A second door in the library that led into a corridor was also sealed in the same way. Then they turned to the electrical apparatus and circuit.

Recognizing that a medium could obviously try to beat the galvanometer through faking her presence by inserting some kind of appropriate resistance into the circuit, Galton and Huggins dipped a handkerchief into a bucket of brine, a potassium iodide solution, then tied it between the brass handles that the medium would later hold. With a series of careful adjustments, which required the help of Crookes in the laboratory giving out readings from the galvanometer, a scale deflection and resistance equivalent to a human body in the circuit was eventually achieved.

Though convinced of the impossibility of an unaided medium's succeeding in duplicating their experiment, Huggins, without first informing Crookes, nailed the brass handles to the table at the widest possible points, 24 inches apart, to ensure that they could not be moved, and that the handles would be beyond the reach of a stretched handkerchief. According to Cox, writing four years later,[6] each of the investigators in turn sat in the chair, their hands previously soaked in brine, holding the brass handles and then releasing their grip to confirm the immediate responsive action of the galvanometer in the laboratory. After about forty-five minutes of preparation, the committee called Annie Eva Fay down to the library.

Once seated before the nailed brass handles, Annie was asked to first dip her hands into the brine solution, then to grip the brass handles, each of which had been tightly wrapped with two layers of brine-soaked linen. Crookes adjusted the shunt resistance to properly center the galvanometer light for later readings, and made other adjustments in the resistance box to record Annie's initial body impedance. This would

Annie Eva Fay, ca. 1874. Courtesy: TCS 1. Harvard Theatre Collection, Houghton Library, Harvard University.

5. The Crookes Galvanometer Tests

be the number the committee would refer to in order to verify that the test conditions had not been changed, that Annie *and only Annie* was still in the circuit. Again according to Cox, with some of the investigators surrounding her and others watching the instrument, the medium was then asked to release her grip for a last check of the galvanometer action. The light immediately swept off the scale. She again seized the handles, which brought the light back to its correct central starting position.

With the hands of the medium confirmed in place, the gaslights in the library were then extinguished, except for one which was kept turned low. A small flickering coal fire still burned in the fireplace, throwing odd shadows about the room.

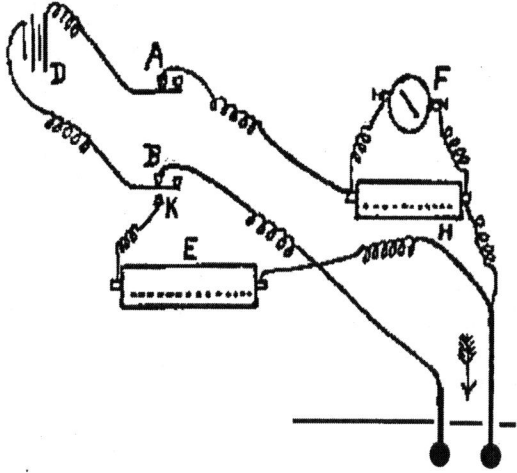

Adapted from William Crookes, "A Scientific Examination of Mrs. Fay's Mediumship," *The Spiritualist*, March 12, 1875, pp.126–28. D, battery; F, galvanometer; H, shunt to cut off more or less of the current in order to regulate the deflection of the galvanometer; E, box of resistance coils; A and B, keys to make and break contact. (A) is always closed, and is used only to correct or check zero. (B) pressed down to K, puts the resistance coils in place of the medium. The two wires on each side of the arrow go to the medium.

Before leaving the library, the committee had carefully noted the position of several prominent objects: a music box was on Crookes' desk at a distance of about four feet from the medium; a violin on a table at eight feet; a library ladder leaned against the bookshelves about twelve feet away. The table and Crookes' desk were otherwise clean, and Crookes' desk was confirmed locked.

At 8:55 P.M., each man made one last observation of the room and took one last look at Annie seated tightly gripping the handles, her eyes closed, apparently beginning to enter the trance state, her face serene. The committee then retired behind the curtained doorway into the dimly lit laboratory to watch ... and wait. Crookes took up his station at the galvanometer, preparing to record whatever might happen.

The initial deflection of the galvanometer light was 211°, and the medium's body resistance was 6,600 British Association Units (BAU).

At 8:56 a hand-bell began to ring in the library.

At 8:57 a hand came through the curtained doorway on the side farthest from the medium, a distance of three feet.

At 8:58 the deflection was 208°; at 8:59 it was 215° at which moment a voice identical with that of the medium said, "I want to give you something." A hand thrust through the curtain handing Harrison a copy of his newspaper, *The Spiritualist.*

At 9:00 the deflection was 209°. The voice said, "Serjeant, I have got something for you; come here." A hand came through the curtain to give Serjeant Cox a copy of his book, *What Am I?*

At 9:01, the voice said, "Here's something for you, astronomer." A copy of Huggins' book, *Spectrum Analysis,* was given to him by the hand appearing again.

At 9:02, the voice said, "Come here Traveler, I have a present for you." When there was hesitation among the committee, the voice repeated its request. When Galton approached the curtain, he was given a copy of his book, *Art of Travel,* with a 214° deflection recorded by Crookes.

At 9:03, Ionides asked, "Have you got nothing for me?" "Here," said the voice, "is something you will like better than a book." A box of cigarettes was thrown through the curtain onto Ionides' lap, the only guest who smoked. Crookes was shaken. He was positive that the cigarettes had been securely locked in his desk before Annie Eva Fay had entered the library.

At 9:04 a small ornamental clock, which had been standing on the mantle-piece five feet from the medium, was handed through the curtain. The deflection was 213°, and Annie's body resistance measured 6,500 BAU.

9:04:30: Cox and most of the other observers, but not Crookes who was watching the galvanometer, saw a full human form standing at the opening of the curtain.

At 9:05 the galvanometer light swept instantly across the scale — the circuit was broken!

The committee, led by Crookes, rushed into the library, one of the men turning the gaslight up full. Annie had collapsed back in the chair in a faint or a trance, her still moist hands hanging loosely, her head slumped over on her shoulder. She did not stir for almost thirty minutes.

Having quickly called up the stairs to Mrs. Crookes to minister to Annie, and while waiting for the medium to recover, the committee was startled to discover that more had been happening in the ten minutes of the séance than what they had recorded in the laboratory.

Crookes unlocked his desk to check the carton of cigarettes in one of the drawers. The pack thrown to Harrison matched the one empty space in the carton. He had no explanation for how his locked desk could have been opened in the dark.

5. The Crookes Galvanometer Tests

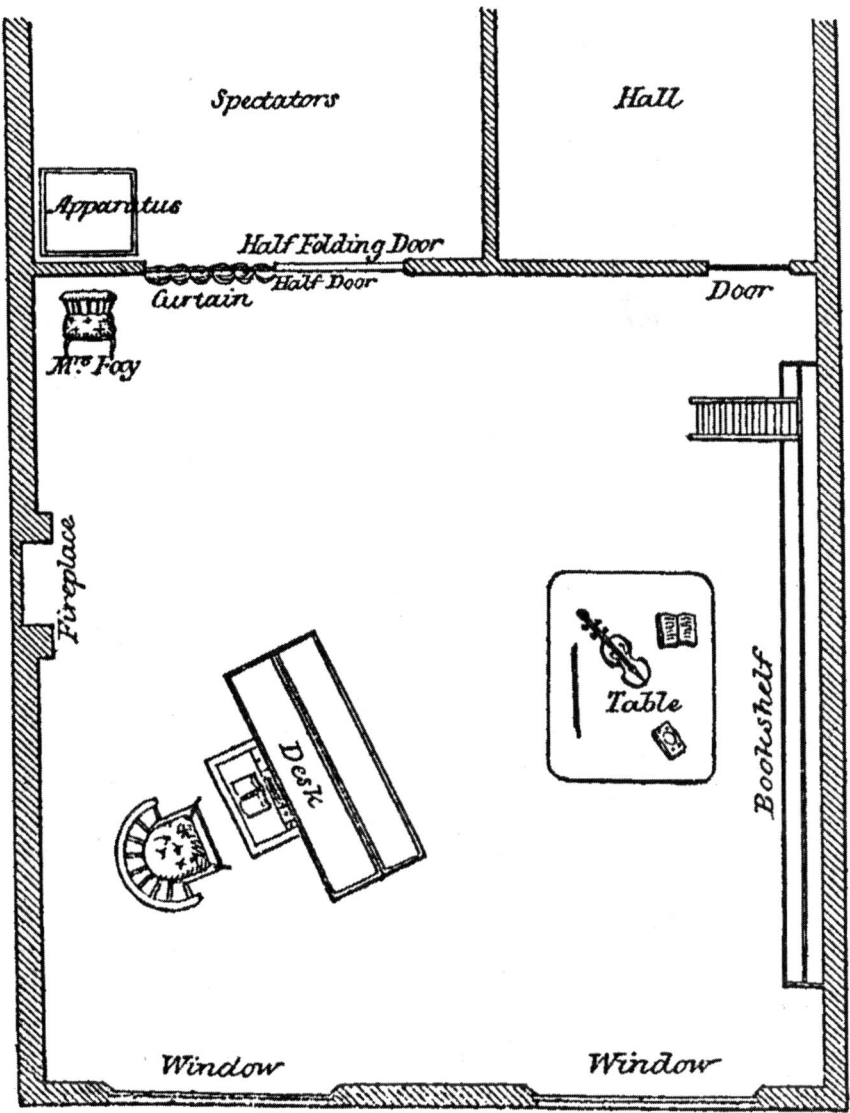

DIAGRAM OF MR. CROOKES'S LIBRARY.

Sketch of Crookes' library and laboratory taken from "A Scientific Séance — The Electrical Test for Mediumship," James Burns, *Medium and Daybreak,* March 12, 1875. A description of the final galvanometer test of Fay on the 25th of February, 1875. The artist drew the chair for Fay backwards. This séance will be discussed in more detail later.

A piece of old china in the shape of a plate was found on Crookes' writing-desk. In the drawing-room upstairs, there was a plate-rail all around the walls, about eight feet from the floor, which held several pieces of matching old china on display. Annie had never been alone in the drawing-room and no one in the family had touched the china for weeks. Galton was certain that nothing had been on the desk at the beginning of the experiment. The committee was nonplused.

Before her arriving, Crookes was certain that Annie had known the names of only two of the guests who would be present. The resultant knowledge demonstrated by the spirits of the works of all the members of the committee astonished each of the men involved. In fact, Crookes wrote in his public report that he did not know with certainty where the copy of *Spectrum Analysis*, a book without a title on the spine, was in his library, but he was certain that he could not have found it in the dark. The books in Crookes' library were organized by size, the smallest on the highest shelf, which would require the use of the ladder, which had been leaning up against the bookcase before the séance started, but was now lying on the floor. Crookes later stated that he had no reason to believe that Mrs. Fay even knew that such a book existed.

Edward W. Cox wrote in more detail later in 1879, commenting on the structure of the experiment and its results:

> The perfection of this instrument [the mirror-galvanometer] as a detector of any removal, however slight, of either hand of the person holding the handles, was vouched for, after personal trial and careful examination, by all the eminent Scientists present. They were agreed that by no means known to Science, as the machine was set, could the Psychic quit it for an instant without instant detection.

Cox then observed sardonically:

> It [the Crookes electrical experiment] was designed for the purpose of enabling the experimentalists in the one room to be assured that the Psychic did not move in the other room, entirely obviating the use of ropes and other mechanical binding, said to be inefficient, inasmuch as skill and practice are supposed to enable any person to escape from any knots however ingeniously complicated — a feat, by the bye, never yet performed by criminal prisoners, who are invariably incompetent to secure their freedom by the means said to be so easily discovered and resorted to by Psychics.

Cox then described the experience much as Crookes had earlier, until the moment that the spirit called him to the curtain. He wrote:

> I went to the curtain and received the first volume of this treatise [*The Mechanism of Man*, 1874 edition]. In doing this I separated the curtains about a foot, and there in full view stood the Psychic, or an exact duplication of her — the same satin dress, the same lace, the same long curling

5. The Crookes Galvanometer Tests 55

hair. As the book was given to me, the hand touched mine; it was warm and moist and fleshy, and the same rings were upon the fingers. Looking, I saw another form, like that we had left upon the seat, grasping the handles, still there, still in the same posture, but too much in shadow to enable me to note the dress.

After describing, as Crookes had, the astonishing results of the committee's examination of the library, Cox concluded his recall of the Crookes experiment:

Whatever the agent, it certainly was *not* a Spirit of the dead. It was undoubtedly the *living* Psychic (or a duplicate of her) we saw and spoke with. If a Spirit, it was the Spirit of the *Quick* and not of the Dead. But one query remains. Did some other *non*-human being maintain the needful contact, while she moved about? Certain it is that *no* human being did so.

The ladies waiting upstairs were silenced by the men's description of the events that had just occurred only a few feet below them. They all looked nervously up at the gap in the display of china on the molding high on the wall. Mrs. Crookes, at first, wouldn't touch the plate brought up from the library.

Annie was given tea, though something stronger was suggested by Ionides, to help her recover her strength. Once she could safely walk without assistance, a cab was called. She politely declined the offer from each of the gentlemen to escort her back to her hotel in Bloomsbury Square — she would leave alone, the way she had arrived.

Only a ten minute experience — but without any explanation. Crookes published a detailed description of the séance in *The Spiritualist*, March 12, 1875, as well as summaries published in various newspapers including London's *Daily Telegraph*— he later stated, in agreement with Cox, that no human agency could have achieved the effects observed.

Anna had faded from public memory in 1927. She was by then 76 years old, three years past her retirement as a result of breaking her ankle in a fall. At that time the reigning American psychic phenomenon was Margery, the Blonde Witch of Boston. Margery's real name was Mina Crandon, the wife of prominent Back Bay surgeon and Harvard lecturer Dr. Leroi G. Crandon. Young, attractive, intelligent, and vivacious, Margery drew international attention with her dazzling séances, sometimes given semi-nude, a novel approach which certainly leavened the intense academic investigative fervor.

However, in the final paragraph of a public summary of the then ongoing Margery investigation, a key examiner and respected colleague of Harry Houdini, Dr. Walter Franklin Prince, Research Officer of the Boston Society for Psychic Research, made the following concluding remarks:

> There is living today a lady, Anna Eva Fay, who under control apparently more exacting than any to which Margery has submitted, by greater wonders than have occurred in connection with Margery, outwitted the electrician Varley and the great scientist Crookes, who were utterly unable to conceive of any normal mode of production. Only the other day (if I may be permitted for once to speak from personal knowledge), under the most casual circumstances, she produced for me in three minutes a "phenomenon" more mysterious than anything I saw in eleven sittings with Margery.[7]

No conjurors, including J. N. Maskelyne and Houdini, have ever duplicated the Fay — Crookes galvanometer séance under the same conditions as described by William Crookes. The "exposures" given over the years by various magicians in the press and books only revealed their lack of any understanding of the actual test conditions of the Mornington Street séance.

The final galvanometer test of Annie Eva Fay on February 25, 1875, ended William Crookes' investigations into the reality of Spiritualist claims, essentially leaving unanswered the question posed by his biographer, E. E. Fournier d'Albe, "Was Crookes the founder of a new science of the supernatural, or was he an eminent physicist gone awry?"[8] (The author's description of how the February 19, 1875, Fay séance most likely was done is given in Appendix G.)

On August 1, 1874, Crookes responded to a letter from Madame Boydanof of St. Petersburg, Russia, who had inquired regarding the possibility of contacting a deceased member of her family. After a brief resume of his work the past three to four years, giving some of the names of the most prominent mediums whose manifestations he had investigated, he wrote,[9] "During this whole time I have most earnestly desired to get the one proof you seek — the proof that the dead can return and communicate. I have never once had satisfactory proof that this is the case."

Following an SPR Council Meeting in November 1895, E. T. Bennett, assistant secretary, quoted Crookes as saying that among the hundred or more mediums he had had to do with — with hardly any exceptions — all more or less at times resorted to trickery. But, Bennett noted, Crookes ridiculed the idea of doubt being thus thrown on phenomena well observed and attested under different conditions. Crookes anticipated that his mediums would try to cheat. In *The Spiritualist,* June 19, 1874, he explained, "I notice that with every new medium one or two séances only leave suspicion on the mind. It was so in the case of Home, Williams, Herne, Miss Fox, Miss Cook and Miss Showers." The prospect of trickery was always a part of Crookes' thinking and preparations.

As someone with an occult predisposition,[10] who apparently had come to believe in invisible though non-human intelligences, Crookes would still be involved in proving the existence of a psychic force, the ability to move solid objects without physical intervention by the medium or similar non-material concepts. But after almost five years of arduous, sometimes bitter industry, he still had no proof of the fundamental claim of the Spiritualists, and only suspect proof of a psychic force, largely through D.D. Home, and the galvanometer tests of Annie Eva Fay.

But it wasn't his critics, like Dr. W.B. Carpenter, who had so soured Crookes on continuing his research into psychical matters. It was the ingratitude and unreasoning mind-set of the spiritualists themselves. As he wrote in frustration to D.D. Home, November 3, 1875,[11] "I have worked hard and sacrificed more than anyone would believe for the cause of spiritualism, and I have been met with little but calumny, slander, backbiting and abuse from spiritualists," and again to Home on November 24, 1875,[12] "I am so disgusted with the whole thing that, were it not for the regard we bear to you, I would cut the whole Spiritual connection, and never read, speak, or think of the subject again."

Ellen Crookes, also writing to Home, January 11, 1876, "We have seen nobody connected with spiritualism for some time past, for we have had so much annoyance and insult from so many persons that I prefer cutting the whole set.... In my humble opinion, *if a medium is made to cheat by bad spirits* (the usual excuse) he or she ought to be avoided as much as though they were found cheating of their own will; it is nonsense to expect the public to believe such an explanation.... I hope Willie [Crookes] will keep to his resolution to keep away from public mediums and never print anything on the subject again [emphasis original]."[13]

Clearly it was time for William Crookes to fold his hand and again focus exclusively on the game he knew better than most, the mysteries of the material universe. Though he would continue to sit privately with a few mediums in his later years, and retain the friendships of even fewer, he kept to his resolution. Crookes never retracted any of his public statements regarding spiritual phenomena and the Psychic Force, and the mediums he had publicly endorsed never, at least publicly, admitted to tricking him.

6

Muscle Reading?

> "...reasoning deductively from the known relations of mind to body, I had established conclusively to my own mind that the so-called mind-reading was really muscle-reading."
> — George M. Beard, 1877

Uneasy with the Yale public endorsement of the genuine nature of the powers of J. Randall Brown, Dr. George M. Beard was quick to publicly dismiss the copper wire demonstrations as "only conjuror's tricks," but when pressed by reporters he could not provide a viable explanation for the tricks. Beard's only speculation was that a confederate must have somehow been used — a circumstance impossible under the conditions established at Yale.[1]

In an 1877 article, "Physiology of Mind-Reading," Beard, after crediting Brown with "brilliantly successful demonstrations of his skill," wrote, "...reasoning deductively from the known relations of mind to body, I had established conclusively to my own mind that the so-called mind-reading was really muscle-reading." That term is still used today, along with "contact mind reading," to describe the thought reader act.[2] Also in the article Beard admits that the conditions of Brown's performances and the integrity of the subjects "rule out at once the possibility of collusion."

In a pamphlet, *The Study of Trance, Muscle Reading and Allied Nervous Phenomena*,[3] published eight years after his experiences at the Sturtevant House and the Yale investigation, and shortly before his death in 1883, George M. Beard wrote of Brown: "For weeks this young and unknown adventurer, without education, without a history, held the American people by the nape of the neck, controlling the press as absolutely as a Napoleon or a Czar." But Beard had still publicly complimented Brown on his willingness to be tested and his positive cooperation.

At his New Haven performance, following the Yale investigation, before an audience of one thousand, which included Dr. George M. Beard, Randall Brown asked a member of the stage committee to look about and concentrate

6. Muscle Reading?

on a single person anywhere in the theatre. Blindfolded and holding one hand of the subject, the thought reader then led the committeeman on a quick tour of the hall up one aisle, across and down a second to return to the stage.

Throwing his blindfold aside and without hesitation, Brown then marched back into the audience and within seconds placed his hand on the shoulder of the thought-of person to the utter astonishment of the audience, the committee, and Dr. Beard.

Writing in 1877, Beard described his reaction:

> In a wide hall, in the presence of a large audience, where the subject had the right to think of any object he chose, Brown once found, after considerable searching, so limited an area as a capital letter in the title of a newspaper pinned up on the wall and barely within reach.... I could not believe, until the above-named experiments had been made, and frequently repeated, that it was possible for even the most expert operator to find such small objects; and no physiologist, I am sure, would have believed such precision in these experiments conceivable.

Beard had no explanation for Brown's "double test," speculating without evidence that the minute nervous tremors of the subject, to which the physiologist ascribed all the observed phenomena, were somehow transmitted directly through the intervening neutral human being to Brown — and without error.[4]

While Beard and his professional colleagues attempted to duplicate in their laboratories what they had witnessed in theatres, J. Randall Brown moved on to other venues, audiences and obstacles.

Naturally not every show went well. After his well-publicized triumphs at Yale and the New Haven theatre, Randall Brown's failures during a subsequent performance a few days later at Danielsonville, Connecticut, were remarkable in their consistency, more complete than he had ever experienced in the past. Simply put, nothing succeeded, which was largely because the local committee had read about unconscious muscular motion and had planned to try to thwart the thought reader at every turn — but short of outright cheating — if, in fact, that was the actual secret underlying Brown's remarkable phenomena.

Their study of the reports of Brown's performances had suggested concentrating on an object on the person of the thought reader himself; or on the subject's hand being held by the thought reader; or on a location at a great distance beyond the performer's knowledge. Any or all of these techniques could lead to confusion and failure on the part of the thought reader.

With the audience's loud jibes of his repeated failures ringing in his ears, J. Randall Brown finally took the hand of a committee member concentrating on a distant location and led him out of the theatre into the night, trailed by the committee and many members of the audience. Brown led his subject through the streets, across the town and finally into the lobby of a hotel. It was, the amazed committee member confirmed to the reporters and others who had followed them, the precise location that he had been thinking of.

Taking the major risk necessary to overcome the evening's failures, Brown had turned a pending public disaster into a triumph — which at the same time strongly implied that his powers were genuine. Again, the fact that J. Randall Brown, with his still limited performing experience, displayed such self-confidence and sense of showmanship is impressive — though a sense of desperation may certainly have been an element.

From Connecticut, Brown moved on to Boston to appear for two days starting January 8, 1875, at Redpath's Lyceum.

Noting that Randall Brown's manager, Mr. Pugh, was distributing a leaflet with Professor Crocker's statements on it, Professor Persifor Frazer, Jr., speaking before the Social Science Association of Philadelphia, on May 12, 1875,[5] challenged Professor Crocker's conclusion as unproven even though Frazer agreed that Brown was undoubtedly honest.

"But," Frazer insisted, "asseverations of good faith, even though supported by circumstantial evidence, can be of no value in a scientific inquiry into facts."

One of the sobriquets applied to Brown was "the human telegraph." If, Frazer reasoned, Brown could detect thoughts at the end of several feet of copper wire, could he in fact detect thoughts at the end of a telegraph copper wire running between Philadelphia and New York?

Brown with his manager met Frazer and others at the Philadelphia Western Union Office for a test to run as follows: Two "experienced operators" had cut ten slips of paper with the numbers from thirty to forty written on them. They then sent a message that requested the New York operator get ready to hold the telegraph wire in his fingers and to intently think of one of the numbers which represented his age. Everyone in the room watched Brown in silence and intense interest.

Finally a tap-tap was received indicating all was ready. J. Randall Brown, blindfolded and tightly holding the wire with both his hands, bowed his head over the table where the slips with the numbers were laid. He commenced to move slowly to and fro, at times lowering his forehead to actually touch the slips directly. Finally he pulled off the blindfold and handed a slip to one of the operators. The number was 37.

A quick request went to New York for confirmation. The answer, when it finally came, rendered the experiment a farce. It was: "Battery put on the wire by mistake. Sorry."

6. Muscle Reading?

Smiling, one of the operators commented that he didn't think they had any batteries 37 years old.

Three other attempts were made, this time between Philadelphia and Wilmington, but were all failures.

Frazer concluded his paper: "from the facts known in connection with this new form of mind reading ... there is nothing to justify the inference that the results are obtained by the agency of any unknown or occult force." A conclusion which, in effect, refuted the earlier Yale conclusions.

Scientists were agreed, however, that J. Randall Brown was genuine, but they still could not agree on just what that meant.

Though the telegraph stunt was an initial and embarrassing failure, years later Brown would return to it as he readily recognized its publicity prospects. He just had to figure a way to ensure success, which he subsequently did, as will be described later. The wire stunt became Brown's signature effect. It is interesting to note that none of the other early thought readers, including Washington Irving Bishop, Stuart Cumberland, Alfred Capper and others, ever attempted the telegraph stunt.

In October 1875, in Davenport, Iowa, J. Randall Brown participated in a bizarre competition at the home of Mrs. Bleik Peters.[6] Described by the reporter as "the daughter of a high official in the court circle of Davenport" and as middle-aged, Mrs. Peters had also demonstrated thought reading capabilities before local gatherings, but instead of holding the hand of the subject, she needed to touch the *lunar plexus*, the region between the eyes, of the subject.

In each of the competitive experiments, both Brown and Mrs. Peters succeeded. It was the joint test which caused a local commotion.

With both the lady and Brown out of the room, a piece of flagroot was placed under an upturned champagne glass on a plate; then everything was covered with a napkin. It was resolved by the observers that the test would be: Brown to remove the napkin; the lady to lift the glass; Brown to take the flagroot; and finally Mrs. Peters to lift the plate.

Recalled to the parlor, Brown, blindfolded, and the lady joined hands; then the designated subject, or transmitter, placed his fingers on the brow of the lady and took the hand of Randall Brown. After only a brief moment, the two thought readers then moved quickly, without hesitation carrying out the entire test without a mistake. The committee and reporters were stunned.

Finally, the two thought readers were placed at opposite ends of a long drawing-room with alphabet cards hanging from a wire before each thought reader. A person in the middle of the room opened a Bible at a random page and fixed his thought on a single word in a passage.

The transmitter held a copper wire connecting with Brown and extended his other hand out toward Mrs. Peters. Immediately, the two thought readers began to strike letters simultaneously to spell out the thought-of word. The test was repeated with a different man selecting another random passage from the Bible with equal success.

Mrs. Peters was never mentioned again in the press, and J. Randall Brown moved on to his next engagement. No public explanations or speculations were ever offered by observers for what they had witnessed.

7

W. I. Bishop and W. F. Barrett

> For my own part, I am inclined to believe other mental phenomena—such, for example, as the possibility of the action of one mind upon another, across space, without the intervention of the senses ... that cases of such mental action at a distance do really exist.
> —William Fletcher Barrett, Professor of Physics, Royal College of Science, Dublin, *London Times,* September 22, 1876

A major underlying problem with the performance of thought reading from its beginning was that some curious members of the audience discovered in private experimentation after the show that they too could perform some of the same stunts as those of the professional thought reader. Not as quickly, perhaps, or with the drama, or frequent remarkable successes of the professional, but the inquirer could do some of it.

A few of the curious experimenters also counted the house, as Brown himself had once done, and decided to step on the stage themselves. Within the first two to three years of Randall Brown's first public performance in Chicago, he began to encounter a growing number of variously talented competitors who mimicked with widely uneven success various elements of his routine, while sometimes even improving on Brown's own presentations.

The thrilling suggestion, even public awareness of walking at the far edge of human capability, of experiencing the scientific interest in the unknown that had so surrounded and energized Brown's early performing experience, was steadily being eroded through increasingly inept, and lower priced, repetition—except for a small young man named Bishop.

J. Randall Brown appeared only once at Chickering Hall in New York City in 1877. It was Thursday evening, February 1, 1877, before a capacity audience. In an article in the *New York Times*[1] the following day, the reporter briefly described Brown's opening remarks:

Before commencing his experiments Mr. Brown made a short address, in which he stated that he could not account for the power he possessed of divining the thoughts of other persons. He would, therefore, show what he could do without attempting to explain anything, leaving each one to draw his own conclusions. At his request a committee of eight gentlemen was appointed by the audience, to name the persons who were to assist in the performances of the experiments.

There followed Brown's successful and quick finding of a key hidden with someone in the theatre. With the applause still sounding, the thought reader just as quickly found a person in the audience only thought of by Assistant District Attorney Russell. Several other experiments followed, frequently interrupted by applause, with the *Times* reporter stating that the last test was the "most interesting."

Brown, blindfolded, walked through the audience with a member of the committee after asking the gentleman to fix his mind on one individual seated somewhere in the theatre. Making a second and then a third tour of the rustling, active crowd, some of whom began to stand to watch the movements of the thought reader, Brown returned to the stage, doffed his blindfold and walked up the aisles, "closely scanning the faces before him." He stopped before "a well-known member of the press" and, smiling, said, "This is the

---

MIND-READING.

A PSYCHOLOGICAL ENTERTAINMENT AT CHICKERING HALL—INTERESTING EXPERIMENTS BY MR. J. R. BROWN.

Mr. J. R. Brown, the mind-reader, gave an exhibition of his peculiar power at Chickering Hall last evening. Before commencing his experiments Mr. Brown made a short address, in which he stated that he could not account for the power he possessed of divining the thoughts of other persons. He would, therefore, show what he could do without attempting to explain anything, leaving each one to draw his own conclusions. At his request a committee of

New York Times, February 2, 1877.

> SPIRITUALISM AND ITS AGENCIES ON TRIAL.—IN accordance with an invitation from leading clergymen, physicians and lawyers of this city, Mr. W. Irving Bishop will give a public exhibition of the means by which many of the characteristic phenomena attributed to Spiritualism are performed, at Chickering Hall, Thursday, May 18, at 8 P. M. Introductory address by Wm. A. Hammond, M. D. Mr. G. W. Morgan will presided at the organ. Tickets can be had at Schuberth's, 23 Union square, and at Chickering Hall on the evening of the entertainment. Admission, 50 cents; reserved seats. $1.

New York Herald, Sunday, January 16, 1875.

gentleman." The committeeman on the stage loudly confirmed that Brown was correct to an explosion of applause.

A young man named Washington Irving Wellington Bishop was in the Chickering Hall audience that night. (His full name is confirmed from a letter written by his mother, Eleanor Fletcher Bishop, to President Abraham Lincoln, June 21, 1864, when Bishop was eight years old. In June 1864, Lincoln was preoccupied with the Battle of Cold Harbor where 7,000 Union soldiers were lost in 20 minutes, the last clear victory for General Lee and the Army of Northern Virginia. And the Siege of Petersburg under General U.S. Grant was just beginning. Thus, it is highly unlikely that Eleanor received any response to her letter.[2])

W. I. Bishop (he never used Wellington as an adult) had been described by a Boston reporter as "a slim frail-looking little man, with blue-green eyes, a small face and delicate limbs." Other reporters had commented on his effeminate features, but also on his quick engaging wit and elegant style.

That night Chickering Hall was filled to capacity, 1,247 seats. A full Chickering Hall for one performance (at 50 cents a general ticket and $1.00 for reserved seats) provided approximately $800-$1,000 in box office receipts to Randall Brown for about ninety minutes of work.

W. I. Bishop had most recently been the business manager for three months for the renowned spirit medium Annie Eva Fay, before leaving her in April 1876, over a money dispute. Following the appearance of a full page illustrated article that claimed to expose the tricks of the "notorious Annie Eva Fay" in the *New York Daily Graphic*[3] (Bishop had posed for the illustrations used), Bishop himself had also once filled Chickering Hall, May 18, 1876, by presenting a widely promoted exposure of Annie Fay's mediumistic tricks — but that money was now long gone. Bishop's most pronounced personal talent was spending money far faster than he could obtain it, leaving him in perpetual debt. He had also inherited his mentally unstable mother's penchant for occasional collapses into a deathlike cataleptic trance, where all evidence of pulse or breathing was apparently erased. On one occasion, a year or two earlier, Bishop had been apparently dead for twelve hours before he suddenly regained life.

Bishop had taken to carrying a card that pleaded:

> To Whom It May Concern
>
> If I am found dead, do nothing to me for forty-eight hours. I occasionally fall into a state which resembles death, but is merely a trance. Get me to bed; keep my body warm; and have patience. Under no condition let a surgeon's knife touch me, do not apply electricity to my body and do not place my body on ice.
>
> W. I. Bishop

Bishop presented his mediumistic exposures again on Saturday, November 4, 1876, to a filled Music Hall in Boston as part of a high-profile charity drive to save Old South Church from demolition. With engaging guile, Bishop induced a number of prominent Massachusetts men, including the Massachusetts governor, the Boston mayor, Dr. Oliver Wendell Holmes, Everett Edward Hale, and other prominent citizens to sponsor his presentation, even to actually appearing on stage with him — a pattern that Bishop would effectively utilize several times in the following months.

However, of the $1,100 raised at the Music Hall for the Old South campaign, Bishop had appropriated all but $80 of the proceeds for himself and his unnamed male assistant as "personal expenses." When the great men of Massachusetts realized they had been cleverly gulled by Bishop, they were finally too humiliated to publicly challenge him. To their threat of exposing his cupidity, Bishop had contemptuously commented that their action would

W. Irving Bishop at 21. Courtesy TCS 1. Harvard Theatre Collection, Houghton Library, Harvard University.

In Aid of the Old South Church.
W. IRVING BISHOP,

AT the request and under the auspices of His Excellency Governor Alex. H. Rice, His Honor Mayor Sam'l C. Cobb, Rev. Edward E. Hale, Rev. Phillips Brooks, Rev. W. H. H. Murray, Rev. M. J. Supple, Rev. S. Cabot, M. D., Rev. Geo. O. Lorimer, Prof. E. N. Horsford, Oliver Wendell Holmes, M. D., R. M. Hodges, M. D., E. Ellis, M. D., and O. H. Storer, M. D.,

Will Perform and Explain

SPIRITUALISM

At MUSIC HALL, SATURDAY, Nov. 4, at 8 P. M.
N. Y. Times, June 10.—"Mr. Bishop's exposure leaves the Spiritualists without a leg to stand upon."
Box office now open. Secure your seats.   1t‡   n1

BOSTON MUSIO HALL.

Boston Herald, November 1, 1876.

only serve to advertise him even more widely. Beaten, the "Solid Men" quietly retired. Consequently, the Boston papers were filled with glowing reviews of Bishop's presentation and accolades for his generous support for the cause.[4]

It was in Boston that Bishop was photographed dressed as a woman[5] — supposedly to fool spirit mediums whose pernicious fraud he was so diligently investigating, though no image of Bishop had been published in Boston up to that time.

In the *Boston Herald* article, in which Irving Bishop was referred to as "Miss" Bishop, the reporter was more intrigued by the antics of older men trying to pick up Miss Bishop than he was with the evening's desultory "mediumistic investigations," which had revealed nothing, fraudulent or genuine. But public interest in exposing mediums promised only an erratic cash flow and Bishop had nothing else to offer the paying public to support his high-spending habits.

Born March 4, 1856, in New York City, Bishop had been an indifferent student at St. John's College and had worked only as a clerk in Hudnut's

Drug Store in New York prior to joining the Annie Eva Fay enterprise. His mother, Eleanor Fletcher Bishop, had become a well-known medium whose most prominent client was the millionaire Commodore Cornelius Vanderbilt, to whom she provided stock tips from the spirits. Eleanor's connections in the New York Spiritualistic community had led Bishop to the Fay opportunity. His father, Nathaniel Coney Bishop, had been an alcoholic traveling salesman who had died in 1874, though Bishop would always claim his father had been a prominent New York attorney.[6]

Always emotionally unstable, Eleanor had thrown herself into the open grave as her husband's casket was being lowered. That bizarre behavior was in spite of the fact that Eleanor had tried to divorce Nathaniel in 1867, claiming that her husband had tried to murder her. She had been separated from him for seven years.

It was a knotty family.

Magic folklore has it that W. I. Bishop traded J. Randall Brown details of his Fay exposure in return for Brown's instruction in thought reading. However, there is clear evidence that Bishop was already using a limited form of muscle reading in his mediumistic exposures in 1876 before seeing or meeting Brown; and further, Brown did not begin to incorporate anti-spiritualistic exposures in his act for almost two years.

During Bishop's

W. Irving Bishop, November, 1876, Photograph by Warren's Portraits. Courtesy TCS 1. Harvard Theatre Collection, Houghton Library, Harvard University.

exposures of mediumistic trickery at the Boston Music Hall, he claimed to reveal the billet reading techniques of the Salem Seer, the medium Charles H. Foster. Bishop demonstrated how the Seer could determine which one of several folded billets held the key name by holding the wrist of the inquirer and detecting the unconscious tremor in the wrist when the inquirer's hand was over the right billet. In his demonstrations that night, Bishop was successful several times.

Foster, who had been in the Boston audience, later publicly ridiculed Bishop's "exposure" by pointing out that he, Foster, never touched his clients at any time.

A more likely development is that Bishop counted Brown's take at Chickering Hall and in observing Randall Brown's routines became confident that he could perform the same act. Brown's growing national reputation as a mind reader seemed to point the way to a longer term positive cash flow than repeated exposures of the spirits. Bishop ultimately went on to combine his Spiritualist exposure routine with Brown's thought reading and returned to the stage for the rest of his short life.

Bishop privately practiced thought reading for about three to four months. His advertisements for his anti–Spiritualist show do not mention thought reading until May 1, 1877, when he billed himself for the first time as "The Renowned Anti-Spiritist and Mind-Reader."

Still relying primarily on his spiritualist exposures occasionally complemented with a limited thought reading routine, Bishop performed for several months through the mid-western states.

In Ireland in the mid–1860s at the

AMUSEMENTS.

FRAKER HALL,

Wednesday & Thursday,

MAY 8th and 9th

W. Irving Bishop!

THE RENOWNED

ANTI-SPIRITIST

—AND—

MIND READER!

Who created such an excitement in Chicago, will positively appear, duplicating and performing all the world-renowned Mediums' greatest tests, in his

Great Light Seance!

ADMISSION, 50c.& 35c.

W. Irving Bishop first advertisement as Mind Reader, May 1, 1877.

County Westmeath estate of W. E. Wilson, William (later Sir) Fletcher Barrett, about 23 at the time, was deeply puzzled, yet excited by what he saw demonstrated in a number of mesmeric experiments conducted by Wilson on a sensitive young girl. Initially incredulous, Barrett then conducted his own experiments on children from a nearby village. He discovered that when led properly into a mesmeric trance one or two of the children could achieve what appeared to be a heightened sensory state apparently not documented by such prominent physiologists as Dr. William B. Carpenter and others on altered mental states.

One girl, blindfolded and entranced by Barrett, could experience the emotions or sensations of the operator without any audible or visual communication. She also named the suit of a card or the value of a banknote that Barrett had concealed in a book that he held near her head. She apparently successfully read his thoughts in order to describe the interior of a place on which Barrett was concentrating. It was a place he was confident that she could never have seen, William Ladd's scientific instrument shop on Regent's Street, London. She had never left Westmeath in her life. Her description was correct in every detail, even to the clock outside the shop. How was it possible?

Though having started as a doubter, Barrett was coming to believe that, in the mesmeric trance state, information could be transferred from one mind to another without the use of the normal senses—that thoughts could be transferred directly from mind to mind. Could that also happen in a normal state, without whatever it was in the mesmeric trance that seemed to facilitate such an occurrence?

Barrett did not discuss his personal mesmeric experiences publicly until some ten years later when he delivered a cautious yet controversial paper to the Anthropological Sub-Section of the British Association for the Advancement of Science (BAAS) meeting at Glasgow, September 1876, "On Some Phenomena Associated with Abnormal Conditions of Mind."[7] The paper's topic was received with some contempt by many of the scientists present, who felt such a subject had no place in scientific discussions.

Typically, no scientist was more vicious in his criticism of Barrett than Dr. William B. Carpenter, who had brutally attacked William Crookes' earlier experiments with D. D. Home and other mediums. Carpenter wrote to Barrett,

> ... my medical education, my psychological enquiries, my experience of the dodges of the deceivers and in the unintentional assistance given to them by incautious victims of their arts, and in the extraordinary self-deception of those who go into the enquiry prepossessed with an idea, give me a qualification which you do not possess, and that you must first gain a position as an expert in this particular line of investigation, before anything

you say will carry in the least conviction to those who have earned the rights to be considered as experts [underlining in the original].[8]

A devout Christian, born in Jamaica as the son of a Nonconformist Congregationalist missionary, Barrett held his religious belief at the center of his life, a belief that he would never question. Barrett felt as well that the transference of thought he was observing resembled incidents described in the Scriptures. As a result, the claims of the Spiritualists, a system of belief in 1876 that was almost twenty-eight years old, of communicating between the minds of the living and the minds of the dead, also rose in importance in Barrett's estimation.

Between January 1864 and July 1866,[9] Barrett had worked as the assistant to the renowned physicist, John Tyndall, Professor of Natural Philosophy at the Royal Institution,[10] As a result, he encountered, on an almost a daily basis, other prominent scientists and philosophers, including Michael Faraday, George Gabriel Stokes, Thomas Henry Huxley, Herbert Spencer and others. Each of them was unfailingly courteous and friendly to Barrett, though at times a bit condescending to the young man. Tyndall's assistant, however, was never invited to join their private and sometimes animated philosophical discussions.

One position was very consistent, in all of their philosophical and scientific deliberations, as Barrett later recalled:

> Faraday had published about 1855 his famous experiment on table-turning, showing how unconscious muscular effort accounted for what he saw.... Tyndall[11] also had denounced spiritualism as an imposture. Both Huxley and Herbert Spencer were frequent visitors to the Royal Institution laboratory and both of these eminent men treated all psychical phenomena with contemptuous indifference.[12]

Barrett's scientific training at the Royal Institution had thus been surrounded by a consistently hostile atmosphere toward any suggestion of psychical legitimacy. Tyndall, particularly, was looked on as the leading spokesman for "scientific materialism," a philosophy that insisted that physical laws and principles (including energy conservation and atomism) provided the only trustworthy explanations of the cosmos, and that scientific progress demanded the eradication of the study of metaphysics and the supernatural.

With his family's very limited financial means, Barrett's own early academic training had consisted of attending grammar school and then public lectures given in London in chemistry and physics, by A. W. Hofmann, Edward Franklin and John Tyndall, followed by his earnestly studying the texts suggested at the lectures. It was Barrett's eagerness and intelligent application that had led to Tyndall's hiring him as his assistant with the intent to train Barrett as a competent experimenter. And as part of his training, it was Barrett who constructed the apparatus used by Tyndall in many of his acclaimed public lectures to demonstrate the marvelous effects of heat, light, sound, electricity and magnetism, including the spectacular action-at-a-distance demonstration of igniting a gas-filled balloon at one end of the room with beams of light generated from the other end.

Though Tyndall had publicly praised Barrett, their relationship had begun to deteriorate when Barrett had complained that Tyndall had not given him appropriate credit in an article Tyndall had written on radiation and things got worse after Barrett's negative review of a physics book written by a friend of one of the key financial supporters of the Royal Institution. Tyndall had helped get Barrett published in the *Philosophical Magazine* and in other publications which had begun to enhance Barrett's nascent reputation. But when Barrett refused to retract his book review, his patron's threat of withholding his annual contribution unless he received an apology forced Barrett to submit an apology and his resignation.

As the years passed, Barrett acquired a growing reputation for being vain and querulous with a penchant for self-advertising,[13] a reputation that would strengthen throughout his life. Though later elected a Fellow of the Royal Society and knighted, Barrett never achieved any scientific distinction, despite having been surrounded through much of his career by some of the most prominent scientists of the late nineteenth and early twentieth centuries. The proximity of greatness, without his participating in it, often galled Barrett intensely, as becomes apparent in some of his private correspondence.

In spite of their growing conflict, Tyndall obtained a teaching position for Barrett at the London International College, and was later (in 1873) to help obtain Barrett's appointment at age 28 as Professor of Experimental Physics at the Royal College of Science, Dublin. In his new position, Barrett began to present public lectures which mimicked the successful theatricality of those of Tyndall. Barrett's lectures rapidly became popular in Dublin. However, by 1874 Tyndall and Barrett were arguing in public regarding claims of priority in acoustical demonstrations. Finally, in annoyance, Tyndall deleted Barrett's name from his standard textbook on sound. Though the two men never reconciled their differences, Barrett's position at the Royal College of Science was never at risk.

What Barrett did put at risk, in his paper at the BAAS Glasgow meeting in 1876, was his emerging scientific reputation. Even getting permission to give his paper had caused a serious commotion, and it was only the deciding vote of the chairman of the Anthropological Sub-Section, Alfred Russel Wallace, co-discoverer with Charles Darwin of the theory of evolution by natural selection and himself an avowed Spiritualist, that created a time in the meeting schedule for Barrett.

After describing in detail his experiences with the mesmerized girl in Westmeath from the mid–1860's, Barrett wrote:

> I convinced myself that the existence of a distinct idea in my own mind gave rise to an image of the idea in the subject's mind; not always a clear image, but one that could not fail to be recognized as a more or less distorted reflection of my own thought. The important point is that every care was taken to prevent any unconscious muscular action of the face, or otherwise giving any indication to the subject.

This power of "thought reading," as it has been termed, has often been described by writers on mesmerism, but little credence has been given to it by physiologists or psychologists.

Certainly, Barrett pointed out, the girl's remarkable description of Ladd's shop could not have been communicated to her through muscular actions of any kind. After suggesting that a committee be formed by the BAAS to investigate the phenomena he had described, Barrett concluded by urging scientists:

> to be careful lest in a too hasty rejection of phenomena that seem incredible and inexplicable, according to received opinion, we are not laying ourselves open to that same spirit of bigotry that persecuted Galileo. Surely the motto of every man of science ought to be found in Sir John Herschel's words, "The natural philosopher should believe all things not improbable; hope all things not impossible."

In suggesting a possible mechanism for the phenomena described, Barrett had utilized the language from the developing field of electromagnetism, avoiding completely any appeal to the Spiritualist or supernatural regions for explanation.

In a letter to the *Times* a few days later, he wrote:

> For my own part I am inclined to believe other mental phenomena — such as, for example, the possibility of the action of one mind upon another, across space, without the intervention of the senses — demand a prior investigation. That cases of such mental action at a distance do really exist, I, in common with others, have some reason to believe; but before they can be generally accepted the evidence must accumulate and be thoroughly sifted.[14]

Barrett closed his September letter by requesting that anyone having experienced such action at a distance, should communicate directly with him at 18 Belgrave-square, Monkstown, Ireland.

Though no action was taken by the BAAS on Barrett's suggestion of forming an investigating committee, Barrett himself continued during the following years to investigate, as he found the time, reported instances of thought transference sent to him as a response to his *Times* letter. He also cooperated occasionally with individuals at Cambridge University interested in psychical research.

But the question remained, was mind to mind communication possible in a normal state, or was an entranced mesmerized condition necessary? A letter Barrett received in early 1881 from a clergyman in Derbyshire, the Rev. A. M. Creery, describing his work with his four remarkable daughters, seemed to suggest an answer.

8

The Greatest Rascal

"It is well that Mr. Bishop is an honest man, for, with his gifts, he might have been the greatest rascal amongst us."
— Professor Thomas Henry Huxley, 1879

In order to avoid close comparison and direct competition with the more established J. Randall Brown, as well as with other less skilled thought readers, W.I. Bishop embarked in September 1878 for England, where the thought reading act had never been experienced — and the spirits had not yet been subject to relentless scrutiny by professional exposers.

That British disembodied spirits remained untouched at so much per ticket was largely due to the low number of professional public mediums practicing in England in marked contrast to America. The Spiritualist movement developed in Great Britain based principally on the family circle where the medium was either a family member or close friend, who was not paid but who received a meal or boarding for her work. The movement, as a result, had a wide presence in the upper levels of British society that was not then the case in America.

British mediums, generally, did not advertise themselves, relying on word of mouth almost entirely. Thus when American mediums, like Annie Eva Fay in 1875, arrived with their American promotional techniques, the British Spiritualists were shocked at the aggressiveness of supposedly spiritual people, calling their activities derisively "the rogue and vagabond" method of promotion.

Because his delicate, even effeminate features suggested too young an age for a learned investigator, Bishop adopted pince-nez glasses and the restrained manner and conservative fashion of a scholarly investigator. He began as well to grow sideburns to further alter his features.

Bishop, again following Randall Brown's example, presented himself first as an investigator, not as a music hall entertainer; as a concerned educated gentleman (he modestly suggested Harvard, when asked) disinterested in money. He was, the British press assured its readers, nobly committed to supporting worthy causes and protecting the public from soulless spiritual predators. And, being a foreigner, W. I. Bishop did not face any of the strict social barriers of Victorian England that a later Bishop competitor, Stuart C. Cumberland, would strive to overcome in his own way. Thus, as an American with no awkward social status, Bishop could gain access to the homes and manor houses of the upper classes and ultimately, the aristocracy itself, including members of the royal family.

He only had to find the way.

Upon his arrival in London with his unnamed male assistant, W. I. Bishop, alone, first called on naturalist, physiologist and ardent anti-spiritualist, Dr. William Benjamin Carpenter, F.R.S., to establish his bona fides as a fellow anti–Spiritualist. Bishop presented Carpenter with letters attesting to his abilities from prominent men of science, business and the academic world; his New York and Boston press clippings; and documents from his Chickering Hall and Music Hall presentations. Professor Thomas H. Huxley, the naturalist famous as "Darwin's Bulldog," was also present.

William B. Carpenter was described by a colleague as "a tall, spare man, elderly but not aged, with the gray of his naturally light hair hardly discernible at a little distance." Carpenter received Bishop cordially.

After their examination of Bishop's documents, the American performed demonstrations for the two professors of what Bishop called thought reading, finding a hidden pin, reading the serial number of a pound note and other quick, simple tests.

Intrigued, Carpenter acceded to the American's request for an introductory letter to similarly minded

W. Irving Bishop with sideburns, 1881.

8. The Greatest Rascal

English gentlemen. In his Bishop letter, Carpenter expressed his desire "to obtain for him (Bishop) an assemblage of gentlemen specially qualified to appreciate the importance of experiments of great value to the Physiologist and Psychologist."

But, remarkably, instead of thought reading wonders, it was a Bishop *card trick* that had most puzzled Carpenter, capturing his close attention. Bishop repeated the effect three times with Carpenter and members of his family as subjects with acclaimed success at each occasion.

The effect was a simple one in which Dr. Carpenter selected a card and returned it to Bishop, who inserted it back into the pack, shuffled the cards and dealt out sixteen cards "*with their faces downwards*" (italics Carpenter's)[1] in four rows as below:

Carpenter stood at the table with Bishop to his right. Taking the professor's right hand with his left, Bishop said, "Drop your left hand down on either row, vertical or horizontal, that you want taken away."

This procedure was repeated two more times leaving one row, C, in place.

"Now," said Bishop, "drop down upon either the two upper or the two lower cards of the remaining row." The upper two, 3 and 7, were selected and removed, leaving only 11 and 15 still on the table. "Now drop down on either of the two remaining cards."

Carpenter selected the lower card, 15, which was removed. Bishop gestured at the remaining card, 11, which Carpenter turned over. It was his originally selected card! The scientist was profoundly astonished.

"I could not," Carpenter wrote later in 1881, "tell how I was led to make the five successive selections of the cards to be taken away, so as to leave behind the card I had originally drawn." He continued, "This experiment is of great psychological interest, as by showing the large measure in which we may be guided in our choice among things 'indifferent' by *influences of which we are ourselves unconscious*" (italics in the original).

Carpenter acknowledged that conjurors were known for being able to "force" a choice on a subject, "as Robert-Houdin had forced a card on Emperor Louis Napoleon after

	A	B	C	D
E	1	2	3	4
F	5	6	7	8
G	9	10	11	12
H	13	14	15	16

Diagram from letter to the editor, W. B. Carpenter, *Nature*, June 30, 1881.

Napoleon had defied the magician to do it. The card Houdin forced was the Caesar." However, Carpenter emphatically denied that there was any opportunity for W. I. Bishop to play the conjuror.

Several days later, Bishop called on William Crookes at his home at 20 Mornington Street. Crookes' mediumistic investigations three years earlier, particularly of Annie Eva Fay, had been the target of William Carpenter's sustained and vituperative criticisms, that reached even to the point of Carpenter suggesting that Crookes' election as a Fellow to the Royal Society for his discovery of the element thallium had been "premature."

Describing his previous work with Fay, Bishop declared his ability to duplicate all the manifestations of Mrs. Annie Eva Fay and to explain to the scientist how Fay had duped him. Crookes declined the offer.

Two weeks later, Bishop went to 38 Great Russell Street to visit the British National Association of Spiritualists to apply for membership, giving as his reference the name of a well known trance medium. Unlike more prominent personages in America and Great Britain, the BNSA did investigate Bishop's claimed reference. A few days later he received a letter stating: "Mr. W. I. Bishop is deemed *not* eligible for membership to the National Association of Spiritualists."[2]

He and his assistant then traveled north to Edinburgh to follow up on the promotional letters he had been sending, which sought to enlist the sponsorship of prominent Scottish politicians, clergy and scientists in his crusade against "the pestilence of Spiritualism." In the letters, Bishop provided the names of prominent New York and Boston politicians and clergy, and the name of William B. Carpenter, as references. Bishop offered his talents and experience, without remuneration, for worthy charities in a just cause.

W. Irving Bishop, as an unknown American, needed valid British credentials before trying to break into the London theatre market, and thus followed the path of other American performers: north to Scotland first, then south to London.

Bishop first presented his spiritualistic exposures January 16 and 17, 1879, at the Edinburgh Music Hall in support of the city's unemployed; and later, February 25 and 26, at the Glasgow New Public Hall in support of the Western Infirmary. There is no reference to thought reading at either location.

At both locations, Bishop followed his familiar pattern. In Glasgow, for example, at the end of January, Bishop appeared at the office of Henry Johnston, a prominent businessman. Bishop presented his testimonials, which included the letter from Dr. W. B. Carpenter, which stated in part: "Mr. Bishop is a young gentleman of New York, of excellent social position, his father being a very eminent lawyer, and Washington Irving having been his god-father." Mr. Johnston received Irving Bishop as a respected gentleman.

8. The Greatest Rascal

"Mr. Bishop told me," Johnston wrote a few days later in the Glasgow *News*,[3] "that he had given two expositions of Spiritualism in Edinburgh, the proceeds of which had been handed to the city in aid of the unemployed, and showed me opinions of the press speaking highly of his performances. He also expressed his desire to aid similarly some Glasgow charity."

With Johnston's involvement and the Western Infirmary as the designated charity, the august committee sponsoring Bishop's proposed two performances quickly came to include the Lord Mayor, the Lord Provost, the Principal of the infirmary, and one of the greatest scientists of the nineteenth century, Sir William Thomson (later Lord Kelvin), which led to expanding the committee further to include university professors, senior clergy, and "several medical gentlemen." The committee issued a gracious public invitation to Bishop to present his Spiritualistic program, to which Bishop issued an equally gracious public acceptance.

Johnston had quickly agreed to Bishop's proposal that after covering his expenses all the proceeds should go to the infirmary. Bishop cautioned Johnston that his experiences in New York, Boston and Edinburgh had shown that expenses could be heavy, running to over half of the total receipts.

To help bring expenses down, Johnston assured Bishop that, as the performances were for charity, the Public Hall would be available at half the normal cost. Bishop further assured Johnston that he wanted nothing to do with handling any funds. Johnston agreed, saying that as the performances were "voluntary on his part" the committee had no right to dictate Bishop's expenses.

Expecting Bishop and his assistant to act as the gentlemen that they had been presented to be, Johnston was quickly astonished to discover that Bishop and his assistant had taken over everything. They created and placed the advertising, designed the stage settings, superintended the sale of the tickets and, to Henry Johnston's ultimate horror, "even cast their coats and took money at the door!" No real gentleman in Johnston's experience would have done such a thing, even in support of a public charity.

Following the performances and the settling of accounts, Johnston found that the Western Infirmary had received only £153 9s 1d while Bishop and his assistant had left with over £455 — over 75 percent of the total.

The morning following the second Glasgow performance, Bishop insisted to reporters that the basic agreement had been 25 percent of receipts to the infirmary, and that he, Bishop, had clearly carried the entire financial risk of the presentations.

Johnston immediately wrote to refute all of Bishop's statements.

The performances themselves were dismissed by some writers in the Glasgow papers as mere demonstrations of "sleight-of-hand and sleight-of-body."

J. Page Hopps, a Glasgow businessman who had attended a number of séances but did not consider himself a Spiritualist, wrote in the *Glasgow Herald* of March 6, that "Mr. Bishop exposed a Spiritualism of his own imagination" and that "the actual spiritual phenomena of common experience was left untouched."[4] He commented that the most wonderful thing about Bishop's performances was "his success in inducing such 'potent, grave, and reverend seigniors' to help him play the fool."

When Bishop was threatened by some of those same savants "to post him as a cheat," Bishop turned on them coolly with the intimation that they were merely advertising him and would help him by so doing. And so, as in Boston, New York and Edinburgh, the prominent men of society simply slunk away, saying nothing.

Most reporters writing of the presentations, however, were enthusiastic: "Mr. Bishop is quite young, but speaks with a fluency and a great self-possession, and his bright merry-twinkling eye, and his 'my good friends' put him on the best of terms with his audience at the very beginning" (*Glasgow Evening News*). And, "On both evenings a hearty vote of thanks was awarded to Mr. Bishop for his very interesting and successful entertainments" (*The British Medical Journal*). "The Chair was occupied by Professor Sir William Thomson, who, in a few suitable words, introduced Mr. Bishop" (*Glasgow Herald*). Thomson later joined Bishop in the spirit cabinet where the "spirits" grasped the scientist about the neck.[5]

Several reporters wrote praising W. Irving Bishop's "scientific presentations" largely because of the presence on the stage of noted scientists.

While in Scotland, Bishop sought a private secretary to help handle his growing correspondence and complex scheduling. In early 1879, on the recommendation of the proprietor and editor of a Scottish newspaper, Irving Bishop hired Charles Garner, the son of Robert Garner, a clerk at John Weblin's butcher shop on St. Giles Road, East Oxford. In less than 4 to 5 weeks, Bishop reneged on his agreement to share profits with Garner and left for Malta, ostensibly a first stop on a trip to investigate the mysteries of India.

In a letter written to his printer in New York while passing through London during the summer of 1879, Bishop commented that his pockets were "becoming comfortably full of pound notes."[6] In the same letter, Bishop contemptuously dismissed his various competitors including "Mind, the Brown Reader" as unimportant. He reserved his most venomous comments for his cousin, T. Brigham Bishop, a successful song writer!

En route, Bishop found another charity in need of his unique touch in Gibraltar on May 18. This time it was money for the widows and orphans of British soldiers killed in the Zulu wars. *The Gibraltar Chronicle* wrote: "Mr. Bishop deserves the thanks of the entire community for the treat he provided

8. The Greatest Rascal

for them, and for his exertions in the pursuit of so laudable an object as the relief of distress."

And in the fall, Bishop returned again to Scotland, in Aberdeen, September 18, and in other places. As long as he could effectively gull the pillars of society, there was no need to alter his obviously successful charity scam.

Returning to Glasgow, at St. Andrew's Hall on February 10, 1880, Bishop gave a presentation without a charity involvement. It consisted entirely of an exposure of the illusions and tricks of the famous magician Robert Heller, repeating a performance he had first given several days earlier in Dundee "because of a letter requesting him to explain the works of Heller."

In anticipation of the Dundee booking, Bishop had hired Frederick Wickes to ghost-write a 78-page pamphlet, *Houdin and Heller's Second Sight Explained,* published in Edinburgh, which was sold for one shilling at his Heller exposure shows. (In 1907, Wickes would publish an expanded version of the pamphlet under his own name called *Thought Reading Explained*.)

Though Bishop had continued to bill himself as "Mind-reader and Exposer" there is no mention of thought reading in any of the newspaper accounts of his public performances. However, Bishop may have privately demonstrated thought reading as a means of augmenting his reputation as an adept and mystery worker. He continued to prosper primarily through exposing the creative work of others — but principally for charity, of course.

The first of a three part series on mediumistic tricks under Bishop's name was published in the January 1881 issue of *Leisure Hour Magazine.* The second part appeared in February and the third in April. The series was probably ghost-written as the writing reflects a polish and a literary background that Bishop never manifested. The series was immediately attacked in the Spiritualist press as misleading and inaccurate in the portrayal of séance conditions.

In April, Bishop circulated an invitation to prominent scientists, clergy, and politicians which again included a copy of the Carpenter letter, to investigate his powers of thought reading.

Twenty-one prominent men gathered on Monday evening, May 9, 1881, at Bedford Square, London, to experience and evaluate what Dr. Carpenter had written were "powers worthy of their professional time."

9

Proof! The Creery Sisters

> Our worst experiments before strangers have invariably been when the company was dull and undemonstrative; and we are all convinced that when mistakes are made the fault rests, for the most part, with the thinkers rather than with the thought-readers.
> — The Rev. A. M. Creery, B.A., July 17, 1882

First originating in the United States, and then spreading to Great Britain from the Continent in the late 1870s and continuing for some years a parlor amusement called the willing game achieved great popularity throughout the British Isles. In the game, a subject, usually a woman, was invited to leave the room while the remaining people decided on a specific simple action that the absent person should perform when she returned. No questions were allowed, no audible clues; the people were to remain quietly seated, thinking of the proposed task. One of the people, the medium, or willer, would explain upon the subject's return to the room that she was to make herself as passive as possible, to close her eyes, and *not to guess at anything* She was to stand still for a moment — then to act on the first pronounced inclination she feels, whatever it may be. The medium, while concentrating on the secret task, would take the subject lightly by her wrist, placing his other hand against her forehead, or placing his fingers against the nape of her neck, whichever technique seemed to work. With some false starts, indecision, usually with some giggling, in many instances the woman trying to sense the will of the group would successfully perform the thought-of action. The game rapidly became a popular way to spend an hour or two on a winter's evening.

An unemployed clergyman, fifty-year-old Andrew Macreight Creery, living in the town of Buxton in Derbyshire, had apparently taken the willing game to new heights with four of his five daughters, aged ten to sixteen — and the family's twenty-year-old maidservant. The Rev. Creery presented a paper at the July 17, 1882, meeting of the SPR,[1] where he said,

> In the month of October, 1880, my attention was called to the phenomena of the "willing game," but being unable to determine how much of the results were due to simple willing, and how much to involuntary pushing, I resolved to thoroughly investigate the whole question of mind on mind.

Creery then described the various experiments with cards, objects, names of towns, and so forth, carried out "night after night for several months" for "an hour or two each evening." In each experiment one of the girls would go out of the room while the other girls with the Rev. Creery decided on an object, a name, a card or something specific. When the girl was recalled to the room, the "thinkers" would will the information to her with remarkably high success rates. The remarkable aspect of the Creery experiments was that, unlike in the willing game, the subject *was not touched* by any of the "willers."

Creery then briefly described several of the family experiments. All of his four daughters and Jane Dean, the twenty-year-old maidservant, were used as subjects. The subject would always know the general description of the object, (a playing card, a location, a name) before leaving the room. Once the subject was out of the room, the specific object was chosed; for example, a card would be selected from a deck. After each of the family had looked at it, the card was replaced in the deck and the deck put out of sight. The subject was recalled, and with the willers concentrating on the identity of the card, the subject would successfully announce the card with a cumulative accuracy well above that expected from just guessing. All of the girls exhibited to a greater or lesser degree the ability to sense, *without contact*, the will of the willers. In all of the Creery experiments, if the first announcement by the subject was wrong, the subject would be given a second chance without any indication being given of how close her first statement was to the actual truth. In most cases, where necessary, the second statement was accurate. On rare occasions, a third attempt was allowed.

Creery's paper continued:

> When the children were in a good humor, and excited by the wonderful nature of their successful guessing, they very seldom made a mistake.[2] We soon found that a great deal depended on the steadiness with which the ideas were kept before the minds of "the thinkers," and upon the energy with which they willed the ideas to pass.
>
> When we began to investigate these curious phenomena we had no idea that the result of our little amusement would ever come before the public. But having been asked to deliver a lecture on some popular subject before a small philosophical society in Derby, I volunteered to give an account of the experiments in "Thought Reading" with which I was then engaged. A short report, which appeared in the local papers, I forwarded to Professor Barrett, who I knew was interested in such matters. He at once took it up, and paid us his first visit on Easter, 1881, the results of which he afterwards

published in *Nature*[3]; from the experiments that I commenced it will be mainly to him that science will be indebted.

The Creery letter was one of a large number of responses that Barrett had received from his request for information given in his September 1876 letter to the *Times*. Though there were a number of other potential cases investigated, the Creery letter drew immediate and sustained interest not only from William Barrett, but from Frederic W. H. Myers and Edmund Gurney. The case of the Creery family would come to provide the most important basis for the proof of thought-reading, thought transference, or, using the term later coined by Myers in 1882, telepathy, as a fact of human nature. That proof became central to William F. Barrett's professional ambitions.

Barrett arrived in Buxton on Easter, April 17, 1881, to spend "three long evenings" testing the Creery family.

10

Truth! Barrett and Bishop

> Of his thought reading power there can be no question or dispute. Mr. Irving Bishop's exemplifications were most wonderful, and sufficient to convince the most incredulous that he actually possesses the powers he claims.
> —Douglas Blackburn, editor, *The Brightonian*, August 6, 1881

Accounts of the Bishop meeting May 9, 1881, at Bedford Square, London, appeared in the next issues of *The Lancet*,[1] *The British Medical Journal*[2] and *Nature*.[3] Mr. Edward Hart, the editor of the *British Medical Journal*, who was present, wrote:

> ... to ennoble a common parlour-trick by the title of "thought reading," is to indulge in an unpardonable hyperbole. And this was really all that Mr. Bishop had to show a large audience of scientific and literary men, whom, by the magic of a great name and seductive promises, he drew from their laboratories and studies, and social engagements to Bedford Square. Mr. Bishop performed two tricks.

The first effect was the pin-finding demonstration, and the second was spelling out a name or word thought of through the use of alphabet cards. The two tests were repeated with various men taking part and with widely varying results.

After finding pins hidden by three of the men, Bishop then first succeeded in identifying the location of Professor Lankester's thought-of pain, a toothache; but then after several minutes trying to locate the pain on which Dr. Pye-Smith was concentrating, Bishop, crawling on his knees, finally located the pain in the doctor's right foot—when, in fact, the thought-of pain was in the left hand that Bishop had been holding to his forehead throughout the test.

Nothing of Bishop's performance had resembled the scientific promise Dr. W.B. Carpenter had described in his letter, and in Hart's opinion, had Carpenter himself been present, he would have never written the letter at all.[4]

Bishop had begun his opening speech by disclaiming any knowledge of what powers may be at play in his demonstrations, explicitly dismissing the theory of unconscious muscular suggestion. As the evening progressed, Bishop came even to claim that he could literally read the minds of people by gazing into the retinas of their eyes. He could read their soul "in the secrets of the brain-cells behind."

Hart continued, "He is possessed, he declared, of a power that is inexplicable even to himself."

The *Lancet* wrote: "We imagine there must have been some feeling of disappointment at the result of the séance among those present; they had come to see something mysterious and inexplicable.... But they did not."

Even then, two further meetings were held at the home of Professor Croom Robertson to arrange for more detailed examination of W. I. Bishop's capabilities by four men from the group present on the May 9. One meeting was on May 28 and the second on June 11. The results were the same as in the earlier meeting. A single Bishop success in a non-contact experiment in thought reading, followed by several complete failures, was dismissed by the scientists as only accidental.[5]

Biologist George J. Romanes writing of the two later meetings in *Nature* on June 23, was concerned that Bishop's much publicized "scientific" encounters were taking the press and the public by storm. The scientific endorsement of men like Huxley, Carpenter and other scientists resulted in the achievement of even greater public credibility for Bishop, which led to his being invited to exhibit his powers privately to the Prince of Wales — an event that granted Bishop a social imprimatur that exceeded even the scientific one.

"This is to be regretted," wrote Romanes, "because the result was to endow the powers, which were afterwards exhibited, with a fictitious degree of importance in the eyes of the public."

But the presence of scientific men convinced the press and the public that the results were scientific, even if the experiments themselves were not.

Bishop's pockets continued to fill with pound notes, and over the succeeding months, highly publicized appearances before the titled aristocracy and members of the royal family became almost commonplace.

> At almost the same time, in Buxton, Derbyshire, William F. Barrett tested the Creery children. In his July 7 letter to *Nature*, Barrett stated that all of the Creery children, ages nine to fourteen "are able to go through the ordinary performances of the 'willing game' rapidly and successfully, *without the contact of the hands or of any communication besides the air between the person operating and the subject operated on* [emphasis original]."

The Reverend Creery had assured Barrett that just prior to his Easter arrival the children had called seventeen consecutive playing cards drawn at random from a pack "without a single failure," a stunning event far beyond any possibility of chance or coincidence. Barrett further assured his readers that the Christian clergyman in question was an old graduate of Trinity College, Dublin, whose "integrity was above suspicion." Barrett, along with other psychical researchers like Gurney and Myers, placed a great deal of weight on the social position of the operators as evidence of inherent honesty — an attitude that carried over into the subsequent investigations of the SPR.

With the child sensitive out of the room or behind closed doors, Barrett would write the name of an object not in the room, in order to prevent any unconscious direction to the subject from the children looking at the object. The paper would be shown to all of the family, then hidden in Barrett's pocket. The child was then recalled and then asked to identify the object — to remarkably consistent success. Barrett noted that the father was found to be preeminently the best willer, and to be in fact almost as necessary for success as the sensitive "guesser." He further discovered that "a battery of minds" all fixed on the same word was always more successful than just one or two members of the family alone.

After three nights of testing, of dozens of experiments, Barrett was convinced that he had found what he had been seeking so diligently: solid proof of mind to mind communication without the use of the sensory organs.

Working with each of the children had been almost uniformly successful, the failures being about one in ten of his experiments. He discovered that even the twenty-year-old maidservant, Jane Dean, was as sensitive as the children with a success rate the same as theirs, a situation that Barrett found to be "very curious"— a situation that seemed to neuter the proposition that the telepathic sensitivity was hereditary. What then was it?

In publicly announcing his results, he called for others to go to Buxton to confirm or refute his findings.

In late June 1881, the Duke of Beaufort acted as master of ceremonies for W.I. Bishop's performance at St. James Hall in Piccadilly. It was noted by the press that Bishop acknowledged the Duke's presence at every possible moment. His Grace even joined Bishop in the spirit cabinet to the delight of the audience, reappearing disheveled and laughing.

But of Bishop, a reporter of the London *Cuckoo* wrote:

> He was a grievous disappointment. His manner of speaking is irritating from its conceit, and the manner of it impertinent, while his feats cannot compare with those of Messrs. Maskelyne & Cooke for originality, nor with those of the Spiritualists for mystery.[6]

But the pound notes kept flowing. In addition to possessing thought reading talents that reached beyond even those of J. Randall Brown, Bishop also possessed a talent for showmanship that exceeded that of Randall Brown, that sense of process and variety that attracted sustained public interest and money.

Unlike Brown's more calm, professional performing style, Bishop's frenetic performances were unpredictable and exciting, but were skeptically characterized in the *British Medical Journal* regarding the May 9th gathering:

> ... as Bishop interrupted his waltz around the room with Professor Croom Robertson, Bishop staggered, rubbed his eyes, looked around bewildered and did not seem to understand what was said to him for a few seconds, creating the idea that he had just awakened from a trance or state of unconsciousness.[7]

Edward Hart regarded Bishop's trance state as simply a theatrical artifice, when in fact it was legitimate — a threatening characteristic inherited from his equally mentally erratic mother.

Reporters noted that while the process of thought reading seemed a debilitating burden to the thought reader,[8] the subject was completely unaffected by the experience; which caused one reporter to muse: "Why would anyone want to be a thought reader?"

One observer who did not believe that W. Irving Bishop's wonders were legitimate, scientific endorsements or not, was radical Member of Parliament and publisher of the journal *Truth* Henri du Prè Labouchère.[9] Though initially open to an investigation of Bishop's alleged powers, "Labby" had said in 1881, "The facts are not denied; and I must request science to explain them, or to avow them inexplicable."

But after witnessing some Bishop performances and the little man's public behavior, Henri Labouchère began writing a number of vitriolic articles on Bishop in his journal. The publisher declared: "He (Bishop) can no more see what is passing in another person's mind than I can."

Finally, in May 1883, Henri Labouchère wrote in *Truth*:

> Mr. Bishop is a citizen of a country where, when a person asserts his belief in being able to do something improbable, he is met with the practical reply: "How many dollars do you believe in it?" I believe one thousand pounds that he cannot reveal by any process of thought-reading the number of a bank-note in an envelope. He evidently does not believe one hundred pounds that he can.

The number was to be known only by a third party who would hold the envelope. The publisher nominated Bottomly Firth, M.P. from Chelsea, as the third party. If Bishop failed, then he would pay Labouchère £100. Firth spoke of "one Bishop, who indulges in charlatan experiments and has a particular line of humbug," to which Bishop called Firth "a narrow minded Quaker."

Following days of bitter correspondence in the *Times* in which Bishop rejected Firth's involvement, Bishop accepted the challenge providing that Labouchère would give the £100 to the Victoria Hospital for Children if he lost. Labouchère refused, insisting his own exchequer needed the money as much as the hospital.

Bishop refused to accept any person nominated by Labouchère, and the publisher, in disgust, withdrew the challenge. But Bishop announced a special challenge to be added to his performance at St. James Hall already scheduled for June 12, 1883, with the proceeds, Bishop announced, to go to the Victoria Hospital for Children. Labouchère refused to attend.

With the publicity from the Labouchère challenge, the spacious St. James Hall was filled to capacity at the high ticket prices of one guinea for the front stalls and half a guinea everywhere else.

Performing some preliminary demonstrations such as a handcuff escape and a bandage-tie escape, Bishop then demonstrated his pin-finding abilities. At that point he pointed to the empty chair on the stage and invited the publisher of *Truth* to occupy it, knowing that Labouchère was not present.

Amidst the confusion that ensued, two other critics, Charles Russell (later Lord Russell) and Professor E. Ray Lankester, stood and offered a five-pound note sealed in an envelope, and an unidentified man threw an envelope containing a "fiver" onto the stage.

Refusing these challenges to the loud antipathy of the audience, Bishop finally accepted a pound note provided by Colonel Trench of the 20th Lancashire Volunteers. The serial number was concentrated on by Mr. Statham from Manchester.

With a handkerchief tied over his eyes and his hand closed around Stratham's wrist, Bishop, with his typical frenetic style, first drew a rectangle with five slots for each digit on the blackboard, then finally after several false starts, wrote the number 66894. When Stratham loudly confirmed that was the correct serial number, the audience exploded in applause. A fire-balloon was released outside the theatre to signify Bishop's success to all of London.

Departing St. James Hall, the thought reader asserted to reporters that, as he had met the challenge, Labouchère should give his thousand pounds to the hospital, not Bishop.

The performance drew massive publicity with a full page of drawings in the *Illustrated London News* devoted to it.

A few days later, Bishop wrote a public letter regarding the performance and concluded by saying, "It is my intention shortly to discontinue my public life, in order to resume my investigations of the mysteries of the East."

But what of the Victoria Hospital for Children? What did they receive after being so extensively exploited in the Bishop publicity? With ticket receipts totaling well over £300 in his pocket, Bishop graciously presented Captain W.C. Blount, R.N., secretary of the Hospital, with a check for £19. Disgusted, Blount refused to accept it. The charity scam had paid off again.

With typical audacity, Bishop even continued to publish the two letters that Blount had sent to him prior to the performance that had praised the thought reader for his generosity and kindness in supporting the Victoria Hospital.

Bishop further claimed, in referring to this episode in all of his subsequent publicity, that he had successfully met Labouchère's challenge, which was not true. Labouchère had specifically challenged Bishop to read the serial number *without touching* the holder of the note — which Bishop had not done and could not do.

Several days later, on July 26, 1883, conjuror J. Nevil Maskelyne[10] discovered that Bishop had saturated London with an eight-page spurious facsimile edition of *Truth,* subtitled "Mr. Henry Labouchère, M.P., versus Mr. W. Irving Bishop," in which Bishop accused Labouchère and Maskelyne of conspiring to defame him and to destroy his reputation. And, in practice, the attacks in *Truth* had begun to interfere in Bishop's career

Labouchère had published several letters from Maskelyne in his journal *Truth*, letters that had accused Bishop of fraudulently claiming supernatural powers. Maskelyne had called the thought reader a humbug, a swindler, a cheat and an impostor — among other considerations.

Responding furiously to the Maskelyne letters in his facsimile of *Truth*, Bishop declared that "on the odium of public opinion" he would crucify Henry Labouchère and J. Nevil Maskelyne as "a villainous brace of scoundrels." He further stated that the magician, Maskelyne, was "devoid of honorable instincts," and with "the proofs of infamy in my possession" the little thought reader said he would hold the magician "criminally liable and make Justice punish him for his villainous conduct."

Labouchère, uncharacteristically, declined to take legal action against Bishop. J. Nevil Maskelyne, however, promptly sued Bishop for libel.

Neither Bishop nor his attorney appeared in court in the first hearing in January 1885 to defend against Maskelyne's libel charges. Instead of the conventional sixpence token penalty, the jury awarded a £10,000 judgment against Bishop (about $1.2 million in 2010 U.S. dollars).

On appeal to the Divisional Court that the damages were excessive, the case was re-considered July 9, 1885, at the Sheriff's Court, London. After a short deliberation, the jury re-assessed the damages at £500.

In a third hearing held December 2, 1885, Bishop's third attorney, Digby

Seymour, argued that the judgment should be reduced even more since the court had seen clear evidence that Bishop had never, as alleged by the plaintiff, claimed supernatural powers, and that Bishop's angry statements, though possible to construe as libelous, had been intolerably provoked by Maskelyne's unbridled attacks.

But their lordships ruled that the award had already been moderated sufficiently and declined the application, without requesting comment from Maskelyne's lawyers. The Maskelyne libel proceedings were finally closed.

J. N. Maskelyne never received a penny of the £500 final judgment.

11

J. R. Brown and His Telegraph Test

> I have no doubt when this operation is done again and again the objectors will get tired of it, and the laugh will then be turned against themselves.
> — Professor Balfour Stewart, July 17, 1882.

Accepting William Barrett's suggestion that others travel to Derbyshire to test the Creery children and to challenge his own conclusions, Balfour Stewart, a professor of physics at Owens College, and Alfred Hopkinson, a law professor at the same school, visited the Creery home in November 1881 and again in February 1882. Edmund Gurney and F. W. H. Myers also traveled to Buxton. Later experiments with the children were also done in Dublin and in Cambridge.

Speaking at the General Meeting of the SPR with the Reverend Creery in the audience, Stewart noted that during their visit, though working at the home and with the same group as Barrett had, that he and Hopkinson had not obtained equally conclusive results as Barrett, but of their results "...neither of us was able to account for by any received hypothesis."[1]

Stewart briefly described their experiments: the child was outside the door (he does not say if the door was closed, nor does he say there was silence during the tests). He wrote the object or thing to be thought of on a piece of paper that was passed to all the family present and returned to him. The child returned and within a minute called out what had been written on the paper. The topics were changed from cards, to locations, to numbers. Though there were errors, there were few. They then changed to what Stewart called "fancy names" like Bluebeard and Tom-Thumb. All of the fancy names were called the first time. Stewart was impressed when the maidservant called Cinderella correctly, as she professed not to know the name.

To tighten the conditions, Hopkinson proposed that the thought-reader face the wall when she returned to the room. The percentage of success was the same as before. The tests of the Creery children by Gurney and Myers brought the same results. For Barrett, who had become the Honorable Secretary of the Thought-Reading Committee of the SPR (Gurney and Myers were the other members), the evidence was well nigh unshakable: Thought transference without the use of any sensory organs was a proven fact. Increasingly to Barrett's mind, it was exclusively due to his work and insights that thought reading as a scientific topic had been discovered.

Barrett, Gurney and Myers wrote an article for the public[2] describing the Creery results with restrained enthusiasm, concealing the family name as "C___."

In the following issue of *Nineteenth Century*, Dr. Horatio Donkin dismissed the Barrett, Gurney and Myers conclusions as "inadequately supported by trustworthy facts."[3] For those who have investigated thought reading with care and "with minds free from mystical bias, any aid towards the extinction of what must then be regarded as an *ignis fatuus* of pseudo-science carries with it its own justification."

Donkin pointed out that the authors even denied Stuart Cumberland's own explanation of his performances, a position he says is "perhaps as unwarrantable as the 'further inquiry' that they suggest.'" Donkin further dismissed the authors' insistence on weighing the personal integrity of participants by virtue of social position or occupation as an important factor in the investigation. He stated on page 132:

> Half of the evidence which has propped up the spiritualist craze is based on the results obtained through mediums of "unblemished character" in private families, whose virtuous reputation has been largely sustained by the fact that they did not take money for their trouble; no regard being paid to innumerable other motives and tendencies to deception.

In concluding, Donkin points out that some of the errors recorded by the observers are more suggestive of errors in the thought-reader's interpretation of the various codes that might be used by the family, rather than errors caused by an unclear mental image projected at a distance across the room. In a final blast, Donkin discredits all of the "C___" experiments as having been "superficially conducted."

But William Barrett refused to retreat — his prize was at hand.

Barrett received a letter from George John Romanes shortly after the First Report of the Committee on Thought Reading appeared in the *PSPR*.[4]

> If you can maintain such a quality in the material and such a tone in the style of our subsequent issues, I think that your new Society is bound to make a serious impression upon the science and the philosophy of our generation.

But the biologist had serious reservations with the Creery work.

> I do not see it stated that the conditions under which the experiments were made were such as <u>absolutely</u> to exclude the possibility of deception. For in all the cases of marked success it appears that Mr. Creery was present, if not also some of his daughters, besides the one selected to guess. Although it is stated that no words were spoken, signs might still have passed unobserved by the experimenters.
>
> I make these remarks not in a hostile spirit, but rather in a friendly one, because I feel what kind of criticism is likely to arise in the minds of those who have not witnessed the experiments, and, on the other hand, if the facts really are genuine, I should like to see their evidence ... the best that can be brought into court [emphasis original].

Romanes' uneasiness was shared over the months by other sympathetic and interested onlookers. Meanwhile, in America, within three years, J. Randall Brown had to begin to offer higher box office splits to local theatre managements along with lower ticket prices to ensure steady bookings. Though Brown could still make more than a workman's wages in a single night — when he worked — his annual income was beginning to slide down the scale toward the average and, at times, even below. Scientific curiosity was fading as well.

With the growing competition and the limited range of effects possible in thought reading, Brown attempted to spice up his act with spooks. Beginning in 1878, Brown began to expose mediumistic tricks, much as other exposers had already been doing for a number of years. It is likely that Brown had witnessed any number of those exposers, both magicians and non-magicians, who were traveling the country claiming to save the public from the infernal grasp of the predatory mediums — for a nominal entrance fee.

When news of a new spiritual stunt by some well known medium was published in the Spiritualist press as further proof of Spiritualistic claims, the exposers would focus on debunking that as their new spark to revive the fading public interest.

At times, an exposer would challenge a medium to a public on-stage face-to-face competition, with the audience at the end of the evening to determine who had won and therefore who would receive the box office receipts. Often, however, there was a previous agreement between the combatants to split the take regardless of the audience.

And like many other exposers, as public interest in the methods of mediums declined, Brown crossed over to claiming to be a medium himself. In 1882, Brown described himself as "The Monarch Among the Mediums with His Religious Illustrated Lectures."

Brown claimed to be traveling under the auspices of the United Society of Spiritualists, an organization that never existed. To further his spiritual credentials, Brown had the printing of his handbills attributed to The Banner of Light Publishing Co., Boston. This circumstance proved too much for Luther Colby, the respected editor of the *Banner of Light,* the premiere Spiritualist newspaper in America. He vigorously attacked J. Randall Brown in his columns, warning his loyal readers and followers against "the sometime fake thought reader and former exposer." He added Brown to his list of "peripatetic humbugs," the professional exposers and frauds which included some former mediums.

In spite of Colby's anger, Brown with his attractive wife, Lillie May, continued to combine the spirits with thought reading for the next several years.

Brown was exposed himself on occasion when caught on-stage trying to manipulate billets, and was embarrassed on more than one occasion, like other stage mediums, to discover that a spirit he was struggling to contact was actually sitting in the front row of the theater, laughing with the rest of the audience.

In 1886, following a retirement of a few months to rest from his travels and unable to obtain rewarding bookings, Brown left America to tour Europe and India for the first and only time in his career. The tour was financially successful.

Claiming he now presented "Occult Mysteries of the Orient," Brown later incorporated enthusiastic quotations from newspapers in England, India and Germany from the tour on his letterhead stationery, with the dates of the quotations periodically updated.

Beginning at the Bijou The-

J. Randall Brown, the Man of Mystery, ca. 1901.

atre[5] in New York, June 9, 1889, through the balance of his career, Randall Brown used "the Wire Test" as the signature stunt to close his show.

Standing on the stage at the Bijou, Brown held one end of an "electric telegraph wire," while Professor Cromwell, a well known lecturer, held the other end of the wire several hundred yards away at the Western Union Office at Thirtieth and Broadway. Cromwell was to concentrate on a number known only to him and project the secret number to Brown by concentrating on the wire he was holding.

Brown, blindfolded, pressed the wire against his forehead for a moment or two. He then turned and wrote the number 742 across the blackboard for the audience to see. He rotated the blackboard to conceal the number. The audience waited in silence.

A few minutes later Professor Cromwell returned to the theater, mounted the stage and announced to the expectant audience the number on which he had been concentrating. It was 742. The audience and the *New York Times*[6] were nonplussed. Later Cromwell insisted there was no means by which Brown could have known the number that had been only in his mind.

The means ultimately became known as a result of Brown's regularly repeating the wire test at his subsequent shows.

The thought reader would invite a prominent local personage to go to the balcony or the rear of the theater and, in seclusion, note the serial number of his watch. Then, with Brown on stage holding one end of the wire pressed to his forehead and the subject holding the other end, the thought reader would receive the brain wave and write the correct number on a blackboard — usually to rousing applause.

At one point in his publicity, to restore some semblance of scientific aura to the act, Brown claimed that the well known scientist Samuel Gross, now sadly deceased, had proposed to insert a galvanometer into the wire in order to measure the brain force flowing through it. Gross, naturally, was not available for comment.

However, on one occasion, the subject changed watches, unknown to Brown, which led to an embarrassing failure. On another, after a successful test, Brown refused to repeat the test with another gentleman and another watch in spite of loud audience insistence — an insistence that finally led to all the ticket money being returned.

But the ultimate blow came many months later when, the day after a successful test, the subject recalled to a curious reporter that Brown had asked him to write his watch serial number down in order to clarify it in his mind. The thought reader had solicitously expressed concern that the public test had in the past proven to be a serious strain to the mental faculties of some volunteers, and he wanted to ensure a positive experience for all involved.

Brown had then courteously offered a pad of paper to facilitate the subject's writing. The subject insisted to the reporter that Brown could not see him write and that he had personally retained the slip of paper with the number afterwards.

Finding a pad similar to the one used by Brown which was of soft paper, the reporter proved that the written number could be impressed into the underlying sheet of soft paper, to be recovered later by lightly rubbing a dark pencil lead over the second page of the pad — and, of course, the subject could retain his original slip of paper. The reporter was impressed with the simple subtlety of the cheat.

The method of the wire test began to spread from newspaper to newspaper wherever Brown and his wife appeared. The Brown annual income, once so impressive, had finally declined to the workingman's average level with 35 cents general admission and no reserved seats, and the local theatre management taking half or more of the total box office receipts.

During the last decade of the nineteenth century, Brown's career had begun to fade as a result of increased competition, exposures and the changing public entertainment interests. With the dates of his European and Indian tour now updated to 1899 on his stationery, he attempted to prop up his publicity by appropriating the title of "the White Mahatma" in 1904 from its originator, Samri S. Baldwin, who was still actively performing. Baldwin responded by billing himself as *The Original and Only Real White Mahatma.* Some stage press criticized Brown for taking another performer's property, but that activity was too common in the show business of the time to be noticed.

However, in spite of imitators, both amateur and professional, throughout the course of his travels, J. Randall Brown had continued to draw the attention and public approval of such American celebrities as author Mark Twain, inventor Eli Whitney, General Lew Wallace (author of *Ben-Hur*), and others.

One of his strongest early admirers had been the famous Salem Seer, Charles H. Foster. When Foster was quoted in the Boston newspapers, after viewing a Brown performance, as attributing Brown's results to "the spirits all around him," Foster adamantly denied it, saying Brown was a genuine mind reader "pure and simple." However, once Brown had stepped across the line to claim mediumship for himself, the Foster quote was never used again in the Brown promotional materials.

But all the triumphs were diminishing memories when, after making sporadic attempts during the early 1900s to regain public attention, Brown finally closed down his stage career in 1923. He began instead to take local jobs as a photographer and printer in Minneapolis, Minnesota.

John Randall Brown died in Minneapolis on July 3, 1926, at the age of seventy-five. His last words to Lillie May were, "Get me out of here."

12

Stuart C. Cumberland, Thought Reader

> For what is called society loves to patronize, and, as a matter of course, hates to be patronized; and it goes without saying that it will never receive as an equal any one whom it can hire.
> — Stuart Charles Francis Cumberland, 1888

Left in April 1879 without immediate income by W. Irving Bishop's sudden departure for Malta, and certainly no fool, 22-year-old Charles Garner could count the houses as well as Bishop, Randall Brown or anyone else. Those few weeks he spent observing W.I. Bishop had revealed a lucrative life that Garner had never before realized existed.

With experimentation and determined practice Garner recognized that he could, initially at least, approximate Bishop's thought reading performance and with continued diligent practice perhaps equal it — and, obviously, the sooner the better. He found mimicking Bishop's spiritualistic exposures to be much easier.

But Charles Garner wasn't a foreigner who could move easily in British society, immune to Victorian social restrictions. The son of a butcher shop clerk simply did not rub shoulders with the upper classes. Garner had to create and daily live a new persona with an appropriate somewhat vague flutter-finger back story — and push the butcher shop as far out of sight as he could.

He first tried the name Charles Stuart, then decided on Stuart Charles Francis Cumberland (Cumberland, he found, had a suitable euphonic tone). Finally, in June 1880, Garner-as-Cumberland embarked on his new career as an anti–Spiritualist. At some appropriate point, he planned also to become a "renown" thought reader.

T.H. Green, professor of moral philosophy at Oxford University, stated on June 28, 1880, "So far as I am able to judge, Mr. Cumberland has remarkable skill in exposing the tricks of 'Spiritualism' which I venture to think a very useful object."

Professor Green thus became the first person to publicly endorse Stuart Cumberland's capabilities in the thought reader's subsequent long career. Green was a neighbor, living at 14 St. Giles Street near the butcher shop.

Cumberland gave several private demonstrations of fake medium tricks closely following Bishop's routines. His principal gathering was held in a reception room at Charing Cross Hotel in London, September 3, 1880. Attendance was by invitation only, but Samuel C. Hall, an ardent Spiritualist, had obtained an admission card and thus found a seat in the crowd.

Cumberland ensured that several reporters were present, with the result that news of his exposures of the mediums' light and dark séance tricks received wide coverage in several London and provincial newspapers.

A reporter for the *Whitehall Review*, writing on September 9, said, "In the room I found Mr. S.C. Hall, a rampant spiritualist; and a posse of the curious of both sexes; also the 'gentlemen of the press' were in force. The 'operator' was Stuart C. Cumberland, who may possibly make by his crusade against the followers of Mr. D.D. Home what he would never realize by paragraph-writing — a fortune."[1]

The reporter summarized Cumberland's tricks and demonstrations, including one with the spiritualist Mr. Hall as the volunteer in which Cumberland demonstrated how unreliable the human senses are in various situations in determining the direction of noises. Hall agreed to be blindfolded. Cumberland then clicked two coins together close to Hall's head, and asked from what direction Hall heard the sounds. The volunteer was, in the words of a reporter, "invariably wide of the mark." Throughout the soirée, Hall continually made loud comments on Cumberland's actions, primarily claiming that nothing that Cumberland was doing resembled the actual manifestations experienced in a séance room.[2] He declared Cumberland's "imitations to be as much like the originals as a pea is like a plum-pudding."

The *Whitehall* reporter concluded his article, "It is pitiful to see educated people, keen as knives in all besides, surrender themselves to the wiles and fascinations of 'mediums' whose characteristics are frequently dirty fingernails and inability to use the letter H with precision"—a characterization that was disturbingly close to a description of Charles Garner only a few months earlier. Cumberland still spoke with a broad Cockney accent. He worked to acquire an upper class pronunciation, but was never to fully succeed.

Each reporter writing about the Charing Cross experience had urged Cumberland to use a more popular forum to advance his crusade against the guile and deceit of the Spiritualist impostors, assuring him confidently that a large, appreciative and profitable public awaited him.

For his first professional foray, Cumberland booked Steinway Hall in Portman Square, London. He puffed up his handbills and publicity with the endorsement letters and newspaper write-ups he had thus far accumulated. One awkward observation was that the bulk of the publicity referred to only one experience, the Charing Cross Hotel demonstration of the previous month.

However, the fact that Stuart Cumberland had successfully attracted the invited press and personages to Charing Cross, though he was completely unknown, was an illuminating measure of the still vigorous public interest in the claims of Spiritualism.

The public eagerness assured by the reporters at Charing Cross, however, did not materialize. Cumberland was deeply disappointed with the mediocre financial results of the two poorly attended Steinway performances.

Still needing to continue to build his anti–Spiritualist credentials, Cumberland looked for a suitable new target for his exposures. He visited a healing medium, Miss M. A. Houghton, in London, claiming that he was suffering from neuralgia. The medium prescribed a remedy for which Cumberland paid her 2s 6d. At the time, she had openly informed him that she was a spirit-medium.

Cumberland then brought charges October 9 against Houghton in the Marlborough Street Police Court in London under the 1824 Vagrancy Act, claiming she had taken funds from him under false pretences.[3]

Under close questioning by Houghton's attorney, Mr. Abraham, Garner gave his name to the court, under oath, as Stuart Charles Cumberland. He stated that he was a journalist and a lecturer, and that he had advertised to give a startling exposure of Spiritualism at Steinway Hall on October 4 and 5.

Quoting from Cumberland's handbill, Abraham also showed that Cumberland had warned the public in his advertisements that "to prevent disappointment and the consequences of a crush ... it is particularly requested that purchasers will take an early opportunity of securing seats," to the loud tittering of the courtroom since both performances at Steinway Hall had been weakly attended with equally poor newspaper reviews. One newspaper commented, "The attendance was miserably thin on both occasions, although several were present with free orders."

At that point, the Houghton case was adjourned to the following morning.

The next morning, October 10, Cumberland had instructed his attorney, W. H. B. Pain, to drop all charges. The reason given the court was Mr. Cumberland's solicitous regard for Miss Houghton's illness.

Houghton's attorney responded strongly to the court that his client was

IMPOSITION DETECTED!
SPIRITUALISM EXPOSED!

In response to repeated requests

Mr. STUART C. CUMBERLAND

Will LECTURE at

STEINWAY HALL,

LOWER SEYMOUR STREET, PORTMAN SQUARE,

MONDAY & TUESDAY, OCTOBER 4th & 5th,

At 8 p.m., on

SPIRITUALISM

And

CLAIRVOYANCE,

REPRODUCING AND EXPLAINING MANY STARTLING

"SPIRIT-MANIFESTATIONS."

· Prices—Reserved Seats, 5s.   Front Seats, 3s.   Balcony, 2s.

SPECIAL NOTICE.—Tickets may be purchased at Austin's Opera and Concert Ticket Office, St. James's Hall, Piccadilly, W., and at Steinway Hall, and in order to prevent disappointment and the consequences of a crush, it is particularly requested that intending purchasers will take an early opportunity of securing seats.

DOORS OPEN AT 7.30.   CARRIAGES AT 9.45.

Steinway Hall Program, October 1880. Courtesy Peter Lane Collection.

perfectly healthy and ready to continue. "Cumberland, or rather a person who calls himself by that name," said Abraham, "but who really appears to be a Charles Garner of Oxford, has come here and made a number of statements which this lady, Miss Houghton, is prepared to contradict. We were quite prepared to go with this case to the very last."

Abraham had informed Pain the previous afternoon that he was determined to vigorously cross-examine Cumberland again under oath. Cumberland feared that would fully expose his butcher shop background and his perjury from the previous day. Either way, Abraham, potentially, could kill his struggling newborn career. Cumberland's amateurish play to hurriedly hang up another mediumistic scalp had badly backfired.

His funds depleted by the deficit from the Steinway Hall adventure and his career badly misfiring, Cumberland had to revise his strategy. Should he continue with the spirits? They could still pay, but he had to begin to emphasize the thought reading in order to revitalize public interest. W. I. Bishop was frequently in the London papers doing more thought reading as well as continuing his séance exposures. As of the end of October 1880, over six months into his new career, Stuart Cumberland had not yet performed a public demonstration of thought reading.

But within a few days that changed.

Though still emphasizing the spirits, Cumberland began to add thought reading to his routine as he promoted small public and private bookings.

W. Irving Bishop was present at three of Cumberland's earliest shows in different small public venues, standing at the back, an amused expression on his face. Leaving early on each occasion, he smugly dismissed his former secretary as irrelevant.

Through 1881, Cumberland's performances began to gain additional public attention with his thought reading drawing more positive reviews. Cumberland's thought reading included versions of most of the Bishop stunts, like pin-finding, reading banknotes, the murder scenario, and so on. Comments were made in reviews contrasting Cumberland's more gentlemanly behavior on stage versus Bishop's bizarre and even wild antics; but the comparisons were not always positive, as Bishop often pushed his performance envelope, sometimes failing spectacularly, while Cumberland appeared to be overcautious, even, to some, timid.

In his performances, Bishop had often claimed he could not explain his powers, implying there was an undefined occult aspect in his capabilities. In contrast, Cumberland claimed only that he could discern his subject's thoughts through practiced intimate perception of physical clues. There was nothing, Stuart Cumberland emphasized, nothing supernatural about anything he did.

In response to Bishop's three-part article on Spiritualist fraud in *Leisure*

Hour, Cumberland published a long letter two months later in the July 1881 issue of the more academic *Journal of Mental Science* titled "Illusionary and Fraudulent Aspects of Spiritualism." This letter was immediately condemned in the Spiritualist press as inaccurate and exposing only conjuror's tricks, not séance manifestations. A second Cumberland letter appeared in the July 1882 issue of the *JMS.*[4]

Unlike the more generalized descriptions of mediumistic fraud by Bishop, Cumberland identified mediums by name and their specific techniques. Exploiting prominent names whenever possible, Cumberland quoted noted physics Professor John Tyndall's comment to him: "One might as well attempt to place a new core in a rotten apple as put new thoughts into committed Spiritualists."

Stuart C. Cumberland, 1881. Courtesy William V. Rauscher Collection.

In his *Journal of Mental Science* letter, Cumberland took credit yet one more time for exposing Harry Bastian and his partner as a fraud during a Bloomsbury séance.

Bastian and Taylor were materializing mediums. When a glowing materialized spirit form appeared moving around the dark circle at the Bloomsbury residence, Cumberland had squirted red cochlea into the "spirit's" face. Crying out, the spirit ran back toward the cabinet with Cumberland in pursuit, just escaping the exposer's grasp through the curtains into the cabinet.

When the lights went up, the medium was discovered with blotches of red cochlea on his face. The Bastian exposure[5] in Bloomsbury gave Cumberland's early career the key cachet it needed.

On Saturday evening, May 6, 1882,[6] with Dr. James Crichton-Browne presiding, Cumberland gave a private demonstration of thought reading to a select group of scientific and literary men at the Marlborough Rooms. The demonstration consisted of his standard routine of pin-finding, spelling words thought of by various members of the group, and disclosing the dates of birth of several of the men present. At the conclusion of the evening's performance, one of the men present, Professor Edwin Ray Lankester, who had been present when W. I. Bishop had performed at a similar venue twelve months earlier, commented that Cumberland had been "correct in his interpretations or readings in a larger proportion of instances than Mr. Bishop"—and in sharp contrast to Bishop, who claimed that he was aided by some occult force that he himself could not comprehend, Cumberland acknowledged that he was aided in all his revelations simply "by naturally quick and highly trained perceptive faculties." Dr. Crichton-Browne complimented Cumberland on his work in exposing "the impositions of charlatans and the superstitions of weak-minded enthusiasts." The few Spiritualists present during the meeting, in spite of Cumberland's own statements and those of others, were still disposed to consider the thought reader as a genuine clairvoyant.

Cumberland's improving public stature attracted American impresario Major James B. Pond,[7] when he visited England in July 1882 looking for acts to import to America. Of the many acts he witnessed, Pond selected humorist and sketch artist Walter Pelham and the thought reader Stuart Charles Cumberland. Cumberland left Liverpool for New York on the mail packet *Arizona*, paying $30 for a cabin. He arrived in New York City on Tuesday, November 28, 1882, at 10:30 A.M., at Pier 38, at the foot of King Street.

That afternoon at the Everett House hotel, Cumberland presented a private demonstration of thought reading to an invited group of nineteen men from the New York press, academic world, clergy, physicians and theatrical managers. Present among the group were Dr. George M. Beard and the Rev. Henry Ward Beecher. The invitations had been arranged by Pond and his partner, Maze Edwards, both of whom were also present. When in New York, Pond always stayed at the Everett House.

Cumberland was styled by Pond in the invitations as a scientific investigator of the claims of Spiritualism and a pioneering thought reader. Pond included some London clippings and letters endorsing the Englishman's prowess.

Cumberland was described in the *New York Daily Tribune* as, "a young man with rosy cheeks and a blonde mustache."[8]

In his short introductory speech, Cumberland disclaimed any belief in Spiritualism, attributing all phenomena to thought reading and trickery. He suddenly stopped and asked the Rev. Beecher to think of any object in the room. Cumberland took Beecher's hand and immediately went to touch the eye-glasses of one of the physicians, which was the correct object. Beecher was astonished.

The reporter from the *New York Times* noted, "The Cumberland experiments were very much like those with which the public has been made familiar through the experiments of Brown and Bishop, who call their experiments 'mind-reading.'"[9]

A piece of white paper was pinned to the wall as Cumberland asked the Rev. Beecher to note the date on a coin in his pocket. Taking Beecher's hand, Cumberland wrote, "1870."

"You're wrong," said Beecher, "and you're right, and there's something strange about this." Cumberland stopped him and changed the number to 1879.

"That's right," said Beecher, "but singularly enough when I first looked at the coin I thought the date was 1870, but a closer inspection showed a tail to the cipher and the date to be 1879."

Dr. Beard closed the thought reading portion by putting the thought reader to two tests that the physician said were "the supreme tests of this kind of work." In the first, the Englishman immediately found a selected pin among fifty stuck into the table in the front of the room. In the second, Beard said he was thinking of an object. Cumberland took him by the hand and led Beard around the parlor, making multiple circles around the table, then about the room and finally back to the table again in the front of the room.

Dr. Beard, in acknowledging that the route was exactly as he had thought of it, and that he had had no actual object in mind, said that "the test has been better by Mr. Cumberland than he (Beard) had ever seen it done before."

Demonstrating two simple mediumistic stunts, Cumberland closed his demonstration. It had been a productive forty-five minutes.

In London, E. Dawson Rogers, one of the original founders of the nascent Society for Psychical Research in February 1882 and the editor of the popular Spiritualist journal *Light*, received a letter from Brighton, a resort town on the south coast of England. As published by Rogers on August 26, 1882, the letter began:

> The following details of the latest and most remarkable development of that form of Thought-reading popularized by Mr. Irving Bishop may prove of interest to your readers. In conjunction with Mr. G.A. Smith, a Brighton mesmerist, not unknown to readers of this and other Spiritualist journals, I have had the satisfaction of experiencing some demonstrations of mind-sympathy which are, I believe, almost without precedent. The modus of Mr. Smith's experiment is this: He places himself en rapport with myself by taking my hands; and a strong concentration of will and mental vision on my part has enabled him to read my thoughts with an accuracy that approaches the miraculous. Not only can he, with slight hesitation, read numbers, words, and even whole sentences which I alone have seen, but the

sympathy between us has been developed between us to such a degree that he rarely fails to experience the taste of any liquid or solid I choose to imagine. He has named, described or discovered small articles he has never seen, when they have been concealed by me in the most unusual places, and on two occasions he has successfully described portions of a scene which I either imagined or actually saw.... Mr. Smith has exhibited marked power as a thought-reader through the mediumship of other persons, but on no occasion has he attained to anything like the power he invariably displays when en rapport with myself.[10]

The letter closed with: We would be happy to receive a visit from any Spiritualist or scientific enquirer who may be at Brighton in the ensuing month.

The letter was signed: Douglas Blackburn, editor of *The Brightonian*.

With their firm belief that the experiments with the Creery children had confirmed the fact of thought transference without contact, Edmund Gurney and Frederic W. H. Myers immediately wrote Blackburn for more details, and then to schedule a visit to Brighton for December 1882. The resulting apparently successful experiments would, in later years, come back to haunt the SPR.

With his first public performance in New York scheduled for Chickering Hall on Saturday, December 10, 1882, Stuart Cumberland began to visit local mediums with reporters in tow in order to build his American reputation by exposing the native spiritual phenomena.

On Saturday, December 3, with reporters from the *Times*[11] and the *Herald*[12] accompanying him, Cumberland called on A. J. Phillips at his home at 161 West 36th Street.

Phillips,[13] a 25-year-old sensitive noted for his quiet temperament and scholarly demeanor, was at first reluctant to demonstrate his capabilities before three clearly hostile visitors, but finally assented.

Working first with the *Times* reporter, who was himself a skilled amateur conjuror, Phillips took him into a room bare but for a deal table and two chairs. Phillips left several slips of paper on the table. He instructed the reporter that after the medium had left the room and the door was closed, he was to write names on nine or ten of the papers, one of which should be that of someone known to the reporter to be dead. He was then to roll the slips into small pellets and mix them until the reporter himself could not know which pellet held the dead name.

Once Phillips had closed the door behind him, the *Times* reporter closely examined the room for peep-holes or anything else that the medium could use to observe him. There was nothing. Still then carefully covering his writing

12. Stuart Cumberland, Thought Reader

with his hand, and tightly squeezing the slips down into small pellets, the reporter was ready.

Outside the room, Cumberland and the *Herald* reporter watched Phillips closely. The medium only stood silently and waited.

The *Times* reporter called the medium back into the room. Seating himself, with Cumberland and the *Herald* reporter watching over his shoulder, Phillips quietly touched each of the pellets with the tip of his forefinger, finally pushing one toward the reporter.

"Do you know the name inside this pellet?" he asked.

The reporter admitted he had no idea.

Phillips then wrote a name on another slip of paper and told the reporter to open the pellet. The name inside the pellet matched that written by Phillips. It was the correct dead name.

The medium successfully repeated the test with the *Herald* reporter.

Phillips then invited Stuart Cumberland into the room. After an initial failure by Phillips, an argument ensued between the medium and the thought reader regarding proper conditions.

Another test was done with Cumberland that also failed, then a third and final test which partially succeeded, with Phillips writing down one of the names in the pellets but not the dead name.

On leaving, Cumberland tried to explain that Phillips had somehow caught a glimpse of the reporters writing the names, but both reporters emphatically stated that was impossible.

The *Times* man wrote, "Cumberland reluctantly admitted that Mr. Phillips possessed 'cleverness' not equaled by any other medium he had ever seen."

Commenting further, he continued, "The upshot was that the visitors, with the exception of Mr. Cumberland, were convinced that Mr. Phillips possessed powers even more remarkable that that of the one who aimed to expose him."

Phillips had disclaimed any spirit power, but simply gave his demonstrations for what they were worth. He, like the thought reader, insisted he was only a dedicated investigator.

Cumberland quickly issued a public denial and challenged Phillips, saying that he would give the medium $10 for every correct name and $10 for each correct date of birth or death. Phillips never responded.

In a front page interview in the *New York Evening Post*,[14] arranged by Pond, Cumberland described his sessions with Phillips as having occurred over several days. His descriptions of Phillips' tests bore no resemblance to those described in the *Times* and the *Herald*, but were rather standard billet reading methods familiar to every magician. He closed the interview by claiming that Phillips did table-rapping by dislocating his big toe, when Phillips had not performed any table raps at all. Clearly, the medium had completely baffled the thought reader.

Phillips was in the audience for Cumberland's first public performance before a large audience, but made no public comment.[15]

The second performance[16] was also well attended. As with the first, Pond had liberally distributed free passes. Nevertheless, some Spiritualists made the familiar claim that Cumberland was not exposing genuine séance phenomena, just doing conjuror's tricks.

W. Irving Bishop had been infuriated when he learned that his former American manager, Major Pond, was now Cumberland's manager. Bishop wrote a circular to denounce Cumberland and Pond, detailing Cumberland's butcher shop background.

To the delight of Spiritualists who relished the sight of one exposer exposing another, Bishop sent hundreds of copies of the circular to various New York periodicals and ticket sellers which were widely distributed after Cumberland's first performances. The Bishop circular was printed in full in the December 26, 1882, issue of the *New York Times*[17] — and a few days later in the *Banner of Light*.

In response to Bishop's attack circular, Cumberland declared in the New York *Times*[18] that Stuart C. F. Cumberland was his name, that his father was a farmer, a landed proprietor, in Leicestershire, and that he had studied for the military before becoming a journalist, during which time he had discovered his preternatural talents as a thought reader.

Pond, who, with Charles Frohman and M. B. Leavitt, was one of the premier American theatrical managers, for his part, detailed his contempt for W. Irving Bishop as an unreliable professional performer who rarely met his commitments. Pond disclosed that he had finally, after much frustration, paid Bishop $50 to cancel their contract and that he, Pond, never wanted to see Bishop again.

Bishop's bitter attack did not derail Cumberland's American tour, as he had hoped, but did attract a comment from the *New York Dramatic News*, January 1883[19]:

> And now the scientific exposer, Mr. Stuart Cumberland, has woke up Mr. W. Irving Bishop, another exposer, who sends to this country printed circulars denouncing the exposer of the first part. This is lively. If these two scientific gentlemen, who really cannot tell the difference between a psychic force and a sardine, will hereafter devote all their occult powers to exposing each other, they may be of some service to the community, and really become entertaining.

Even then, Stuart Cumberland's career and earnings continued to climb. Cumberland's tour then continued south to Baltimore, returned north to Boston, and turned west to Worcester, Massachusetts. In March 1883, the tour went south to Troy, New York, where the situation turned strangely sour.

After performing all his proven techniques to create public excitement for two days, Cumberland opened at the Troy Music Hall. The *Troy Standard*[20] described Cumberland walking on stage to "a vista of empty seats and a bleak gallery."

The reporter continued:

> He stood with a puzzled expression on his handsome countenance, standing motionless until a bevy of late-comers had become settled.
>
> Then Cumberland said, "In all of my travels, and I have traveled much, I have never performed my experiments before so small an audience. I think if I were to divide my smallest audience by about ten I would have a larger number of spectators than I have here tonight."
>
> The thought reader performed a short program and stalked off the stage.

The attendance at the second evening was similar. His exasperation was easily read by the audience members even if their own minds went untouched. Writing with some smugness, the reporter quoted Cumberland:

> "For the first time in my life I have had to wait for an audience," said Mr. Cumberland in that peculiar style of utterance which prominent papers say is now fashionable in "cultured society," but which to an uncultured ear is pure Cockney.

Cumberland then moved on to Toronto and traveled extensively over Canada with improving notices at each new venue including meeting the Governor-General at a reception at Rideau Hall. As part of Cumberland's demonstration, the Governor-General proposed a special test. Speaking to the gathering, the Marquis Lorne said, "I wish you to try a more difficult experiment than those you have just accomplished. You cannot possibly know anything about it, and if you succeed it will certainly be the most extraordinary thing I have yet witnessed." Blindfolded and taking the Governor-General's wrist, Cumberland walked quickly through the halls, going outside the building with the people following behind, and, without hesitation, led the Marquis directly to the pet moose of the Princess Louise in its specially built stall. The people and the Marquis were astounded. The moose became a regular topic in Cumberland's future handbills. It was also noted in the press that Stuart Cumberland and the Governor-General could have been twin brothers.

Finally, Cumberland returned to Great Britain in early 1884 to prepare for his first tour of Europe. He had been kept aware by friends of Bishop's travails with Henri Labouchère and J.N. Maskelyne.

13

Thought Reading Extraordinary: Blackburn and Smith

> "Starting with a crude set of signals produced by jingling of pince-nez, sleeve-link, long and short breathing, even blowing, [our codes] grew to a degree little short of marvelous."
> — Douglas Blackburn, *John Bull*, 1908

For a few weeks, George Albert Smith, eighteen, a short, handsome young man with curly brown hair had been presenting mesmeric performances with modest success at the Brighton Aquarium. When asked, Smith explained that it was a means of supplementing his widowed mother's boarding house income.

Douglas Blackburn,[1] twenty-five, who had been the founding editor of the weekly gossip sheet *The Brightonian* two years earlier, found that his articles exposing the various occult frauds involved in Spiritualism, mesmerism and thought reading were proving to be very popular with his readers. He later claimed that his "great score" was when he had been the first, in 1882, to discover the secret of W. Irving Bishop's thought reading performances — a statement which was manifestly false.

Blackburn noted that Bishop's "bold advertisements and the janglings of believers and skeptics made sufficient noise to stir Europe, and Thought Reading became the craze, and with reason."[2]

Sensing "another subject for my witch hunt" in exposing George Smith's mesmerism, Blackburn attended two or three of Smith's mesmeric performances. Describing his experience later, Blackburn said:

> It was the usual mesmeric entertainment, in which a number of lads were put under the influence and made to do ridiculous things. I was a little bit surprised to find my own office boy among the "subjects" and when I learned from him that he was paid a shilling a night, the bogus character of the business became obvious. But before "showing up" Mr. G. A. Smith I

made his acquaintance.... Smith had absorbed a vast amount of knowledge of the conjuring business, and was most ingenious in inventing new tricks or discovering the secret of old ones.

Blackburn noted later that he realized that he had discovered "a genius in his line" and that he was also the most ingenious conjurer that the journalist had met outside of the magic profession.

Blackburn gave Smith a rousing review in the June 1, 1882, issue of *The Brightonian*:

> The most amusing remarkable entertainment in Brighton this week is that being given by Mr. G.A. Smith, the Brighton mesmerist, at the Town Hall.... For a young man Mr. Smith has marvelous control over his subjects, and it is astonishing that anyone after witnessing his experiments can doubt his genuineness.

Finding they had a joint interest in occult matters and particularly in thought reading along the lines of W. Irving Bishop, Blackburn and Smith began to privately experiment, duplicating what they had seen Bishop accomplish. Smith, particularly, was anxious to add additional wonders to his mesmeric show as his audiences were becoming thinner, with some patrons beginning to notice that the same young boys kept reappearing as subjects on stage. Within a week or two, the two young men created a conjuring act that included mesmerism and second sight demonstrations. Following a few weeks of preparation, Blackburn-Smith performed successfully at numerous charity bazaars and gatherings in Brighton and Hove, and other resorts in southeastern England with Smith taking the lead billing, keeping Blackburn in the background so as to protect his guise of journalistic impartiality. At times, Blackburn would not be mentioned at all in advertisements.

The two young men had determined that their powers would encourage greater public credibility if they refused payments for many of their performances, maintaining throughout their exhibitions that they were dedicated private unpaid demonstrators and scholarly investigators. "Our plan," wrote Blackburn some thirty years later in 1908, "was to bamboozle the 'scientific investigators' thoroughly, and then let the world know the value of scientific research."[3]

As with all second sight acts, Blackburn and Smith developed unique techniques of coding the information which Blackburn obtained from casually walking through the audience. He subtlely communicated the information to the blindfolded Smith on the stage while, with his back to the medium, Blackburn appeared only to be speaking quietly with a spectator.

A *Brightonian* competitor, *The Dolphin*, had earlier (October 16 and 30, 1880) published two brief articles, "Second-Sight Exposed by an Ex-Medium," by a writer who claimed that he had become the second member of a second sight act years earlier at the age of twelve. "The 'system' of my chief," he wrote, "was simplified so as to embrace every variety of article classified in sets, one question, with a word or two added, sufficing to elicit a correct answer for ten different articles." The second *Dolphin* article described an awkward coding system. The article promised "to be continued," but never was. All that had been revealed in the two articles could be easily found in more useful detail in any number of cheap contemporary pamphlets on amateur conjuring. Whether the ex-medium's insights became any part of the later Blackburn-Smith thinking is very doubtful.

W. Irving Bishop's pamphlet ghost-written for him in 1880, *Houdin and Heller's Second Sight Explained,* contained much more useful information on coding at the price of one shilling (see also Appendices B, C, D and E), but there were many others for sale.

Blackburn had written a review of a famous second sight act, "Little Louie" with Professor Heriot, in his paper on December 3, 1880:

> "Little Louie," the marvel of second-sight as the advertisement has it, is at the Aquarium this week this being her third appearance here.... The thing does not draw, however, for the general public understands that sort of thing too well now.

W. I. Bishop appeared at the Brighton Pavilion in July and August 1881, helpfully promoted by Blackburn's enthusiastic write-ups. When Bishop returned to the area, on December 2, 1881, Blackburn gave a dinner in Bishop's honor at the offices of *The Brightonian.* It was attended by the mayor and numerous town officials. During Bishop's performance after dinner, the thought reader ragged and teased the most senior city fathers of Brighton to the loud delight of their colleagues.[4]

Blackburn observed[5] that *thought-reading* was "a very comprehensive title, and whilst it actually describes Mr. Bishop's

※ ※
※

Next week the scientifically disposed will have an opportunity of testing the phenomena more closely. Mr. Smith proposes giving a series of seances in the Lecture Room of the Aquarium, when he will produce some of the higher phenomena of mesmerism, and in conjunction with Mr. Douglas Blackburn give demonstrations of Thought Reading.

※ ※
※

These experiments have received the attention of the British Society for Psychical Research, and a paper on the subject is to be read by Professor Barrett at the next meeting of the society.

※ ※
※

The Brightonian, September 30, 1882.

strange acquirement, it is likely to give the general public an erroneous and exaggerated idea of his capabilities"—capabilities that Douglas Blackburn and George Smith would later claim for themselves.

As they worked together the summer of 1882, Blackburn and Smith refined their coding systems to allow the efficient transmission of increasingly complex descriptive information, including the most difficult information, coding random drawings.[6] Thus they developed a more convincing demonstration of the mysterious powers of the mind, which enabled the two men to create demonstrations of apparent non-contact thought reading. As Blackburn later wrote, regarding the codes, "Starting with a crude set of signals produced by jingling of pince-nez, sleeve-link, long and short breathing, even blowing, they grew to a degree little short of marvelous."

The pair had moved away from the overly familiar area of obvious spoken codes or using the Morse code to key memorized sets of items. To be successful, Blackburn and Smith recognized that they only had to convince an audience that they *might* truly be the real thing, which would start people talking, while the performers themselves made no evident claims to subtle preternatural powers. Blackburn would write positive notices of the pair's appearances in his columns, oftentimes not mentioning his own involvement.[7]

With growing confidence in their operation as it was steadily honed in several performing venues, Blackburn and Smith certainly became aware of the work of the SPR through the article "Thought Reading" written by Barrett, Myers, and Gurney that had appeared in the June 1882 issue of the popular magazine *Nineteenth Century*, which had extolled the positive results of their testing of the Creery children. Rather than write the SPR directly, Blackburn wrote a letter to the Spiritualist journal *Light,* which was published as "Thought-Reading Extraordinary," August 26, 1882. Blackburn described the wonders worked by Smith and himself and invited investigation by scientific inquirers. Blackburn also surely had been aware when he wrote his letter to *Light* of the highly critical article "A Note on 'Thought-Reading'" in the July issue of *Nineteenth Century* by Dr. Horatio B. Donkin, which described the weak aspects of the SPR experimental procedures, suggesting the benign, and, in Donkin's opinion, unprofessional test conditions that Blackburn and Smith might likely encounter.

Professor Barrett acknowledged Blackburn's letter in his "Appendix to the First Report on Thought-Reading."[8] "The following extract from a letter published in *Light* shows that a Mr. Smith, of Brighton, has powers analogous to those claimed by Mr. Bishop," Barrett wrote. Barrett then described how Bishop, with the aid of an unnamed male assistant, had demonstrated to the scientist how information could be subtlely transmitted using simple verbal codes. Bishop then demonstrated his own thought-reading capabilities, repeat-

> **ST. JAMES'S HALL, Grand Parade, Brighton.**
>
> Every Evening,
>
> Mr. G. A. SMITH'S Experiments in
> **MESMERISM AND THOUGHT READING,**
> Admission: Reserved Seats, 2s.; Second Seats, 1s.;
> Back Seats, 6d.
> To commence at Eight o'clock.

G.A. Smith Advertisement, *The Brightonian*, December 2, 1882.

ing several stunts from his regular routine — all of which deeply impressed the scientist.

Frederic W. H. Myers and Edmund Gurney traveled to Brighton, Saturday, December 2, 1882, to investigate the apparent telepathic talents of Blackburn and Smith. Professor Barrett, the Honorary Secretary of the SPR Committee on Thought-Transference, could not leave his duties in Dublin. The experiments began the next day, Sunday, at Gurney's hotel room.

The testing of Blackburn and Smith at Brighton was described in the "Second Report of the Committee on Thought Transference," delivered to a general meeting of the SPR, December 9, 1882, under the heading of "Brighton Experiments," and later published in the *Proceedings of the SPR*.[9] The Report also contained the details of the further successful testing of the Creery children at Myers's home in Cambridge and Barrett's home in Dublin which served to further consolidate the views of the Committee as to the genuineness of the Creery phenomena. Thus Gurney and Myers went to Brighton with the firm conviction that very probably mind-to-mind thought transference without use of the sensory organs was "a proven fact of nature."

Douglas Blackburn, who became an associate of the SPR following the Brighton investigation, was described to the SPR audience as "a very painstaking and accurate observer, to the effect that he had obtained remarkable results in thought-reading, or will-impression, with Mr. G.A. Smith, a young mesmerist living at Brighton." In their introductory summary, the committee said, "The results of these trials give us the most important and valuable insight into the manner of mental transfer of a mental picture which we have yet obtained."

Blackburn was allowed to touch Smith's hand or forehead (Smith had blindfolded himself "to aid his concentration") during eleven trials of silently sending colors and numbers. The trials were met with moderate success, some direct hits, some near misses. Throughout the time of the trials no conversation was allowed, nor any encouragement expressed to Smith if his expression seemed close to the target color or number. Several trials of colors and numbers were then tried with Blackburn and Smith in separate rooms, all of which failed. Seven trials with names were then tried with Blackburn holding Smith's hand, which again were moderately successful. Two trials without physical contact failed.

After a brief pause to allow Smith and Blackburn to rest, four trials followed to determine if Smith could discern the location of pain on Blackburn's body caused by one member repeatedly pinching Blackburn in different body locations for one to two minutes at a time. The other investigator held a pillow in front of Smith's blindfolded eyes while Blackburn, seated across a table from Smith, held Smith's hand. All four trials were successes, a result described in the committee report as "very striking."

Moving to designs, Blackburn was required to project a sequence of simple geometric drawings to Smith with Smith describing verbally what he saw. The designs were drawn by one of the enquirers who then held the sketch up behind the blindfolded Smith so that Blackburn could see it. The two investigators noted that Smith's responses were usually reversed from the actual design, top for bottom, left for right, but in general accurate for all four trials. The design reversal was a new phenomenon to the investigators.

That concluded the first day's trials. Both Myers and Gurney were satisfied with the phenomena they had observed and had meticulously recorded. In their joint view, there had been no opportunity for collusion or fraud.

The following day, Monday, all six trials were focused on non-geometrical designs drawn out of sight of the blindfolded Smith, with Blackburn briefly holding Smith's hand and then releasing it. The designs were random in order to eliminate the possibility that Blackburn and Smith were using any coding—such as, specifically, a Morse code.

Smith was seated with his back to the experimenters on the far side of the room from where the two SPR members stood. After a moment or two— and, as explicitly noted by Myers and Gurney, *after* Blackburn had released Smith's hand—Smith drew his impression of the figures, which were, as the investigators noted in their report, "as like the original as a child's blindfold drawing of a pig is like a pig." But clearly, *in silence and without apparent contact*, Smith's scrawled impressions did in fact reasonably resemble the original nine projected designs.[10]

A note was appended after the conclusion of the committee report which referred to additional trials held following the two days at Brighton, under more stringent conditions without any physical contact between Blackburn and Smith. The details would be the subject of the next committee report.

The committee closed their report with: "The burden of explaining these results rests upon those who deny the possibility of thought transference."

On December 30, 1882, William Barrett wrote a letter to the *Yorkshire Post* to challenge the *Post*'s critical statement, in an article on the Thought Transference Committee's activities, that "the inquirers have been too hasty in assuring themselves of results which, if they are realities, are far outside the order of universal experience." Barrett's letter was also published in *Light*.[11] After pointing out that Meyers, Gurney and himself had been investigating the evidence for thought-reading, "or as we now propose to call it ideoscopy," for some years, even predating the founding of the SPR, Barrett then continued:

> Our later investigations—first, with a family at Buxton, with whom we have made over 1,000 experiments, under the most stringent conditions, and now with a gentleman at Brighton, whose ideoscopic powers are the most remarkable we have yet met with—have shown that very much which passes as thought-reading is simply muscle-reading; but that, nevertheless (and in spite of general experience to the contrary) it is in the highest degree probable that ideas can be transferred from mind to mind without the intervention of the recognized organs of sensation.

The scientist closed his letter with the observation:

> I need hardly point out that any conclusions drawn from public performances are utterly valueless, and that private experiments should be conducted with care and if possible in the presence of a medical man, who should testify to the conditions under which they are made.

Barrett failed to explain to his readers that no medical man was present at any of their trials in Buxton or Brighton, or that the interest in Blackburn-Smith had come about in spite of their being hired public performers — and in fact, as advertised, Blackburn-Smith gave a paid public performance at St. James Hall the same night that the SPR investigators had arrived in Brighton.

The committee, which now included Frank Podmore as a member, with Blackburn and Smith, reconvened at the Dean's Yard rooms of the SPR near Westminster Abbey in London on January 19, 1883. The experiments continued for three to four days. Additional trials with the pair were done on April 20, 21 and 23[12] at the same location. In the "Third Report on Thought Transference," presented before a general meeting of the SPR on Tuesday, April 24, 1883, the day after the last experiments, no mention was made of the presence at Dean's Yard of any critical observers other than the SPR Committee itself, a circumstance corrected only much later[13] when it was revealed that as many as possibly twenty other observers were present at one time or another.

It was specifically noted in the Report that as Mr. Blackburn

13. Thought Reading Extraordinary: Blackburn and Smith

came only in answer to the urgent request of the Committee, and at considerable inconvenience to himself, we feel it our duty to mention this fact, and at the same time, to express our hearty obligations to him for the unrecompensed trouble which we have so frequently impressed on him.

Clearly the original youthful plans of Blackburn and Smith to set up the scientists so as to publicly expose their unscientific procedures were undergoing rapid change. Smith was beginning to look for opportunities outside of mesmeric performances in Brighton coupled with a steadier cash flow, while Blackburn was facing potential libel proceedings against himself and *The Brightonian*.

The general procedure followed was to have Smith, as percipient, blindfolded, sitting at a table in one room with paper and pencil, his back to the room, while, in an adjacent room with the door closed, a committee man drew some random design and gave it to Blackburn, who after studying it for one or two minutes returned the original to the committee. At that time, Blackburn, accompanied by the committee, entered the same room as Smith, and stood two to three feet behind the percipient with his eyes either tightly closed or blindfolded ("to aid his concentration"). The original drawing remained outside the room. After a few moments, Smith would begin to draw on the paper. Once Smith indicated that he had completed the design as he saw it, the committee took the paper, attached it to the original and filed it in a secure location for later examination. The report assured the readers that no statements were made *en passant* to Smith regarding how accurate his effort had been before they moved on to the next design.

Over seventy experiments were performed in the January and April investigations, divided into two groups: about 30 using random designs, and 42 using detection of the direction, vertically or horizontally, of an arrow drawn on a piece of paper. Many of the original drawings and Smith's reproductions were reproduced in the committee's report. Cost and time, however, prevented all of them being reproduced.

Contact was allowed between Smith and Blackburn for the first four trials, but from that point on there was no physical contact allowed. In some of the apparent failures, Blackburn complained that he had trouble keeping the original random drawing accurately in mind, and so Smith was actually drawing Blackburn's recollection. The committee, to test this statement, asked Blackburn, out of sight of Smith, to draw his recollection of the original as Smith was drawing his perception. On the two trials done, it was found that Smith's result matched Blackburn's recollection more closely than the original drawing, thus apparently confirming Blackburn's statement.

In the committee's view, and to reassure the readers, the possibility of collusion, however remote it might seem, still had to be acknowledged as an experimental concern. The report concluded:

> At present we will only point out the very great improbabilities which [collusion] involves, quite independently of our reliance on the integrity of Mr. Blackburn and Mr. Smith, which nothing has occurred to shake in the slightest degree.

Then an experiment with a design that became Fig. 22 was set up. All possibility for touch or visual cheating had been eliminated in the earlier trials; and, in the Committee's view, most possibilities for audible collusion had also been eliminated. But there was one more test to be done in which all possibilities for audible cheating were abolished.

The report read:

> However, with the view of removing all doubts that might arise as to possible auditory communications, we on one occasion stopped Mr. Smith's ears with putty, then tied a bandage around his eyes and ears, then fastened a bolster-case over the head, and over all threw a blanket which enveloped his entire head and trunk. Fig. 22 was now drawn by one of us, and shown outside the room to Mr. Blackburn, who on his return sat behind Mr. Smith, and in no contact with him whatever, and as perfectly still as it possible for a human being to sit who is not concentrating his attention on keeping motionless to the exclusion of every other object. In a few minutes Mr. Smith took up the pencil and gave the successive reproductions shown below.

Though some additional trials (not reproduced in their report) were done. Fig. 22 seemed to be conclusive in every way. That no collusion, no system of coding or cheating could explain the satisfactory results.

The committee then turned to investigate the inversion phenomenon observed in the first trials at Brighton. Blindfolded, Smith was seated with his back toward Blackburn and the committee in a darkened room in which a heavy opaque curtain had been hung between the percipient and the others. An arrow was drawn on a piece of paper and shown to Blackburn, who was seated facing the same direction as Smith. A member of the committee would call out, "How is the arrow pointing?" in as uniform voice as possible, Blackburn remaining silent. Smith would call out his impression, which was recorded, and the arrow would be noiselessly rotated to another position.

After the 37th experiment of inversion, Blackburn withdrew from the proceedings and

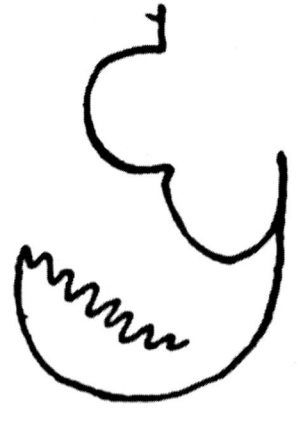

No. 22.
Original Drawing.

Fig. 22

G.A. Smith Reproductions of Fig. 22.

left Dean's Yard. Whether he also resigned his associate membership in the SPR at the time is unknown. Blackburn and Smith never worked together again. The committee continued for five more trials after Blackburn's departure with a member of the committee acting as agent.

Of the 37 trials with Blackburn as agent, 27 were correct, while of the five experiments after Blackburn's departure, one was correct (later changed to two). In terms of coding, knowing that the committee would be using only two basic positions of the arrow, Blackburn had only to code whether the arrow was vertical or horizontal, which gave Smith minimum odds of 50–50 for being correct. That Smith hit on 73 percent of his guesses would be within reasonable expectations.

At the conclusion of the Blackburn-Smith series of experiments, George A. Smith became the paid private secretary for Edmund Gurney until Gurney's death from an accidental overdose of chloroform on June 23, 1888, at the Royal Albion Hotel in Brighton. Smith continued as secretary to Myers.

The "First Report of the SPR Committee on Mesmerism" was also published on April 24 with G.A. Smith as the hypnotic operator. Thus Smith, at the time of the last telepathy experiments at Dean's Yard, had already abandoned the second-sight act for a paid position with the SPR. The fact that virtually all of the mesmeric experiments conducted by the Committee on Mesmerism were conducted with Smith as the mesmerist, and virtually all the subjects used in the experiments were young friends of Smith's from Brighton, did not seem to overly concern the leadership of the SPR. The seven members of the Committee on Mesmerism included all four members of the Thought Transference Committee.

Douglas Blackburn returned to Brighton to continue with *The Brightonian* and to write his second operetta, *Angelo: or An Ideal Love*, to some success. His first, written in 1881, *Disenchantment*, with the libretto by Blackburn, did poorly. Both works were in the style of Gilbert & Sullivan.

In 1884, relying heavily on the Reading Room at the British Library for his research, Blackburn published a small hundred-page paperback book on *Thought-Reading, or Modern Mysteries Explained* (price one shilling), in which, on pages 29–30, he mentions the SPR series of thought transference experiments but without identifying either Smith or himself as the participants. He informed his readers:

> Remarkable though this result is, it still fails to establish actual thought reading; and satisfactory evidence has yet to be produced in support of the assumption that it is within the power of one man to tell in effect the nature of an abstract idea or intention occupying the mind of another.

He concluded his book with:

> The impetus given to the serious study of the Occult by the founding of the SPR has been very great — in spite of a deal of more or less good-natured ridicule, emanating from those who would be the last, and perhaps least capable to rightly estimate the value of such research. The Society has attracted a large number of eminent scientists who do not hesitate to calmly and seriously investigate, in such company, subjects which they would avoid being identified with, singly or on their individual responsibility, through fear of the opprobrium attaching to anything ignorantly supposed to appertain to the supernatural.

Blackburn closed his discussion of telepathy by giving Professor Barrett's name and the Dean's Yard address of the SPR, and invited his readers to communicate any strange incidents or dreams they might have experienced.

On May 17, 1884, *The Brightonian* was forced to close as a result of large libel claims. Blackburn started another newspaper, *The Brighton Figaro*, but it lasted for only a few issues. Further, in 1884, Blackburn had been named as the co-respondent in a divorce case. He moved to London to make his way on Fleet Street as an independent journalist for eight years, then embarked for South Africa in 1892. His return to London in July 1908, however, would cause the SPR considerable uneasiness.

The Committee on Thought Transference closed their "Third Report" with:

> It will, we think, be evident to any candid inquirer who has carefully followed our investigations so far, that our experiments derive much strength and coherence from their very multitude and variety. In a question where the antecedent improbability of our conclusion seems so great, we could not be surprised if any single experiment — even an experiment in which

sources of error were so completely excluded as in the cases where the Creery family correctly told cards, etc., unseen by anyone except the investigating Committee — should leave the reader's mind still unconvinced. But we venture to assert that the *cumulative* character of the evidence which we have now amassed and the extent to which we have eliminated the hypotheses of collusion, chance coincidence, and muscle or sign-reading render our claim to have established the reality of this novel class of phenomena a very strong one [emphasis in the original].[14]

14

W. I. Bishop and "The Secret"

> Oh Mr. Cumberland and Irving Bishop too
> With the pins you try to find I'd like to run you through
> For you have marr'd my happiness and it is very plain
> That all the family now have got, thought reading on the brain.
> —"Thought Reading on the Brain," 1884.

The jokes and songs of the comedians in the English music halls accurately identified the "the rage of the hour," the latest craze, the focus of public attention. In 1884, it was the raucous sensation called "Thought Reading" with the antics of Bishop and Cumberland in all the newspapers — and sometimes in the city streets. The public awareness, additionally, was a benefit to the SPR, bringing letters describing mysterious incidents of apparitions and warnings of death. But it was the laughs that the public wanted at the music halls.

No explanations by the comics were necessary as everyone in the boisterous audiences easily understood what the rapid-fire jokes were all about.

The song "Thought Reading on the Brain" was "rendered with great humour" by comedian Slade Murray. It had three verses and a chorus along with spoken patter and some snappy dance steps between the verses — about a 10 to 15 minute turn. Murray wrote the music. The lyrics, written by T. S. Lonsdale, described a married man with nine children, mostly girls, who have been infected by every disease or fever that has come down their street; and now all the children have come down with "Thought Reading on the Brain." The beleaguered father is particularly disturbed that his girls, even the youngest, prefer to practice their thought reading in the dark with their boyfriends.[1]

Along with the raucous laughs sounding in the music halls, there were also quieter, more somber conversations in other locations about this "thought reading craze."

14. W. I. Bishop and the "THE SECRET"

On June 3, 1884, with stories of a ghoulish East End killing in every newspaper, W. I. Bishop gave a demonstration at the Westminster Palace Hotel to a select group of prominent London men, ostensibly to prove, as reported in the *Pall Mall Gazette*, "the applicability of his system of 'thought reading' to criminal investigation."

The demonstration began with a pin-finding "accomplished without contact." A bank-note reading followed in which on two tries Bishop was able to get only two digits correctly with two different subjects.

Bishop promised to try again following completion of the special experiment of the afternoon — the discovery of an article known to exist within a mile of the hotel, a secret known only to one person present, the Canon Harford. The experiment began at 4:45 P.M.

Bishop went to an antechamber, where he was blindfolded and a black crape bag was placed over his head and shoulders. A copper wire seven feet long was attached to two fingers of his left hand. The thought reader then was led outside the hotel.

With Bishop out of the room, Canon Harford had written the secret location and the secret object at the location on a piece of paper, sealing it in an envelope. He gave it to the chairman of the supervising committee for safekeeping; then he also went outside the hotel where the other end of the copper wire was wrapped around his wrist.

With Bishop's publicity, a crowd approaching four to five hundred people had gathered outside the hotel. They laughed when Bishop immediately "plunged at a headlong pace," dragging Canon Harford behind him. First up Victoria Street, then across it, Bishop and his tethered canon ran down the other side until the little thought reader reached the Dean's Yard. After a moment's hesitation, Bishop charged into the courtyard.

Climbing, stumbling up to the second floor with his staggering, gasping canon in tow, Bishop ran up to a marble bust, pointed at it, breathless, and loudly declared that this was the secret location and the secret object.

The thought reader was correct, even though Canon Harford had never been in the building before.

On Bishop's return to the hotel, he completely failed on another bank note test, getting none of the digits correctly and also failing to detect even the date on a coin. After two more trials to discover the serial number of a banknote submitted by a resident of the hotel, Bishop finally got the number correctly. The afternoon exhibition was concluded.

However, an observer of the proceedings who signed himself "Skeptic" in his letter to the *PMG*, June 4, questioned the entire affair. Why, after all, did Bishop need a black bag over his head when he was already blindfolded, if it was not to allow the performer to push the blindfold away from his eyes at an appropriate moment? The bag looked black to outside observers, but would be almost transparent to Bishop on the inside.

Further, Skeptic noted that Bishop had asked Canon Harford to write his "secret" on a paper and seal it into an envelope while standing in a far corner away from everyone. The place designated by the thought reader was adjacent to a partially opened door, where, Skeptic theorized, a confederate could look over the canon's shoulder and read the secret.

The confederate could then, by any number of means, communicate the secret to the thought reader as Bishop ran through the crowds; even to use so brass a method as to actually running ahead of Bishop to lead him to the right place.

PMG editor W. T. Stead noted that the envelope containing the secret *had* disappeared. While not explicitly accusing W. I. Bishop of fraud, he also noted that Bishop could not reach into the minds of people standing close to him at the hotel in the various banknote tests, failing every time until the last — yet he could succeed in an elaborate experiment which had itself too many loop-holes, too many opportunities for collusion and trickery. As for potential criminal applications of Bishop's powers, nothing further was said.

Within two months and long before Maskelyne's libel trial first opened, Bishop and his assistant left for France, heading east. W. I. Bishop never returned to Great Britain after 1884.

Bishop's tour across Europe extended during the Christmas season to St. Petersburg, where he had been invited to perform before Czar Alexander III and the imperial family. The performance was carefully recorded in the Russian and European newspapers and focused on Bishop's performance of an imaginary assassination of the Czar.

The tour was a major financial success, with Bishop at various venues executing unique stunts like duplicating a drawing thought of by a prominent artist, or playing a musical piece thought of by the composer.[2]

Returning to the U.S. in 1886, Bishop continued to startle audiences with his stunts. In 1886, he originated a wild drive through the city streets in a spectacular hunt for a secretly hidden pin. Bishop, blindfolded, stood in the open carriage to lash on the galloping horses. He ignored traffic and pedestrians, weaving across the streets and even up on the sidewalks in his urgent quest. Finally pulling up in front of the appropriate building, his sweaty horses sliding across the street as they struggled to stop, the little thought reader jumped down with the committee man at his side, and rushed to successfully find the pin — almost every time. Bishop originated the blindfold drive, a stunt which has since become a standard publicity piece for mentalists and magicians using cars, motorcycles and even airplanes.

Bishop also startled the public with his multiple marriages and divorces and increasingly errant personal behavior. There were whispers of cocaine addiction and excessive alcohol consumption, with a mix of absinthe and cognac suggested in the *Chicago Herald* as his "favorite tipple."

Bishop arrived for the first of two performances in Boston, November 30, 1886. Billed in his advertising as "The Enigma of the Nineteenth Century" while declaring that "this would be his only appearance in Boston prior to his retirement from public life," Bishop executed a blindfold carriage drive through the Boston streets and performed before private groups at the Press Club and the Vendome Theatre. The publicity generated great public interest and filled the theatre.

The young, though experienced, city editor of the *Boston Globe,* Charles Howard Montague, arrived early at the Vendome for the first performance. Montague, along with a number of other reporters, was introduced to Bishop.

Montague asked Bishop where he desired the reporters to be during "the exercises." Bishop led them to the very last row of seats, where it was almost impossible to see the stage without standing up, and said to Montague, "Just sit there and keep quiet. That is all I will ask of you."

Though Montague, at that point, knew nothing of Bishop, that curt dismissal triggered a determination in Montague to understand Bishop's tricks. Throughout the show, Montague stood on his chair to watch Bishop's every movement. The editor returned the second night as well. And, while Bishop accomplished what seemed inexplicable feats, Montague, like others, determined to experiment and see for himself.

Montague wrote of his experiments and his growing capability to duplicate Bishop's feats of pin-finding, banknote reading and the murder scenario — at first slowly with mistakes, but then doing private performances for various clubs around Boston. As he practiced, his abilities grew sharper and faster.

On December 19, 1886, a two-part article appeared in the *Boston Globe* with the title "THE SECRET," with sub-titles "How the Minds of Men Are Read" and "A Journalist Who Emulates Mr. Bishop." The first part was written by D. J. McGrath and the second by Montague. It was a detailed exposure of the thought reading act with Montague discussing his experiences detecting unconscious muscular action as he came to duplicate most of Bishop's repertoire.

While Bishop was performing in Washington, D.C., articles exposing Bishop followed by Bishop's rejoinders continued to appear almost daily in the *Globe,* sometimes on the front page.

When Bishop returned to appear at the Boston Music Hall on January 4, 1887, Montague was in the audience once again. Billed to begin at eight, Bishop did not appear until nine. The thought reader warmly acknowledged

Montague's presence and clearly attempted a performance that would exceed anything described in the *Globe* exposures.

In Montague's opinion, the evening was a great success for Bishop. But Montague, who could, best of anyone in the audience, appreciate the real difficulty of Bishop's efforts, recognized that Bishop had pushed himself clearly to his physical and mental limits — and perhaps beyond.

With Bishop's Music Hall engagement over and Montague working on other stories, the *Globe* ran a final article on January 9, 1887, of what had grown to a substantial volume on the issue of mind reading. Written by James W. Clarke, it was titled "Mind Reading: What It May Do for Us By and By."

Using heavy humor, Clarke pointed out how mind reading could facilitate police work, accounting audits, bank examinations, the betrayal of braying politicians, and even dining out (waiters would receive your orders mentally). But he also pointed out the potholes of mindreading: interfering with true romance, and leading to a society in which no one would want to be touched, lest their minds be read.

Bishop's erratic life continued with more marriages and divorces, an aborted tour of Australia and a revolving door of business managers even including managers, of the prominence of M. B. Leavitt. In the summer of 1888, Bishop successfully toured Mexico and Cuba with Harrison Millard, a popular singer.

But the scientific interest that aided and supported the thought reading craze had faded with the growing acceptance by observers that the performer's detection by the performer of unconscious muscular action was the mechanism — a physical, not a mental phenomenon.

And with Bishop's own increasingly unpredictable behavior, his career came to resemble the random motion of a rock rolling steadily and rapidly down a hillside.

W. I. Bishop was performing in St. Louis, March 1889, when his advance man left without giving notice. John G. Ritchie, who at that time had been Bishop's manager for only two months, immediately hired Augustus Thomas, who had himself, that same day in St. Louis, been fired by the manager of the popular actress Julia Marlowe.

It was Tuesday and Bishop was to open in Minneapolis the following Monday. Thomas attended Bishop's Tuesday night performance at Exposition Hall and was stunned by Bishop's thought reading demonstrations. Bishop was ill on Wednesday, so the deal was sealed by Ritchie and Gus Thomas gathered around Bishop's bed.

Thomas, who went on to a highly successful theatrical career as a playwright, writing over seventy plays, recalled in his memoirs in 1922 his initial involvement with Bishop.[3] The thought reader had no posters or advertising paper and only a few clippings for Thomas to work with. When Thomas arrived in Minneapolis, he found the local papers filled with the scheduled hanging of Peter and Timothy Barrett on Friday, March 22, 1889, for the first-degree murder of Thomas Tollefson in 1887. The hanging would clearly dominate all the news. Gus Thomas recognized that to be noticed at all he had to get Bishop "on the band wagon and go with the hanging not against it."

He went to the editor of the largest evening Minneapolis paper and said he had a letter from Washington Irving Bishop for the governor, pleading with the governor to delay the hanging until Bishop could arrive on Sunday to read the mind of the one brother who still claimed innocence, reenact the crime and clarify the boy's involvement. Thomas had read of Bishop doing such a stunt in Portland, Oregon.

W. Irving Bishop at 33, 1889.

The editor asked for a copy of the letter, which Thomas had not yet written, so the advance man "recalled it from memory." The afternoon paper appeared with a ten-line scare headline beginning: "Hope for the Barrett Boys! Thought-Reader Washington Irving Bishop asks a Stay of Execution." The story carried the text of the letter as dictated by Thomas and mentioned that Bishop was to arrive on Sunday preparatory for his week's engagement.

Thomas went to the jail and obtained a signed note from the Barrett brothers that said: "We are willing to wait."

With three reporters in tow, Thomas went from the jail to the governor's office in St. Paul to hand the governor the letter (which Thomas had hurriedly written on Bishop stationery) and pitch Bishop's preternatural capability. The governor was "considerate and non-committal."

The following morning, while all the morning papers issued extra editions to carry the Bishop story, the Barrett boys had been hanged on schedule at 6:08 A.M.

When W. I. Bishop arrived on time Sunday, his opening was sensational, with full houses the entire week. There was special interest in his murder stunt. For his extraordinary work, Gus Thomas received a $25 a week raise.

In his memoirs, Gus Thomas recalled the early part of May, 1889, having dinner with the governor of Missouri, David Francis. That dinner included Bishop, Thomas, and Michael Fanning, the governor's secretary. Following dinner, Governor Francis asked to see a demonstration of Bishop's powers.

Bishop immediately asked the governor to go into his library and select a word from any book. In a few moments, Governor Francis reappeared. Bishop, holding the governor's wrist and followed by Thomas and Fanning, led the group into the library, which contained more than two thousand volumes. With no hesitation, Bishop went directly to a bookcase, pulled down a book, turned to a page and put his finger on a word.

The governor, astonished, exclaimed, "That's it! That's it!" The whole experience took less than two minutes.

Meeting in New York on May 10 at Bishop's hotel, the Hoffman House, Augustus Thomas, W. I. Bishop and popular cornetist Jules Levy had concluded a business deal where Levy would accompany Bishop on tour. Thomas thought it was a good business proposition. They resolved to meet Monday to wrap up the details.

On May 12, Sunday evening, Bishop was the invited guest of actor Henry Dixie at the theatrical season's last Lambs Club Gambol of the year, a gala held monthly during the season at the club's 34 West 26th Street building.

Asked to perform for the assembled members and guests who represented the cream of New York show business, Bishop first demonstrated the murder scenario as he had performed it for Czar Alexander III in 1884, and then repeated the book test as he had performed it a few days earlier for the governor of Missouri by finding a thought-of name in the Lambs Club register book.

The diminutive thought reader became increasingly feverish and chaotic as his performance continued. Finally he collapsed to the floor, unconscious. Dr. John Henry Irwin, who had first met Bishop in Liverpool, assured everyone that it was one of Bishop's cataleptic trances and that the man would recover shortly. Within a few minutes, Bishop improved enough to be, at Dr. Irwin's insistence, carried up to an upstairs bedroom to be put to bed.

Still wide-eyed and trembling, Bishop insisted on repeating the book test again so that everyone could appreciate the difficulty of the feat. The register previously used was brought up to his room. Deathly pallid, Bishop was helped to his feet so that he could locate the name thought of. Then, his body barely functioning, his quivering legs gave way again. The little man fell to the floor in a coma.

Dr. Charles C. Lee, who had attended Bishop in the past, attempted to revive him (which included injections of brandy as well as sending electric shocks through his body), but all efforts failed. Dr. Lee finally left to attend other patients at 4:00 A.M.

Physicians had cautioned Bishop in the past against putting too much stress on his nerves through overwork which could propel him into a cataleptic fit — a caution that the thought reader had always ignored. "The papers may cut me up," Bishop once said, "but the doctors never will."

On Monday morning, a man he passed walking on Broadway stopped Gus Thomas and said, "Your star is sick at the Lambs."

Thomas found Bishop "in a little hall bedroom with an iron cot, where he had been for twelve hours, a tiny electric battery buzzing away with one wet electrode over his heart and the other in his right hand." The thought reader was still comatose. Two doctors sat smoking in the next room, tired from their long vigil.

Sitting beside the cot, Gus Thomas thought that Bishop had every indication of being dead, but then "a deeper solemnity suddenly came over his face." He called the doctors, who agreed that Bishop was dead. It was 12:10 P.M. Within half an hour, Thomas was on his way to Philadelphia to break the news to Bishop's wife. Five hours later he was back in New York with Mrs. Bishop.

Augustus Thomas, out of a job again, went on two months later to stage his first four-act play on the East coast. Called *The Burglar*, it starred Maurice Barrymore. The strong response to the play launched his career as a playwright.

Thomas would return to his Bishop experiences in 1907 in *The Witching Hour*, a four-act occult thriller which incorporated some of Bishop's patter lines with a theme of thought influence that compels a murder. The play was novelized by Thomas in 1908, illustrated with photographs from the play.

But the Bishop story was not over. At four in the afternoon, Sunday, while Gus Thomas was still on the train with Bishop's wife coming back from Philadelphia, an autopsy was performed in which the top of Bishop's head was sawed away and his brain removed for examination.

The thought reader had always insisted in his publicity that his famous thought reading was due to his unique brain. The doctors wanted the prestige of being the first to investigate a thought reader's brain. But the autopsy revealed only that Bishop's brain was darker gray than normal; that it weighed forty ounces, slightly more than the average; and that there were no malformations or other physical indicators that the brain was not that of any ordinary man.

With nothing else to record, the doctors sewed the brain into Bishop's chest cavity and replaced the crown of his head.

Years earlier, Bishop had explained to British novelist Henry Byatt that when he was in a cataleptic state, he could still hear and feel everything and was fully conscious of his surroundings, but could not move or communicate.

Was W. Irving Bishop still alive during the autopsy? If he was, did he hear and feel the doctors sawing his skull open, powerless to stop them? But was he already dead by suffocation when his body was stored in a coffin for an hour before the autopsy? Those gruesome questions have never been nor ever will be satisfactorily answered.

The card was never found that Bishop always carried with him — the one that warned of his cataleptic trances and pleaded for physicians not to perform an autopsy for forty-eight hours. With the hysterical public demands of Bishop's wife and mother, the three doctors who performed the "lightning autopsy" were charged with manslaughter; however, they were never held legally accountable, and all charges were finally dropped by 1893.

The doctors involved continued their careers — even to performing yet another "lightning autopsy" only a few weeks after Bishop was buried. Bishop's death certificate, signed by Dr. Irwin, gave the cause of death as hysterocatalepsy.

Washington Irving Bishop was thirty-three. His extraordinary career had lasted barely twelve years.

Still demonstrating erratic mental imbalance, Eleanor Fletcher Bishop died January, 1918, leaving her imaginary $30 million estate to Harry Houdini. Washington Irving Bishop's only child, Georgina Eleanor Bishop, had died October 7, 1898.

15

The Thought Reader Craze

> Now, I do not profess to give any illustrations of the supernatural. I simply claim that it is possible to read persons' thoughts under certain conditions, not abstract thoughts, mind you, that is impossible, absolutely impossible.
> — Stuart Cumberland, *Pall Mall Gazette* Offices, May 23, 1884

Returning from a successful European tour that included entertaining the wealthy and aristocratic in Vienna and Paris, Stuart Cumberland readily accepted W. T. Stead's invitation to demonstrate his thought reading, Friday, May 23, 1884, at the *Pall Mall Gazette* offices before thirty prominent representatives of Victorian culture.

Of those who did not attend the gathering at the *PMG* offices, several wrote letters to the editor to express their opinions. One unnamed "eminent scientist" insisted that Cumberland should be blindfolded with pads of cotton wool. Henri Labouchère wrote, "Thought-reading may easily be accounted for. It simply means that with certain persons an indication of their thought may be obtained by — or rather through — the muscular action of their hand." The conjuror J. N. Maskelyne said much the same but emphasized in italics "*with practice*." One of the invited guests summed it up by telling Stead, "Mr. Cumberland does all that Mr. Bishop ever professes to do, and makes no fuss about it."

The first subject Cumberland selected was Oscar Wilde, who immediately declined. The thought reader then chose Stead himself. Blindfolded with white silk, though cotton wool pads were available, Cumberland successfully found the object thought of — the pince-nez glasses of the London correspondent of the *Neue Freie Presse*. Cumberland pointed out that he "always desired his subject to think of the direction or route to article rather than the article itself." After some friendly banter, his blindfold back in place, Cumberland found a pain in one finger of the American millionaire, Andrew Carnegie, to warm applause. When he failed the find the pin hidden by naturalist, E. Ray Lankester, declaring the scientist's concentration was insufficient, he took the wrist of Oscar Wilde, who knew the location. The performer immediately went in a straight line to the lapel of another man. After successfully finding an object thought of by an unnamed woman and delivering it to the person she had been thinking of, Stuart Cumberland requested time to rest.

During the half-hour of Cumberland's repose, Oscar Wilde "discoursed in his 'free-and-easy way'" on art, poetry and culture.

For the final test of the evening, an object was thought of by the science writer Grant Allen, which was located somewhere outside the *PMG* offices. With Cumberland blindfolded — and hatless, as he thought wearing a hat might interfere with the exercise — the two men, joined at the wrist, rushed out the door and up North Cumberland Street to the astonishment of police, hansom cabs, and open-mouthed waiters, along with matrons and maids hanging out of windows to watch the odd proceedings.

The procession of the Siamese twins up the street with the crowd following them gained in size. Stopping at No. 17, Cumberland pounded on the door. When the servant opened the door and saw a blindfolded man followed by a crowd, he slammed it shut again. Cumberland paused and asked Allen to concentrate harder; then, dragging the reporter behind him, Cumberland rushed to No. 6, pushed through the door, went up the stairs, straight to the drawer of a desk, paused, then retreated to an ottoman by a window. The thought reader raised the lid of the ottoman, and brought out the hidden object: a carefully preserved hunk of bread, eighteen years old, a relic of a major *PMG* article written on the ugly degrading conditions in work houses that had subsequently brought substantial reforms. The bread was considered too hallowed to throw away, and so had been securely kept in a glass case.

The largely successful thought reading demonstrations, written up in detail on the front pages of the *Gazette*, were still unconvincing to many of the observers. They had begun to accept the explanation of unconscious muscular action as an answer, but still with some reservations.

Responding to a letter written by Edmund Gurney in the *PMG* the day after his reception on the 23rd, Cumberland said:

> With regard to Mr. Gurney, that gentleman, judging by his letter, does not approve of my experiments; evidently, they do not sufficiently savor of the supernatural. "The public," he sadly complains, "go away with the idea that these performances are 'thought reading'!" So be it! My object in life is to prove that none of us possesses supernatural powers, either in the matter of thought-reading or in the working of miracles. All this talk about mental picture-reading and thought transference is so much sheer nonsense. I have seen a great deal of these so-called mental picture-readers, but, somehow, they have inevitably failed when they have attempted their experiments in my presence.[1]

Journalist Grant Allen then wrote in the PMG:

> I should like to mention that, while I quite admit the interest of Mr. Stuart Cumberland's experiments, I still remain personally in a somewhat skeptical attitude. I do no think the conditions at his séance on Friday last were such as to secure scientific accuracy or to guard against the possibility of collusion.[2]

To which Cumberland responded in the *PMG* the next day:

> What would Mr. Grant Allen have? What conditions does he propose? At present he leaves me entirely in the dark as to the requirements of his kindly skepticism. I need hardly say that at the reception on Friday last I was perfectly willing to fall in with any test, in accordance with my professions, that the audience inclined to impose. On that occasion I perfectly succeeded with Mr. Grant Allen in an experiment which was not of my own proposing.[3]

And finally, Dr. Horatio B. Donkin joined in:

> But just what Mr. Cumberland and many others in greater or less degree can do in their way has nothing whatever in common with the pretended experiments of the Psychical Research Society. So-called "thought-reading without contact," or "thought transference," exists only in the minds of mystics and mystery-mongers, and the exhibitions of the working of these alleged "faculties" are either at once stopped by ordinary tests, or are so conditioned by their exhibitors that rigid tests are out of the question.[4]
>
> "Do you not believe in the possible evolution of a new faculty?" said Mr. Oscar Wilde, coquetting for the nonce with scientific terminology, to Mr. Grant Allen, during Mr. Cumberland's séance the other day. "Such a belief," severely and pertinently replied Mr. Grant Allen, "would in no way justify my acceptance of any given faculty you may choose to gratuitously hypothesize."

Donkin closed the extended correspondence on the *PMG*-Cumberland gathering with the observation: "He [Mr. Cumberland] is in no way to be classed with certain charlatans whose success depends on the superstition of the audience they so boldly deceive."

For Cumberland the *PMG* experience created a handsome load of sustained publicity while developing a contact with Henri Labouchère which would, in turn, lead within a few weeks to a further publicity coup. Through an invitation from Labouchère, Stuart Cumberland performed thought reading within the House of Parliament with Prime Minister William Gladstone himself as one of the subjects.

Closely following W. Irving Bishop's publicized performance at the Westminster Palace Hotel on June 3, 1884, with its undercurrent of suggested trickery as outlined in the *Pall Mall Gazette*, Stuart Cumberland appeared before an invited audience of 50–60 personages at the Charing Cross Hotel on June 5. Some of those present had attended the earlier Bishop performance.

Initial tests with several people, with Cumberland trying to find an object, failed. Cumberland commented finally to one subject, a reporter of the *Morning Advertiser*, "Captain Hamber, you give no more indication than a stone; I must give you up." Successes and failures followed until the final key demonstration: the finding of a pin hidden by a committee of scientists within a quarter-mile of the hotel.

With the pin securely hidden, Cumberland, blindfolded, was tied to his subject with a silken rope and the hunt was started.

With crowds following in the streets the hunt was quickly successful with Cumberland returning to the Charing Cross Hotel in triumph. But the possibility of confederacy as in the Bishop case was still suggested as a solution even though the three members of the committee who had hidden the pin insisted they had not been watched.

Barrister and author Angelo Lewis (who wrote as "Professor Hoffman") was in the audience on September 11, 1884, at the Savoy Theatre to watch Stuart Cumberland. Lewis wrote his comments on Cumberland in one of his scrapbooks.[5] He briefly summarized the evening's various demonstrations — but one incident attracted Lewis' admiration and response: when Cumberland wrote down the four numbers of a check known only to Sir John Bennett. Lewis wrote, "This was done instantly and, if really *bona fide*, was very marvelous."

"What times these 'thought-readers' are having!" exclaimed W.T. Stead in the *PMG*: "Here is Mr. Stuart Cumberland, the 'rage of the hour,' in St. Petersburg, experimenting with princes and supping in palaces. His note to us fairly scintillates with Highnesses and Grand Dukes."[6]

But within two-three years, scientific interest in thought reading was fading even as the Society for Psychical Research continued to focus its interest and experimentation on non-contact forms of thought transference. Other physiologists and psychologists had come to accept that the feats of Bishop and Cumberland had been due entirely to their extraordinarily skilled detection and interpretation of unconscious muscular action. Further, with the number of thought readers expanding — male and female, performing in America, Europe and Great Britain — the public novelty of the act itself was declining as well.

In addition to performing thought reading around the world, Cumberland had written about the social conditions, governments and prominent personalities he had encountered in Canada,[7] South Africa,[8] Egypt,[9] and other countries, in books and articles that led, ultimately, on May 3, 1887, to his being elected a Fellow of the Royal Geographic Society.

15. The Thought Reader Craze

Stuart Cumberland solving a chess problem thought of by William Steinitz.

In 1887, Cumberland also began writing "Shilling Shockers" with occult and second sight themes with titles like *The Rabbi's Spell*,[10] *The Vasty Deep*,[11] and *The Fatal Affinity*.[12] All sold quite well, establishing Stuart Cumberland as a popular thriller author.

The story was widely told (primarily by Cumberland) that the wife of Prime Minister Gladstone kept looking under his bed for weeks after reading *The Fatal Affinity*.

Stories of Jack the Ripper filled the London newspapers with the horrors in the East End in 1888. The London *Daily News* Oct 6, 1888, approached thought reader, Stuart Cumberland, who had just returned from a tour of Scotland:

> Though he bates no jot of his pretensions as a thought reader, Mr. Stuart Cumberland, confesses himself unable to be of any use in bringing the Whitechapel assassin to justice "as matters at present stand." Nevertheless, we are assured by Mr. Cumberland that he has on two separate occasions — one in Warsaw and once in Australia — successfully read the thoughts of prisoners in whom nothing could be made in the usual way. He has also, times without number, successfully experimented with imaginary criminals, reproducing in every detail the form of murder which they had in mind to commit.

It was helpfully pointed out by the *Daily News* that imaginary murders were not illegal.

Exploiting the Ripper panic, Cumberland held a demonstration of thought reading and the detection of crime at the Hotel Victoria[13] before a select audience of lawyers, diplomats, authors, and others, with a senior magistrate serving as judge of the proceedings. Opening with quickly finding a person thought of by one of the ladies, Cumberland then performed two variations of his standard "murder scenario" in one of which the killer was the librettist W. S. Gilbert — who, to the delight of the gathering, approached the Baron von Siedlitz, asking, "Will you kindly allow me to murder you, sir?"

The magistrate deferred sentence in each case, commenting on the interesting experiments. "The murdered, murderers, thieves and abetters" then left after a "very pleasant couple of hours."

With the gruesome Ripper killings still in the news, Cumberland claimed in his own newspaper, *Stuart Cumberland's Mirror*,[14] that he had had dreams in which the identity of the Ripper had been revealed. He included a sketch of the Ripper as seen in his dream. He said that seeing the man's face had inspired him to write his "recent weird story *A Fatal Affinity*."

On September 10 a woman's butchered body was found under a railway arch in Pinchin-street in Whitechapel. Her identity was unknown. Two days later the *Times*[15] noted that "Mr. Cumberland managed to gain entrance to the mortuary and viewed the remains but for what object is not known." On September 19, when Cumberland was again interviewed about his dreams of the Ripper, he could speak with authority on the killer's methods used on the latest victim.[16] As the killings drew smaller headlines, Cumberland moved on to other publicity opportunities.

Stuart Cumberland, 1896.

In 1892, Phyllis Bentley, described as a relative of Cumberland's wife, joined Cumberland in many of his subsequent British and European tours. She performed a Magnetic Girl act similar to that of Lulu Hurst, who had retired in 1886. Bentley utilized a number of the crowned heads of Europe as her subjects.

With W. Irving Bishop's departure from Great Britain in 1884, followed by his bizarre death in 1889, Stuart Cumberland became the premier thought reader in Great Britain and Europe. He remained so for the rest of his career.

Unlike Bishop, who had squandered his money faster than he earned it, Stuart Cumberland had preserved and invested his capital. After making an estimated £50,000 ($6.1 million U.S. in 2010) from thought reading plus income from his books and novels, Stuart Cumberland retired from active performing about 1910, appearing later only for charity or at the request of a prominent member of society or royalty. His last book, on Spiritualism, appeared in 1919.[17]

Stuart Cumberland's Dream Sketch of Jack the Ripper, 1888.

The 1880 prediction made in passing by the reporter of the *Whitehall Review*—that Stuart Cumberland could earn a fortune from thought reading—had been fulfilled.

Throughout his career, Stuart Cumberland had always refused to accept fees from the titled and wealthy to ensure he would be greeted as a guest of equivalent social standing, and not just an artiste to be dismissed to the kitchen after performing his wonders. In about 1888, Stuart Cumberland received the title of Chevalier of the Order of Christ from the Portuguese court which had further enhanced his social position. At no time during his career was Stuart Cumberland looked on as a mere music hall artist.

Stuart Charles Francis Cumberland died on February 28, 1922, at St. George's Hospital, London. He was sixty-five. No surviving family is mentioned in the London *Times* obituary, which listed him as "author, journalist and thought reader." There was no reference to the butcher shop where Charles Garner had started.

Other thought readers — like Alfred Capper in England (who started his career after seeing Bishop); and Paul Alexander Johnstone[18] in America (who started his after seeing Brown); and Lucy DeGentry, Maud Lancaster,[19] and C.A. George Newmann and many other performers, never received the scientific and social attention afforded Brown, Bishop and Cumberland. The later thought readers never became the "rage of the hour"; they never became real enough to the public to become the target for jokes in the music halls.

But as the three early thought readers pursued their careers, the world around them was shifting: intellectually, medically, psychologically and scientifically which had, at first, transformed the performers' conventional publicity events into serious "experimental meetings." They were "tested" for unknown evolving human mental capabilities as suggested by Darwin's theories, or as evoked by publicized advances in wireless telegraphy (sending invisible messages across something called the ether) or by other challenging and unsettling technological discoveries.

Ultimately, the passing years of experimentation and investigation erased any serious scientific interest in professional thought-readers. Further, with the growing number of thought readers on the stages, the novelty and the money involved declined. The latest craze moved on, as it always does; and the passage of time transformed J. Randall Brown's initial discovery back into the variety act of its origin on that Monday morning in 1873 at a Chicago saloon.

"My experiments," Stuart Cumberland had insisted at the *PMG* offices in 1884, "are neither mysterious nor unnatural, but are simply the outcome of an extraordinary gift of perception."

The gift that Stuart Cumberland referred to did not relate only to his thought reading talents. His gift of perception, like that of Brown and Bishop before him, was primarily focused on counting the house.

16

"The Willingness to Deceive"

> I have dwelt at some length on our series of trials with the members of the Creery family, as it is to these trials that we owe our own conviction of the possibility of genuine thought-transference between persons in a normal state.
> — Edmund Gurney, *Phantasms of the Living*, Volume 1, Page 29, 1886

The continuous publication from 1882 of the *PSPR* and from 1884 of the *JSPR* was due largely to the energy, intelligence and wealth of Edmund Gurney, coupled with the close support, insights and wealth of the poet Frederic W. H. Myers. Though others certainly contributed in various ways, the society presidency of Henry Sidgewick, Knightsbridge Professor of Moral Philosophy at Trinity College Cambridge, from 1883 to his death in 1900, in particular gave the fledgling organization a credible public standing well beyond financial concerns. It could probably be argued that had Sidgewick not taken the presidency when it was offered at that gathering in February 1882, the SPR would not have come into existence. However, even then, it is doubtful that without the sustained early financial support of Gurney and Myers, the SPR would not have been able to survive solely on members' donations.

This book is not a history of the SPR, a subject already dealt with in marvelous detail by Alan Gauld (1968), Janet Oppenheim (1985) and others, but some mention must be made here of the first major publication of the SPR in October 1886, *Phantasms of the Living*. It was a prodigious work by any measure: two volumes, 1,300 pages which provided 701 case studies of spontaneous telepathic communication of human crisis. The case studies were winnowed from a raw census of 5,705 submissions from the public in response to Society advertisements in many newspapers, the same advertisement that had so aggravated Professor Simon Newcomb when it appeared in American newspapers. The detailed sifting and evaluation of submissions was achieved largely through the labors of Gurney with the assistance of Frank Podmore, as they followed up the most likely initial letters and descriptions, then tried to nail down the reality. Did the apparition really appear before any news of the accident or death had reached the percipient? Did the telepathic message clearly describe what the event was? Was there contemporary correspondence, notes or witness testimony that supported the descriptions of the incident at issue? Or was the apparition just the product of fevered imaginations and faulty memories, a zeal to be noticed, or simply regurgitated family traditions?

Gurney and Podmore, and others as needed, tried to clear out the nonsense and identify, in the end, the best and most reliable cases. In the book, Gurney provided rough calculations of the odds for the episodes included, given various assumptions, to eliminate chance or coincidence, the most likely initial front of attack from probable critics. Millions to one, Gurney calculated, against chance or coincidence — and, given the reality of telepathy as a fact of nature as already proven by the Committee on Thought Transference through their experiments with the Creery children — the results given in *Phantasms*, in the collective opinion of the SPR, were most probably genuine. (It is interesting to note that there is no mention of the Blackburn-Smith experiments in *Phantasms*, even with the high marks initially given the results by the committee.)

Once the final cases were assembled and selected, Myers wrote a 71 page introduction, which he read as a paper to a general meeting of the SPR. Edmund Gurney wrote the entire balance of *Phantasms* — even while acting as editor of the *Journal* and the *Proceedings*, and as the honorary secretary of the SPR, an effort prodigious in its own right.

The journalistic reviews of the book were at first many and widely varied, from a brief respectful notice in *Mind*, to a more prominent review in the *Times*. Many of the write-ups recognized the difficulty of selecting and verifying which cases could be accepted as valid. The issue of adequate reliable contemporary proof was raised more than once. And, naturally, there were a few critics who mocked the "collection of ghost stories" that masqueraded as science — but generally the reviews were polite.

But things changed in 1887 as the unsympathetic attacks took on a more caustic edge. Professor C. S. Pierce, writing in the *Proceedings of the American Society for Psychical Research,* saw no validity anywhere in the 1,300 pages. As in other circumstances, it fell to Gurney to answer all the criticisms — which he did with style and courtesy, but without fully refuting Pierce's criticisms. Then, in August 1887, A. Taylor Innes, writing in the *Nineteenth Century*[1] "Where Are the Letters? A Cross-examination of Certain Phantasms," — attacked the complete lack of contemporary documentation as a fundamental flaw in the entire enterprise. There were, in fact, for all of Gurney's and Podmore's diligent efforts, only three cases of contemporary documentation (one

16. "The Willingness to Deceive"

of which later proved to be a hoax). Innes' criticisms were met by the customary Gurney élan.[2]

But more devastating input came from an unexpected quarter. Henry Sidgwick wrote[3] to William Barrett on October 5, 1887:

> My dear Barrett,
> I am very sorry to have to tell you that we have undoubtedly detected the two Creery girls — Mary and Alice — in the use of a code of signals to produce spurious "thought-transference" phenomena; or rather *two* codes — one of *visual* signals when both the girls were together in the room without any barrier between them, and the other of signals to the *ears*, used when they were separated by a screen.... We agreed that Gurney should go off to Manchester — before the girls returned from Cambridge — and endeavor to find out whether a similar code had ever been used before. He did so: and the result was a confession from Maud Creery, of which I enclose a copy. The signals she describes are exactly the same as those we discovered. So there can be no doubt that the code is of long standing, I fear. Meanwhile we kept Mary and Alice here, without saying anything of our discovery till the evening before their departure, when my wife taxed them with the code, in two private interviews. They at first denied it indignantly, but when she convinced them that she knew the signals they admitted it: but still said that it had never been used before this visit. This, I fear, cannot be believed after Maud's confession.
> Of course, something must be said about this in the *Journal* & *Proceedings*. I think it better that Rev. Creery should say it....

The children's codes were subsequently explained by Gurney[4]:

> When the two girls were in sight of one another, the signals were a slight upward look for hearts, downwards for diamonds, to the right for spades, and to the left for clubs. Further, the right hand put up to the face meant king, the left hand meant queen, and knave was indicated by crossing the arms. It is doubtful there were any signs for other cards. We failed to make out any out clearly. A table showing the degree of success in guessing each card suggests that there were signs for 10 and ace, but that they were either only used occasionally or used with poor success.
> In experiments in which a screen was placed between the two girls, so that they could not see each other, auditory signs were used to indicate suits. A scraping of the feet on the carpet meant hearts, coughing, sneezing or yawning meant diamonds. If there were signs to distinguish between the black suits they were — like the signs for 10 and ace in the visual code — sparingly used or often unsuccessful. The sisters were naturally very restless, which made the movements described less obvious than they otherwise would have been.

Gurney revealed that once he and Mrs. Sidgwick, and occasionally Professor Sidgwick, had detected the codes, they themselves then guessed the card selected (which they had ensured was kept completely hidden from them) from the actions of the two girls. Their consistent success confirmed the girls' codes.

The objective of the Cambridge experiments had been to "strengthen the evidence for Thought-transference" when all members of the Creery family were unaware of the object to be guessed,[5] or when the two sisters acting as agent and percipient were in separate rooms. The experiments using codes were allowed for "amusement and encouragement" to enhance the chance of success in the more difficult tests. All of the difficult experiments ended in failure.

Gurney concluded: "But, of course, the recent detection must throw discredit on all previous trials in which one or more of the sisters shared in the agency." But then Gurney expressed his suspicion regarding the results of all the other experiments "on which we relied," given the girls' "proved willingness to deceive."

Within a few days, Professor Barrett responded[6]:

> I expect the natural alarm which the Cambridge Expts. has caused in our minds is probably apt to make us unjust in our judgment of the Earlier Experiments. For my own part I am convinced that enough entirely trustworthy Expts. exist with the Creery family to make it unwise to expunge the whole of their evidence.

Gurney and the Sidgewicks were not impressed with Barrett's insistence on the legitimacy of the earlier Creery evidence, a development which fed the growing estrangement between the "Cambridge group" and Barrett in Dublin.

The Rev. A. M. Creery responded to the Cambridge evidence on October 18[7]:

> The announcement which appears in the last *Journal*[8] in that my daughters were detected using a code of signals in some thought-transference experiments in Cambridge has given me intense pain; and I have no desire to excuse their misconduct, nor to extenuate their guilt, for which they grieve quite as much as I do. But I do not believe that signs, signals and hints of any kind were used in the earlier experiments.

Creery then earnestly presented a condensed resume of the early experiments conducted in the presence of Professor Barrett to demonstrate that collusion could not have been a factor in the remarkable results.

Creery then concluded his *Journal* letter with the mocking observation:

> If the scientific investigators, all of whom afterwards became prominent members of the "Society for Psychical Research" could have been deceived by a few children practicing a "code of signals," their keenness of vision, and their faculty of "continuous observation" are less than I could have imagined. Than the above statement I know no more, and I can say no less.

Thus finished the Creery family episode of thought reading.[9]

But what of the investigators who later formed the core of the SPR Committee on Thought-Transference? Were they blinded to any alternative explanations for the Creery sisters' and the maidservant's thought reading performances by their urgent desire for confirmation of their beliefs? Certainly it would appear so for William Barrett, for whom his "discovery" of thought reading and transference through the Creery experiments would be his greatest claim to scientific importance, even to the point that he insisted again, "This case is historically of importance, for it led to the first clear evidence of thought-transference in the normal state of the percipient."[10]

It would also appear that the investigators were not only ignorant of conjuring methods—information on which was easily available in inexpensive pamphlet form—but more critically, unfamiliar with conjuring psychology. It was common for Gurney and others to claim in their write-ups familiarity with magic tricks, but any understanding of the application of those tricks seemed outside their experience.

The Reverend Creery, who can be assumed the architect of the Creery phenomenon, also overreached on one hand while supporting the credibility of the sisters' performances on the other. The lack of detailed coding for the values of playing cards other than the face cards and the ace and ten was a step toward projecting the appearance of honesty, and less coding meant less chance of detection. The girls' successfully getting some cards, the most vivid in design, but not the others even with increased effort, implied a genuine phenomenon. After all, the thinking would be, only tricksters would never miss.

But then the Reverend Creery's careless incorporation of the maidservant into the play shattered the most plausible explanation for the sisters' strange skills, i.e., a family inheritance, a unique family capability. He may have thought the incorporation of Jane Dean would make the whole performance more impressive—as it may have been in the neighborhood parlor performances of the girls, when sometimes even other children would be included in the fun. But as Newcomb had objected earlier, there had to be a general cause to explain the results and to allow their replication by others. Mere accumulation of the same data without a defined cause did not prove anything of scientific value.

And what of *Phantasms of the Living*, which relied so heavily on the Creery evidence to validate the 701 cases presented? Innes had already resumed his attack on the book in 1888, but when forty-one-year-old Edmund Gurney died from an accidental overdose of chloroform on June 23, 1888, the most persuasive voice of the SPR was silenced.

17

The Conjuror and the Physicist (Devant and Lodge)

> I should be sorry to deny that there is nothing in telepathy without the use of tricks.
> — David Devant, 1936.

Writing in his 1931 autobiography, *Past Years*, British physicist Sir Oliver Lodge, F.R.S., renowned for his pioneering work in pre-relativity physics, the characterization and control of radio waves, and his demonstration of wireless telegraphy a year before Marconi, recalled his involvement with some of the early tests that probed the reality of thought transference. Lodge had initially dismissed *telepathy*[1] as "a baseless superstition." He had declined to join the SPR when it was formed in February 1882, in order to focus his intellectual and creative energies on his own career of teaching mathematics and physics.

In 1883, while Oliver Lodge held the first endowed chair in physics at University College, Liverpool, the American thought reader Washington Irving Bishop came to Liverpool, as the scientist recalled, "to display what [Bishop] called 'thought-reading' in a public and sensational manner." Bishop performed his thought reading marvels surrounded by spectators in the streets of Liverpool, as well as in the theatres and in the private homes of the wealthy.

Through one of his former students, Edmund Gurney, Lodge had come to count Frederic W. H. Myers and Professor William F. Barrett as friends. Co-founding members of the SPR, Myers, Barrett and Gurney were not impressed with Bishop's widely publicized wonders. They considered his performances as only a highly sensitive form of muscle-reading, remarkable in effect and in showmanship to be sure, but as Bishop's performances apparently relied on his being led by a spectator's unconscious muscular indications it was, in their joint opinion, not true no-contact thought transference. Bishop, naturally, publicly disputed any explanation of his work as based on muscle-reading, also referred to in the press as body-reading, which was looked on by the writers as simply an adult variation on the popular child's game of "willing."

Acknowledging the Myers, Gurney and Barrett insights, Lodge, in his earliest psychical interest, had been drawn to investigations by Malcolm Guthrie, owner of the Liverpool drapery concern of George Henry Lee & Co., where two young female employees, Miss Edwards and Miss Relph, had been engaged in some thought transference experiments. Guthrie had communicated the results of those experiments to the SPR, which, from its day of founding, had widely advertised in the popular media for such contacts.

Cautiously suspecting a code or some other conjuring trick when the two Lee employees worked with each other, and still very skeptical of the basic concept of telepathy, Lodge became more involved because of promising results obtained when others from outside the firm were drawn into the experiments. After a number of tests over several days and under different test conditions with different combinations of personnel, Lodge finally concluded that "it was possible for one mind to act on another directly without any physical intermediary of a known or customary kind." Speculating on the probable mechanism of the demonstrated telepathic talents, Lodge was disinclined to accept physical solutions like brain waves or ether waves as proposed by other scientists, notably the chemist and discoverer of the new element thallium, William Crookes. In Lodge's view, the thought transference process must be of "a kind that might be called purely psychic."

Oliver Lodge first put his name on a public communication regarding the reality of thought transference with a brief letter to the editor of the authoritative scientific journal *Nature*, which to Lodge's undisguised amazement was published as "An Experiment in Thought-Transference," June 12, 1884, p. 145. Lodge's involvement in psychical research continued to deepen throughout the rest of his life, to include not only telepathy investigations but also the more murky mysteries of the darkened séance room and communications with disembodied intelligences — all the while continuing his celebrated original work in physics.

Lodge was knighted by King Edward VII in 1902 in recognition of his many extraordinary contributions to science and to British industry. (Arthur Conan Doyle was knighted the same day.) Through his writings and his highly admired public lectures on physics and the development of modern science, Sir Oliver Lodge had become over the years the public image of an accomplished creative scientist who, in lending his personal professional credibility to the work of the SPR, helped to legitimize scientific investigations of sometimes bizarre psychical phenomena, even in the face of severe and unrelenting criticism from many in the Victorian intellectual community. A tall, graceful man, standing four inches over six feet, with a pleasant, compelling speaking voice, Sir Oliver Lodge could command instant respect from virtually any British audience.

In his article "Thought Transference," which appeared in the popular magazine *The Forum* in 1909, pp. 56–62, Lodge defined what he considered to be the established proof of thought transference as "communication between mind and mind, by means other than any of the known organs of sense."

> Whenever I use the term thought-transference, I never mean anything like the public performances, whether by genuine persons or imposters. The human race is so constituted that such performances have their value — they incite others to try experiments; but in themselves, and scientifically, public performances are useless, and often tend to obscure a phenomenon by covering it with semi-legitimate contempt.

Lodge concluded:

> An attitude of keen and critical inquiry must continually be maintained, and in that sense any amount of skepticism is not only legitimate but necessary. The kind of skepticism I deprecate is not that which sternly questions and rigorously probes, it is rather that which confidently asserts and dogmatically denies.

But then…

One evening in late April, 1909, Sir Oliver Lodge, with his wife and some friends, attended an eight o'clock evening performance at St. George's Hall,[2] Langham Place, Regent Street, in London. On the bill was magician and illusionist David Devant,[3] generally considered at the time to be the greatest British magician — and in the later estimation of many historians of the conjuring arts, perhaps ranked as one of the two or three greatest conjuror-illusionists of all time.

Many years later, David Devant wrote of that remarkable evening in an article published in *Windsor Magazine*, December 1935, called "Illusion and Disillusion."

In the article, Devant revealed the workings of many of his most famous illusions — not with enough detail that anyone could readily duplicate his fabled feats of magic, but enough to clearly establish his priority in the invention of the tricks. Having been forced at fifty-two to retire in 1920 due to a growing disabling paralysis, Devant had seen over the years other magicians claim credit for some of his trademark illusions. It was time to rectify history.

Of one illusion, however, a mind reading routine called *Translucidation*, first premiered at St. George's Hall in February 1909, Devant had another, more remarkable story to tell.[4]

The illusion was a typical baffling Devant creation. His sister, Dora,

17. The Conjuror and the Physicist (Devant and Lodge)

beautifully gowned, walked on stage and sat on a simple cane-back chair near the footlights. A group of spectators came up on stage to form a semi-circle upstage around and behind her. The stage was otherwise completely bare.

Devant blindfolded his young sister, then went down into the audience carrying a black bag and six cards with matching envelopes. He handed the envelopes and cards to a spectator, who then distributed the cards and envelopes to six persons. Devant asked that each of the six write a message secretly on the card without allowing anyone else to see it, to immediately seal the card in the envelope, and to mark the envelope in any manner they wished.

Devant asked the spectator to collect the sealed envelopes in the black bag. As the spectator neared the seats of the Lodge party, the scientist rose from his seat and waved aloft a special colored envelope that he had sealed at home before coming to the theatre. He challenged Dora to read what was in it. The audience went tense with expectancy. Devant could not conceal his surprise. Collecting Lodge's card in the black bag, the spectator moved on until all of the now seven envelopes were in the bag.

Taking the black bag at his fingertips with his arm fully extended upward to ensure that everyone in the theatre could easily follow his movements, Devant mounted to the stage, dropped the bag on Dora's lap, and stepped away.

While Devant said a few words, explaining that they claimed no special powers — only the natural talents within the capability of everyone in the theatre — Dora put one of her hands inside the bag.

She withdrew a sealed envelope from the bag, held it against her forehead and recited the message on the concealed card, her lyrical voice carrying easily throughout the murmuring hall. One by one, the seven cards were read without hesitation by the blindfolded medium — including the special envelope from Lodge.

All seven of the envelopes were then returned intact to the people in the audience who had written the messages. All of Dora's readings were confirmed as exactly correct, including the message of the scientist.

As Devant wrote in 1935, "It seems, on the face of it, unexplainable, and the trick had a great vogue." But there was more to come than just applause.

Professor Lodge carefully examined his sealed envelope, then rose and, raising his hand for silence, addressed the capacity audience. "I do not understand," he said, "by what means this marvel has been accomplished. I know nothing in science that could account for it, and although the lady herself and Mr. Devant may be unaware of the supernatural powers she is exercising, I believe that the intervention of such power alone could offer a solution." The scientist resumed his seat to the stunned silence of the audience. Devant himself was momentarily speechless, but then recovered and continued with the evening's performance.

Devant later recalled in 1935, and again in 1936 in his book *Secrets of My Magic*, "It was indeed an impressive moment and I was placed in an extremely embarrassing position. I had and have always had a great respect for Sir Oliver, and I had no wish to deceive him or to lead him astray in his honest and serious investigations.

"On the other hand, I had my living to earn as an illusionist, and here was one of my most successful demonstrations and I could not afford to jettison it."

Devant and his backstage partner, Nevil Maskelyne, approached Sir Oliver after the performance to confidentially assure the respected scientist that the stage results which seemed so extraordinary had been obtained by trickery — quite clever trickery perhaps, but only trickery, nevertheless.

To Devant's and Maskelyne's utter astonishment, and deep disappointment, Sir Oliver refused to believe them. David Devant then promised the scientist that one day he would reveal the secret to him.

The complete secret of Translucidation, however, was revealed only a few weeks later in *Will Goldston's Magician Annual for 1909–10*, which incorporated a detailed illustration. It was entitled "A Sensational Second Sight Act" and appeared on page 75. David Devant's name was not mentioned. The *Annual* sold for four shillings and six pence ($2 in America plus postage) over the counter at the Conjuring, Theatrical and Entertainment Department at the famous A. W. Gamage department store at Holborn Circus.

Goldston had managed the department since 1905 and had made a practice of publishing books and pamphlets that claimed to reveal the secrets of the most popular illusions of the day — though often the "secret" was just Goldston's best guess, which often would be later proven wrong after the illusion had been withdrawn in favor of a new wonder, and the secret illusion's workings were no longer of value. However, in the case of Translucidation, Goldston was correct in every respect.

The Devant secret: when Dora sat on the chair, a woman below stage reached up through a small trap door in the stage through a slit in Dora's voluminous skirt to connect the end of a speaking tube to another tube attached under Dora's dress, which then led up to a point behind one of the medium's ears. The tube was concealed in Dora's hair arrangement. The woman's hand then moved to immediately below Dora's lap, where Dora pushed all the envelopes down through the slit that was hidden by colorful embroidery.

Standing in a soundproof room below stage, the woman then quickly passed the envelopes to another assistant, who placed the envelopes on a frame backed by a powerful electric light. When he switched the light on, the message in the envelope was easily readable. He read the contents into the speaking tube to Dora and then handed back the envelope to the woman, who then passed it back up through the slit in the skirt into the black bag.

Dora removed the envelope from the bag, held it to her forehead and read out the message written inside. Each envelope was handled the same way.

When a card was encountered that had been folded, thus blocking the light, the envelope was quickly torn open. After the message was read into the speaking tube, the refolded card was quickly placed in a duplicate envelope and the spectator's original marking replicated.

Translucidation continued to be one of David Devant's most popular illusions for several months. Speaking of his sister, he wrote in 1935, "Dora was an ideal assistant, exhibiting all the coolness so essential in action."

Remarkably, even in the face of Devant and Maskelyne's joint insistence that the "envelope trick" was entirely trickery, and only recently having publicly and explicitly stated his own specific criteria necessary before seriously considering any apparent psychical event, Sir Oliver Lodge that night invoked the supernatural as his *first* response, his first explanation to his observation, when a brief moment of considered logic would have suggested a visit to the well-known magic department at Gamage's as his first step of investigation — an option that some in the audience probably exercised.

Responding on May 1, 1909, to a letter from Sir Oliver in which the scientist had propounded several methods for the "envelope trick,"[5] Nevil Maskelyne diplomatically pointed out that none of Lodge's proposals could work given the conditions in St. George's Hall. To Lodge's suggestion that accomplices might have been used, Maskelyne devoted half the letter to emphatically dismissing the use of confederates as "a fraudulent deceit." To Lodge's suggestion that some secret preparations could have been accomplished by Devant and his sister during their "Mental Magnetism" (a two-person mindreading routine) performed just before Translucidation, Maskelyne pointed out:

> Miss Devant has no need to use any liquids, or any other means for rendering the envelopes transparent; nor does Mr. Devant, ever touch them until after their contents have been read. Neither do the "Mental Magnetism" experiments provide him for opening or otherwise dealing with the envelopes. The latter, as you may perhaps recollect, remain in the hands of the audience until Dora has performed the actions suggested [in "Mental Magnetism"], or has finally resumed her seat. Then only are the envelopes collected are laid upon her lap.

Indeed, even Nevil Maskelyne stated in the letter that he did not know how the Devants performed their Mental Magnetism routine, a statement supported by Devant in his 1936 book.

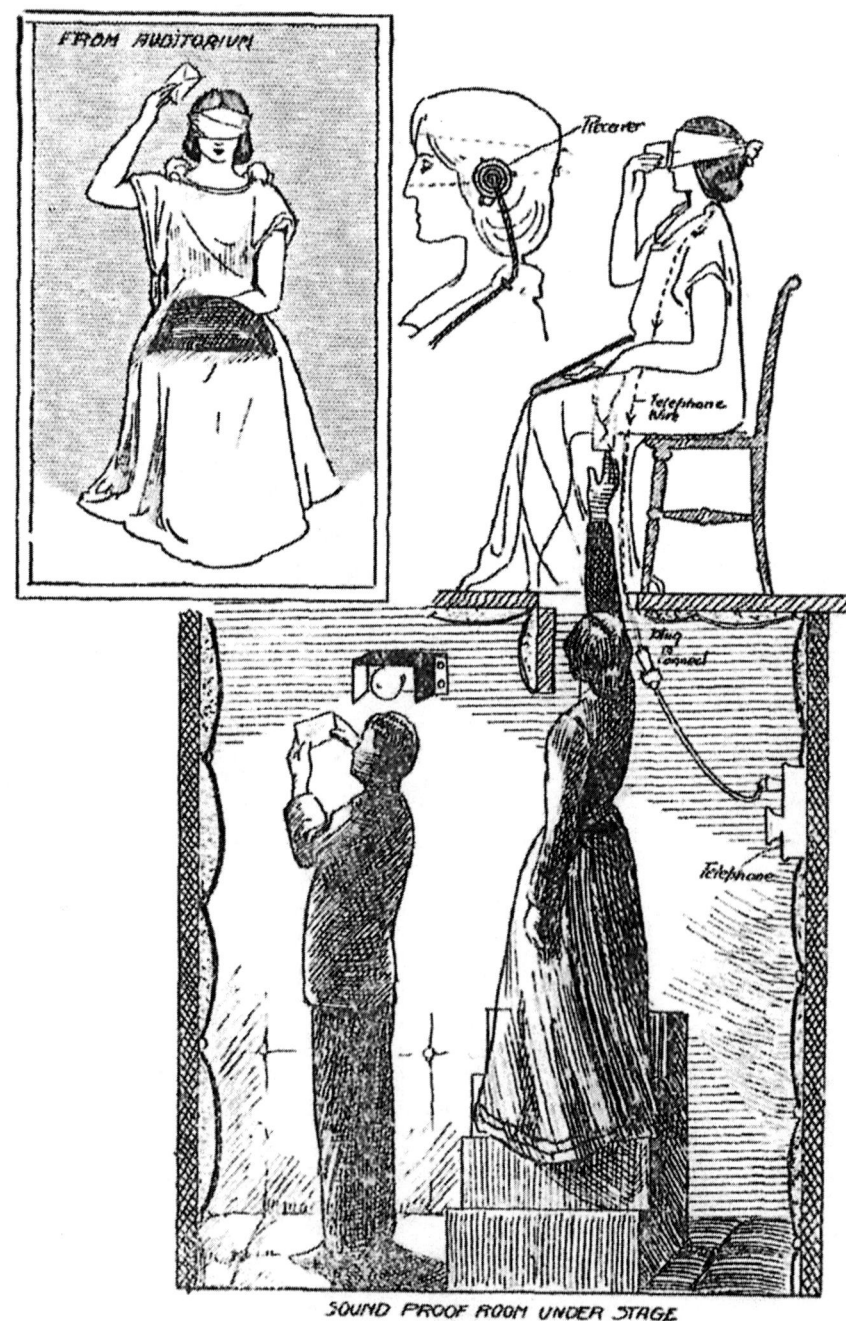

"Translucidation" as depicted in *Will Goldston's Magician Annual for 1909–10*.

17. The Conjuror and the Physicist (Devant and Lodge)

That Translucidation had deeply bothered the scientist is evident from the three page response to the Lodge enquiry. In the letter, Maskelyne suggests that Lodge would know the method sometime in the future, as he and Devant had promised that night.

Anne Davenport has suggested to the author, I believe correctly, that Oliver Lodge wrote to Nevil Maskelyne rather than Devant, as Maskelyne was very active in the nascent British telecommunications and telegraph industry, and Lodge likely felt more comfortable writing to a fellow engineer.

18

The Blackburn Revelations

> Most human evidence is unreliable.
> — Douglas Blackburn, London *Daily News*, September 5, 1911

The experiments of Blackburn and Smith, of which Gurney and Myers in their December 9, 1882, report to the SPR wrote, "The results of these trials give us the most important and valuable insight into the manner of the mental transfer of a picture which we have yet obtained," nevertheless were not included in *Phantasms of the Living*. Nor did they appear in any other SPR publication after the final session at 14 Dean's Yard on April 23, 1883, the session that ended with Blackburn's abrupt departure. Blackburn certainly saw the futility of spending any more of his unpaid time with the SPR, certainly now with George Smith already a paid hypnotist for the SPR. There was no potential payoff for Blackburn with the SPR, and there were issues to be dealt with in Brighton more pressing than thought reading.

After Blackburn's departure, George Albert Smith spent about nine years as a paid private secretary and hypnotist to Gurney and Myers, and assistant to Eleanor Sidgewick in her telepathy experiments.[1] In 1892, Smith left the world of psychical research, his reputation as a genuine telepath still untarnished, to return to the resort entertainment business in Brighton and Hove. He leased St. Anne's Well Gardens in Hove, where he staged a wide variety of exhibitions such as hot air ballooning, parachute jumps, a monkey house, a fortune teller — and, what would be the most important impact on his future career, magic lantern shows in which he incorporated dissolving views that enhanced the storytelling possibilities of the slide shows. Smith also began to schedule the slide shows with lectures at the Brighton Aquarium where he and Douglas Blackburn had started their brief thought reading career ten years earlier. There was no mention in Smith's seaside resort publicity of the SPR or his telepathic experiences.

18. The Blackburn Revelations

In March 1896,[2] Smith attended the Lumière program in Leicester Square, London, and later viewed the films of Robert Paul in Brighton. In 1897, Smith began to produce and manufacture his own films. He claimed to have invented the close-up shot before D. W. Griffith. He patented a double-exposure system in 1897, and, in 1906, patented a two-color additive system called Kinemacolor which became the first successful commercial color film process. With the color films, Smith began a highly successful run in the growing British cinema, until his patent was overturned in 1914, which ended his film career. In his time, Smith became a Fellow of the Royal Astronomical Society, and in 1955 a Fellow of the British Film Academy.

George A. Smith died May 17, 1959, at the age of 95.

Douglas Blackburn worked at the Johannesburg *Star* for three years after his arrival in 1892. With major unrest in South Africa, exacerbated by the Jameson Raid fiasco, December 29, 1895, which effectively acted as a declaration of war on the Transvaal and the Boers under President Paul Kruger, Blackburn's quick pen was utilized in pamphlets, leaflets, and one-man newspapers until he became a roving columnist for the Johannesburg *Standard and Digger News*, in 1899. His first novel, *Prinsloo of Prinsloodorp*, appeared in April 1899, published in both London[3] and Johannesburg, ultimately in three editions. He served as British correspondent behind Boer lines after the formal declaration of war on October 11, 1899, was deported, and by December was serving in the British Ambulance Corps. He was wounded at the Battle of Colenso.

Blackburn went on to write six more novels, all of which appeared in multiple South African and London editions. Through the course of his career, Douglas Blackburn became recognized as the leading British writer in South Africa, and the founder of the South African school of modern fiction.

In addition to the novels and stories, he also wrote non-fiction as well as a prolific stream of articles and columns on the Boer War and its aftermath.[4] In 1906 he returned to London for six months for medical treatment, and then returned to the Natal, where he worked in the Criminal Investigation Department during the Bambatha Rebellion in 1906, an uprising of the Zulus against British rule and taxation. Finally, in July 1908, Blackburn returned permanently to England.

Upon his arrival in London, prominent reviews of his latest novel, *Leaven: A Black and White Story*, appeared in the *Spectator* and in the *Bookman*. Blackburn's *Prinsloo of Prinsloodorp* was issued in its fourth edition, and *I Came and Saw*, another novel of South Africa, was also published. He wrote of socialism in South Africa for *New Age*—and, beginning December 5, 1908, wrote a series of six articles for *John Bull*, "Confessions of a Famous Medium," in which he revealed that the successful telepathy experiments conducted by the SPR Committee in 1882–3 with Blackburn and George A. Smith had been a hoax.

However, a year prior to the Blackburn *John Bull* series, a letter, "Occultism and Common Sense," appeared November 26, 1907, in *The Westminster Gazette*. Its author, Dr. Horatio B. Donkin, observed that there were two occasions in the winter of 1882–3 when outside critics were invited "to witness and apply tests" during the SPR "telepathic" experiments at Dean's Yard. "On one occasion," Donkin wrote, "the tests, applied to prevent possible *auditory* communication, put a stop to the phenomena; on the other, similar prevention of *visual* communication had a like effect." Donkin then points out, "No mention was made in the [published] reports of these meetings of the presence of the critics or of the consequent cessation of the phenomena," a disturbing ethical flaw in the SPR leadership.

Donkin's name had been proposed by friends to the SPR as one of the outside critics to be invited to Dean's Yard to observe the Blackburn-Smith experiments, but his name was turned down — largely, Donkin believed, by Barrett, Gurney and Myers — because of his 1882 article in *Nineteenth Century* in which he had severely criticized the conclusion of genuine thought reading by Barrett, Gurney and Myers, on the basis of the Creery tests.

"I urge," said Donkin, "that the omission of these details from the *Proceedings* gives rise to more than suspicion of the fallaciousness of the experiments in 'telepathy' carried on by the society, and of the candor of those who were responsible for the publication of those *Proceedings*."

A corroborating article, "Occultism and Telepathic Experiments," appeared on January 29, 1908, in *The Westminster Gazette*. It was sent by Dr. Donkin but written by Sir James Crichton-Browne, F.R.S., who had been present at the 1882–3 experiments.[5] At the time of the experiments, Crichton-Browne was the leading British psychiatrist, and was the Lord Chancellor's Visitor in Lunacy, a senior medical position he held until 1922. He had written his article without prior knowledge of the Donkin letter. In this circumstance, Dr. Crichton-Browne was the medical man that Professor Barrett had earlier recommended be present as a necessary condition during all experiments in thought transference. He recalled:

> I was invited to join the conference by George Romanes to witness a remarkable manifestation of thought-reading by a youth who could without contact receive and reproduce, not words but figures, diagrams, or pictures, presented to the mind of an operator with whom he was in some way *en rapport*.

He acknowledged that the events of twenty-five years in the past could not be fully recalled with accuracy, so he would limit his comments to only

18. The Blackburn Revelations

those incidents for which his memory was very clear. The exact dates he could not recall, nor could he could name all those present, but he estimated that about twenty men were present. Many of them he did not know, but he recalled that the group included Francis Galton, George Romanes, Dr. W. Stone (who owned the rooms used), Dr. G. Wyld, and members of the SPR investigating committee: Henry Sidgewick, Professor Barrett, Frederic Myers, and Edmund Gurney. Also present was a woman, whom Crichton-Browne identified as Blackburn's wife. As Blackburn never married, the identity of the woman is unknown. Possibly it was Alice Smith, Smith's sister; however, in all the later articles by Blackburn on the SPR experiments, at no time does he mention a woman being present.

After opening comments by Sidgewick describing the experiments to be undertaken and past successes experienced, all of which were corroborated by Blackburn, the experiments began. Smith was blindfolded with a white handkerchief "being drawn over the bridge of his nose and his eyes, and tied behind his head." He was seated at a table in the middle of the room, facing the windows, with his back to the door leading to an adjacent room. Crichton-Browne recalled that the woman sat across the table from Smith, facing him. The investigating committee was Romanes, Galton, Sidgewick, Myers and Crichton-Browne, while the others present formed an observant audience.

Romanes drew an owl. The drawing was shown to Blackburn. Crichton-Browne recalled "distinctly" that Blackburn stood two to three yards behind Smith, with his hands in his pockets, "and that he contracted his brows from time to time and made faces. This went on for five minutes or so." Smith then finally drew on the paper before him "a crude and clumsy outline of an owl. It was very different from Romanes' sketch, but was undoubtedly suggestive of an owl."

Some other similar experiments were done successfully, at least to the satisfaction of SPR members present, when it occurred to Romanes and Crichton-Browne that some kind of code might be in use. Consequently the next sketch was a "sort of nondescript arabesque, simple enough, but not easily describable in words"—or codes.

Blackburn's face fell on seeing the design, and he claimed that it might be too complicated to remember and send—to which Romanes replied, "Oh, no, we can look at it, turn away, and reproduce it without difficulty."

Constrained to continue, Blackburn stood behind Smith, made some passes with his hands. Smith, after a few moments, drew a few lines on the paper, but they did not resemble the target sketch in any way.

Crichton-Browne believed that Smith was not effectively blindfolded, and that Blackburn was communicating with him both in sight and hearing. Consequently, with the permission of the two "performers," "We proceeded to do so *secundum artem*." Romanes and Crichton-Browne re-blindfolded Smith by first packing his eye sockets with cotton-wool. Then his ears were plugged, and a large dark handkerchief was tied about his head.

All experiments following the change in blindfold were complete failures. "The moment," Crichton-Browne wrote, "that Mr. Smith's senses were thoroughly occluded all transference stopped."

"I was invited to be critical and skeptical, and I was so." But it was clear to Crichton-Browne and Romanes that some of the psychical researchers present still did not believe any tricks were being practiced.

> The last scene of all, or passage-at-arms, I vividly recollect, Mr. Myers, standing in front of the fireplace, said, "It must be allowed that this demonstration has been a total failure, and I attribute that to the offensive incredulity of Dr. Crichton-Browne." To which I rejoined, "I hope I always will show offensive incredulity when I find myself in the presence of patent imposture."
>
> I understood that minutes of that conference were taken, and were to be submitted to all who took part in it for correction; but from that day to this (1908) I have never heard a word about it.
>
> I have no doubt Dr. Francis Galton will be able to confirm or amend my recollections.

The above statements suggest why no dates were given in the committee's third report, rendered on April 24. If the complete failure described by Crichton-Browne, which was never mentioned in the publications of the SPR, occurred on April 21 at Dean's Yard, then there was an urgent need for another set of experiments to provide enough data for the committee report to the open meeting of the society scheduled for April 24, which could not be postponed. This need explains the rushed session on April 23 and the urgent summons to Blackburn (Smith was already in London working for Gurney), and Blackburn's final abrupt departure back to his own problems in Brighton.

Several months later, after the *Westminster Gazette* articles, following the appearance of Blackburn's series of six articles 1908–09 in *John Bull*, Alice Johnson, then honorary secretary of the SPR, issued a four page leaflet on yellow paper, stamped "private and confidential for SPR members only." On page 3, she makes the statement:

> Shortly after these [Blackburn] articles began to appear, I communicated with Mr. G.A. Smith, and then went to see him, to ask for his version of the matter. I was already aware that, for reasons unconnected with the experiments, but which Mr. Myers and Mr. Gurney considered sufficient, they had made no more experiments with Mr. Blackburn after the series published in the *Proceedings*, Vol. 1.[6]

In 1883, the Blackburn-Smith partnership had clearly ended, and Blackburn had no ongoing loyalty to the SPR and thus no need to further inconvenience himself. So it was that he left to catch a train to return to his own problems. Johnson's statement seems an unfortunate attempt, given the roiling of the SPR membership by Blackburn's articles, to privately damn Blackburn with innuendo.

The SPR leaders' suppression of the Blackburn-Smith experiments might have been, not the suspicion that Blackburn had been a cheat and therefore possibly Smith might have been himself at some points, but by the fear that utilizing the Blackburn-Smith data as one of the two key parts of the foundation of *Phantasms* would trigger an immediate response from Crichton-Browne, Galton, Romanes and perhaps others regarding the utter experimental failures at Dean's Yard once all Smith's sensory channels had been blocked. Using only the Creery information may have seemed the safest way to proceed; it was considered conclusive, after all.

Beginning in *John Bull* on December 5, 1908, and each week for six weeks, Douglas Blackburn peeled back the workings of an early SPR investigation into telepathy which had been, for a time, touted in the *Proceedings* by the committee as conclusive evidence of thought transference as "a fact of nature." *John Bull* was a popular gossip sheet (the British Library does not maintain a file of the journal) and so was publicly ignored by the SPR, largely in the hope that the Blackburn issue would go away, that important people would never read *John Bull*. Alice Johnson and others made a great thing of the fact that several points which Blackburn described in his articles could not be found in the *Proceedings* of the time—which, given Dr. Crichton-Browne and Dr. Donkin's recollections, would seem an empty defense.

Douglas Blackburn was writing, as had Crichton-Browne, twenty-five years after the events he describes in his series of articles, so some inconsistencies with more contemporary accounts would be expected.

Blackburn admits in the first of the series, "I was among the many who at this period fell a victim to the vague fascination of various forms of Occultism." Brighton had become "a hotbed of, and the happy hunting ground for, the mystery monger, professional and private."

Blackburn met G.A. Smith, whose interest in the occult matched his own, and the two young men came to focus on the abilities of W. Irving Bishop. They found, "as everybody now knows, that the business is extremely simple when the trick is mastered."

> As editor of a widely-read paper, I was able to boom Smith very effectively, I remaining in the background as the impartial journalist investigator who occasionally assisted at an experiment.
>
> ... we resolved that we should be doing the world a service by fooling them (Gurney and Myers) to the top of their bent, and then showing how easy a matter it was to "take in" scientific observers.

> I have kept my secret for twenty-six years, and only withdraw the veil now because of the disgust inspired by the preposterous alleged communications from the spirit of F. W. H. Myers, in which one of the most refined and cultured of men is made to write and think like an illiterate conjuror.

The second article was subtitled, "The Inadequacy of Scientific Precautions."

> I must explain that our preliminary experiments were genuine in so far that we tried to get *en rapport* by will-power; but the results were often wide of the mark, and only the pronounced friendly prejudice of a Myers would have credited them as successes.
>
> The experiments at first took place at the lodgings of Mr. Gurney at Brighton, and were distinctly elementary. Indeed, in some cases the problems set us were so simple that we purposely bungled them so as not to make ourselves too cheap, just as the astute conjuror will make several "failures" before succeeding in a trick.

Blackburn then described the chessboard technique used by the two partners to "send" a random drawing, i.e., a memorized hundred-square board with a letter-number designation for each square. Sending via code the sequential positions of squares crossed by the lines of the original random drawing would allow Smith, visualizing the board, to roughly duplicate the original drawing (see Appendix D for a simplified version of this approach). Regular geometric designs like triangles and octagons would be easily sent from a memorized list. The "successes" from regular or random designs were considered by the investigators as equivalent in importance.

> Now my point is this. If such a person can convey by genuine Telepathy to another a regular figure, which he visualizes, why can he not with equal success visualize and transfer to the brain a picture of an irregular figure like a splotchy blotch? And is it not strange that while he can accurately describe a regular triangle, he should fail when one side of it curved or wobbly? This is where Smith and I failed in the long run.

In the third article, Blackburn gave examples of unconscious assistance received from the SPR investigators which aided their results. He then turned to the Reichenbach phenomenon, which was also a focus of an SPR Committee.[7] The phenomenon, first announced by the German scientist Baron Karl von Reichenbach, was that certain sensitives could perceive magnetic emanations in the dark, usually blue in color. Smith was one of 45 subjects tested, men and women, and was one of only three who were successful (the other two were friends of Smith). Sitting in the dark, Smith successfully called out when the magnet was turned on and then off, where every precaution was made to conceal the switching action from the subject. Smith was right on almost every trial — as were his friends.

"How did you manage it?" I enquired. For answer Smith opened his mouth and showed me a steel pen nib. By placing his head between the poles of the magnet, the movement of the nib acquainted him when he ought to "see the light." The experiment was regarded as quite conclusive.

In the fourth article, subtitled "Private versus Professional Humbug," Blackburn observes:

> It has, I believe, been the rule of the SPR to avoid the employment of paid or professional agents, the assumption being the not unnatural one that where the agent is making a profit out of his services he may be tempted to imposture. But it by no means follows that the absence of a monetary consideration will ensure good faith.
>
> Every person who has had any experience in sifting evidence is aware that misstatement does not necessarily imply intentional fraud. I am satisfied that many of the witnesses cited by the SPR honestly believe they are telling the truth, but I have so often found the most honorable witnesses touching up the weak points in their stories, and have heard so many otherwise reliable people describing things that Smith and I never performed, that I feel justified in manifesting the utmost incredulity in accepting the testimony of reporters of psychic phenomena when the incidents described are otherwise uncorroborated.

He then describes the circumstances of "Fig. 22," when Smith was blindfolded, his ears plugged, his head encased in a bolster case and a blanket thrown over everything. He also describes a second situation in which Smith was isolated from him in another room, the two men not even seeing each other before the experiment, yet a random drawing was successfully sent. Blackburn left the explanations to the next article.

In the fifth article, "My Masterpiece," Blackburn, after describing the circumstances of Smith's isolation under the blanket again, described how the two had communicated without visual or auditory codes. The technique used was known to stage mindreaders at the time (see Appendix C, effect 39, "Second Sight Through Brick Walls," from an 1895 pamphlet). Once Blackburn was shown Fig. 22, as customary, he drew and redrew the design as he paced the room to apparently impress it into his mind before going into the room where Smith was seated at a table under the blanket. No sound was allowed. In the process, Blackburn drew the design on a cigarette paper, wadded it up and slipped it into the metal protector tube on his pencil, the same pencil that Blackburn had been using throughout the various experiments. Smith, who judged when Blackburn would be given the design, and would be repeatedly drawing the design, waited a few minutes after the door to the room opened, then shouted "I have it!" as he reached out with one hand from under the blanket to search the top of the table. "Where's my pencil?" Smith shouted from underneath the blanket. Blackburn quietly and quickly stepped forward to place his pencil on the table within easy reach. Smith pulled the pencil with its protector tube under the blanket, withdrew the cigarette paper from the protector, opened it out, and drew four increasingly closer versions of the original, but omitted a key factor of the drawing, the wriggling line on the left, to give the exercise more credibility. When he pushed the paper back out from under the blanket it was soaked with sweat. The effect was utterly convincing.

In the second of the isolation tests, prior to the test, Smith had suggested that "we must make Gurney the medium." Blackburn had an idea. The two went to a cornchandler's off Victoria Street to look for burrs which accumulate on the clothing of the harvesters. They found two or three. Their idea was to attach the burr to Blackburn's balled up cigarette paper and then, somehow, attach the burr to Gurney at an agreed location.

Blackburn sat with Myers beside him, while Gurney was with Smith in another room. Blackburn stared at the design given him by Myers, then paced the room again and again. Finally he murmured to Myers that he didn't believe Smith was trying. As Myers stepped to the door and whispered to Gurney, Blackburn drew the design on the cigarette paper. When still nothing happened, Blackburn repeated his complaint, but this time Gurney came into the room to listen to Blackburn directly, at which time Blackburn attached the burr to the bottom of Gurney's suit-coat, in the location previously agreed to. Smith recovered the burr and successfully drew the design.

In the final article on January 9, 1909, "The Master Key," Blackburn observed:

> When the secret of any trick is revealed the tendency of most people is to express astonishment that it should deceive. They overlook the very important circumstance of unpreparedness on the part of the victims. The chances of protecting against fraud in pretended psychic experiments are extremely remote for the all-sufficient reason that the tricksters have absolute control of the conditions. They say in effect, "If you will permit us to perform this trick in our own way we shall fulfill our promise by producing something startling." If the investigators object, then the reasonable retort is: "We do not profess to do this thing under any other conditions than our own."
>
> The only scientific observer who refused to be taken in by Smith and I was Sir James Crichton-Browne. He witnessed some of our experiments at Dean's Yard and expressed himself rather strongly.
>
> The interesting circumstance in this matter was that Sir James actually discovered nothing, but was prompted to denounce the business on suspicion only.

On encountering Sir James, Smith and Blackburn realized that he would be too skeptical to allow them to bend the conditions as necessary. The axiom,

18. The Blackburn Revelations

Blackburn explained, of all psychic phenomena was that the presence of an antagonistic person completely upsets the essential conditions, a response frequently used to bail out mediums and psychics faced with failure.

> Sir James showed his hand too soon, or I am fairly satisfied that he would have caught us out. Thanks to the warning conveyed by his hostile preliminary observations, we were put on our guard.

Closing his series, Blackburn wrote:

> Unquestionably the tremendous hold that telepathy and cognate branches of "enquiry" has taken on intelligent people is largely explained by the circumstances I have endeavored to emphasize, namely, that the player has absolute control of the game, as he makes the rules.

His exposure completed, Blackburn then went on to other literary projects. Alice Johnson wrote to G.A. Smith on December 15, 1908:

> I have seen Mrs. Sidgewick & reported to her our discussion about the Blackburn articles. She thinks it better under the circumstances to take no notice of them—at all events for the present. If some respectable person or paper attempts to endorse them in any way, we might then think it desirable to defend the Society against the charges made. We should of course consult with you in that case before replying; but it does not seem likely that the contingency will arise.

In other letters, Johnson hastened to assure anxious members that G.A. Smith had not confessed to anything, that Smith had insisted that all the experiments had been genuine, and that the Blackburn articles were "deliberately concocted & and are not a genuine confession at all."

Thus, the *John Bull* series was left to fester, with the reputation and competence of the SPR allowed to be quietly questioned. So things continued until September 1, 1911, when an article appeared in the *London Daily News*—one of those respectable papers which so concerned Alice Johnson. The title of the article was "Confessions of a 'Telepathist,'" by Douglas Blackburn. It was for the most part a summary of the earlier six-part series. The focus was not specific trickery, as anyone, including magicians, can be deceived or baffled, but the predilection of the investigators toward substantiating their previously held beliefs—feeding that hunger that Frederic Wickes wrote of so clearly in his 1907 book, *Thought Reading Explained*.

As Blackburn put it in his conclusion:

> Mr. Frank Podmore, perhaps the most level-headed of the researchers—and to the end a skeptic—aptly puts it: "It is not the friend whom we know whose eyes must be closed and his ears muffled, but the 'Mr. Hyde,' whose lurking presence in each of us we are only now beginning to suspect."

> What one desires to believe requires little corroboration. I shall doubtless raise a storm of protest when I assert that the principal cause of belief in psychic phenomena is the inability of the average man to observe accurately and estimate the value of evidence, plus a bias in favor of the phenomena being real. It is an amazing fact that I have never yet, after hundreds of tests, found a man who could accurately describe ten minutes afterwards a series of simple acts which I performed in his presence.

The study of mal-observation in human testimony is extensive. The early work of S.J. Davey and Richard Hodgson,[8] contemporary with the events described in this book, demonstrates how utterly unreliable were the descriptions of séance sitters or audience observers of the effects they had witnessed.

The response to the *Daily News* article was swift. On September 4th, G. A. Smith, whom Blackburn had thought was dead, responded in the *Daily News*: "Let me say at once that Mr. Blackburn's story is a tissue of errors from beginning to end." He then went on to deny any attempt whatever to deceive the SPR researchers.

Blackburn wrote at length on September 5. After expressing his delight that his information regarding Smith's mortality was in error, he continued: "But now to business. Mr. Smith gives a categorical denial to my story; declares that he was a genuine sensitive, and I also a possessor of psychic power. He could do no less, and I cannot blame him."

Blackburn then, step by step, refuted Smith's denials, which were based primarily on Smith's extensively quoting from the SPR *Proceedings* reports on the experiments. Smith's position was that if Gurney, Myers and Barrett said it happened, then it happened. To which in closing Blackburn comments:

> If under the conditions of the blanket and bolster case, an irregular figure can be produced bearing a reasonable resemblance to the original I will not only admit that our great feat was genuine, but will immediately proceed to cultivate that psychic power which Mr. Smith insists I possess, but of which so far I am unconscious.

On September 6, Smith responded with yet another lengthy denial. In the same issue, William Barrett, also to Blackburn's surprise still alive, contributed: "Mr. Blackburn thought Mr. Smith was dead and apparently he thought I was dead too, for he described himself as the sole survivor of those who were present at the experiment.... You may say that not only I, but Myers and Gurney, had the most absolute confidence in Mr. Smith."

On September 8 in the *Daily News*, Eleanor Sidgewick wrote, supporting Smith, but observing that "but little is yet known of the [telepathic] process or of the conditions to ensure success."

Blackburn returned to psychical research in the *Sunday Times* in 1917, commenting on: "the extraordinary gullibility displayed by Messrs. Myer and Gurney." Blackburn concluded:

> I say deliberately, as a result of long acquaintance with and personal knowledge of most of the leading Occultists of the past forty years, that, while I acknowledge their absolute honesty and intent, I would not lay a shilling against a ten-pound note on any one of them not being roped in by the venerable Confidence Trick at the first time of asking.[9]

Douglas Blackburn went on with his journalistic career, writing his last novel, *Love Muti*, in 1915. In 1916, Blackburn joined the staff of the *Tonbridge Free Press*, where he wrote a column called "The Looker On" for the next thirteen years. On February 17, 1920, he started a five-part series called "Ghosts and Mediums I Have Met," in which he implies that he thought the medium Lottie Fowler had genuine psychical powers. He died of pneumonia at Victoria Cottage Hospital on March 28, 1929, at the age of seventy-one. He was buried, at his own request, in a pauper's grave. Blackburn had been a popular raconteur and colleague on the *Free Press*, and a respected member of the local community.

William F. Barrett outlived all of the other early SPR psychical researchers. How important thought transference and the Creerys were to Barrett can be seen in a letter he wrote to Sir Oliver Lodge on April 8, 1900,[10] in which he first complained how five photographs from his report on dowsing had been taken "without any acknowledgement of where they came from; a frank breach of literary etiquette." His querulous tone continued, describing how he was not being properly respected, though softening it somewhat by suggesting some aspects may have been "unintentional." "Of course," he continued to Lodge, "you are in every way a higher man than I am [Lodge would be knighted in 1902, while Barrett would wait until 1912; Lodge had won the Rumford Medal of the Royal Society in 1898 before Barrett had even been elected a member in 1899], but Faraday, Stokes, FitzGerald and others, whom I knew well, never had an air of condescension either. Perhaps I am unduly sensitive." He then turned to his key concern: "You are rightly jealous of your priority of discovery in certain physical additions to knowledge, but you do not realize that I am equally jealous in certain psychical phenomena." Then, to stake his claim of priority, "can you point to any earlier announcement of Thought Transference than my Glasgow paper in 1876 & my letter to *Nature* in 1881." And explicit pride in his determined stout resistance to criticism, accepting "my share of the hostility not only from scientific men, but also from the Sidgwicks," a circumstance that also, in his view, needed to be properly acknowledged. By 1900 Barrett's break with the Cambridge group had become almost complete.

On Saturday, December 20, 1924, long after the thought reader craze had passed, in a letter to the *Times*,[11] William (now Sir William) F. Barrett, F.R.S., still clung to the legitimacy of the Creery family experiments as establishing that "thought transference was a rare but genuine phenomenon." In the letter, he cited Professor and Mrs. Sidgewick, Edmund Gurney, and other deceased former colleagues, who, he claimed, as a result of their own experiments with the Creery family had "confirmed the opinion I had arrived at." Barrett's known pronounced inclination to self-promotion had expanded over the years as those from the earlier days who could have challenged his reminiscences died away.

In short, thought transference was his, Barrett's, discovery — and no one else's. It was a position he tenaciously embraced to his death on May 26, 1925.

Eric J. Dingwall visited George A. Smith in 1954, while Smith, 90 years old, took a break from mowing his lawn:

> I asked him how if, as he asserted, their shows had been genuine telepathic demonstrations, Blackburn had in his writings shown such detailed knowledge of the most ingenious methods of faking and code work — to which I got no satisfactory reply.[12]

19

Truth ... or Hunger

> It is not the friend whom we know whose eyes must be closed and his ears muffled, but the "Mr. Hyde," whose lurking presence in each of us we are only now beginning to suspect.
> — Frank Podmore

It is too easy, and perhaps unfair, these many years later to so easily find fault with the early psychical researchers and the relative ease with which they allowed themselves to be deceived during the period of the thought reader craze. The late nineteenth century was a time of scientific discoveries of major importance that were radically changing the human perception of the earth and the cosmos. Where humanity had always, it seemed, lived securely, surrounded as they were by the Known, only to be discovering that the Known was only the beginning of something else not yet defined.

That the gentlemen of the SPR could be duped by professional thought readers like Washington Irving Bishop, Stuart Cumberland or others is to be expected, just as William Crookes was hoodwinked by Annie Eva Fay several years earlier. Intellectually, Annie Eva Fay was no match for Crookes, but the field on which they battled was not the intellect or the rigors of science. Fay and other mediums and thought readers played on the hunger of human nature, as Frederic Wickes so aptly described it in 1907, to identify and find that enchanted boundary on the other side of which apparently lay the answers to the deepest mysteries of nature — that area that Crookes himself described so well in 1879, and which he admitted he found so seductive.

The SPR researchers' ready acceptance of the honesty and reliability of those of social standing at least equivalent to their own; or of defined social positions that implied honesty, like that of the Rev. A.M. Creery ("a clergyman of unblemished character and whose integrity has been exceptionally tested"[1]) and his innocent young girls; or of "the integrity of Mr. Blackburn and Mr. Smith, which nothing has occurred to shake in the slightest degree," were all emphatically attested to over the years by Professor William F. Barrett because they had so amply fed his own hunger for discovery. It was all very much as Frank Podmore suggested,[2] that the issue to be most aware of and fear is not the trickery of the thought readers without, but the "Mr. Hyde" within.

Epilogue

Sensors Magazine, August 2002, ran a poll of its engineering readers to discover which of the comic book "superhero powers" they would want most to possess. Of those who responded, 51.2 percent wanted to be able to fly, while 48.4 percent wanted to become invisible at will. (Those who wanted to fly were asked a secondary question: Would they wear a helmet? The response was that 58 percent would fly without a helmet while 42 percent would use one.) The remaining 0.4 percent of the engineers chose powers like being bulletproof, being able to run super-fast, create fire with a snap of the fingers, and so on.

Thought reading was not on the list. Telepathy was not considered a "superhero power" in the poll since, after all, no laws of physics needed to be violated to demonstrate it — and, according to the popular press, anyone with a pack of ESP cards and some practice could read minds.

An Afterthought

In the course of gathering research for this book, and exchanging many chatty e-mails, a very helpful British source once questioned: "Even with all the investigations done over the decades, you seem to believe that telepathy is impossible. Is that true?" Certainly a valid question to raise after so many pages and footnotes.

Back years ago when I was a senior in high school I decided that I would stop performing standard magic and become a mentalist, a mindreader. I had been doing children's shows, getting paid and not feeling very satisfied or having a lot of fun. Then, standing backstage, I had watched a mentalist perform before a theater audience of several hundred. With no props, no rabbits, no goldfish, no funny boxes, he simply stopped the show. It was stunning. It was mentalism for me from there on. When I asked the mentalist after the show about the requirements for a mentalist, he only laughed and advised, "All you need is a pencil, some paper and a lot of gall." He left out one or two other items, as I discovered.

I was a competent enough performer, though certainly not a real showman. My audiences, now all adults, with their occasional gasp of surprise, accepted that I was probably close to the real thing. In putting my mental routine together, I had been urged by a semi-pro mentalist to always play any hunches that I might get during a show. After all, nothing was lost if I was wrong; it would just add credibility to my persona — and I just might score big.

In one show, about five or six shows along into my developing career as a mindreader, I was in the midst of bringing a major effect to a climax before an audience of about 35 men and women, when I had the oddest feeling — a feeling of green grass, bright chrome green in fact, and something about mowing a lawn. The feeling had absolutely nothing to do with any aspect of the show — so I stopped, turned toward what seemed to be the general section of the audience from where the feeling had emanated, off to my right as I recall, and described the green grass and mowing a lawn. A woman to my right screamed, her eyes bugged out, and she began to say, louder and louder, "My God! My God! I just thought of that! I just remembered I have to rent a power mower, the grass is too tall!" With a chill down my spine I still remember, I nodded suavely (I hoped) toward her, said something somewhat rational along the lines that these things always happen to me, and closed the show at that point. Obviously, I couldn't top that experience, nor could I stop and point out to the audience that what they had just seen was real while all the rest of my stuff that night had been fake. If I had done it right, the audience shouldn't be able to tell the difference.

But there it was.

But where the green grass had come from I don't know. It certainly wasn't coincidence — and it wasn't a lucky guess. Some days later, when I described my experience to a retired vaudeville performer in the magic club I belonged to at the time, he only nodded sagely and said, "Keep playing those hunches, kid. They will only get better."

I played hunches in later shows but always came up empty.

So, in answer to the question, yes, in my experience some kind of amazing spontaneous telepathy happened once, but never again. I had been in the midst of concluding my closing stunt; my mind was focused on the patter, getting the gimmick out of the way so my hands could be shown empty, and so on.

Where had the green grass come from?

In a well-performed mind reading act, there is likely a growing expectation of something unique on the horizon created in the mind of the audience. That expectation — which is missing or even suppressed, in a scientific laboratory setup — that might somehow enhance a subtle connection. It might be the key to that fleeting, very brief moment when a gate swings open and a ephemeral picture or feeling escapes from a person's mind. What the actual mechanism might be for the transfer of that brief flickering thought, I don't know — a kind of quantum warp, a burst of brain energy, or whatever. William Barrett, even after over forty years' research, had no answer either.

For me it happened once. For the men and women, and innocent girls, described in this book — did it ever actually happen at all? I have to believe that it did — at least once.

Appendices

A: Impossible or Supernormal?

> "We must make up our minds as to what is possible and what is impossible — and not waste time in trying to look for the impossible!"
> — Michael Faraday 1857

In January 1933, in the *Bulletin of the Boston Society for Psychical Research*, Dr. Walter Franklin Prince offered his thoughts on the concepts of "impossible" and "possible."

In 1928, Dr. Prince, then Research Officer of the Boston Society for Psychic Research, had sent two questions to 180 adults, both members and nonmembers of the Society. The two queries were written as follows (italics used are Prince's):

> A number of persons have answered the following questions. Will you please be one to add to the number? Any published result will give no names and neither embarrass anyone who answered nor cause regrets.
>
> 1. If a person grasps firmly the corner of a handkerchief by and between the thumb and forefinger of one hand and the diagonally opposite corner of the handkerchief by and between the thumb and forefinger of his other hand, can he, *without lifting, shifting the location of the handkerchief or relaxing the pressure of any thumb or forefinger in the slightest*, by normal means cause a real overhand knot to come in the handkerchief on the line between the two hands?
>
> Warned by some of the replies I particularize further. The question contains no verbal catch but means what it seems to mean; such a knot would not allow the use of the two free corners; the knot is to be formed with the handkerchief itself and nothing else added; there is to be no knot anywhere on it when the thumbs and forefingers are first fixed in position; the handkerchief is not to be cut or otherwise impaired; and there are no other conditions — the handkerchief may be grasped behind the back or in any other position so long as it is grasped as stated; it is even allowable to tie a knot in one's neck and slip it down on the handkerchief, if anyone can do that.

If the answer is "yes" I shall expect an explanation of the method. If "no," then comes the second question.

2. If, nevertheless, under these conditions, actually and by you admittedly adhered to, such a knot, in the manner described, should actually be formed in and with the handkerchief, would the phenomenon be entitled to be called a supernormal one and, if not, why not?

Mind. I do not say or even hint that the knot *is* possible, unless asking the questions is construed as a hint. It may be that my questions are meant to test their psychological effects, or that I wish to see how certain people distinguish between "possible" and "impossible," "normal" and "supernormal." Nor do I say that the feat *cannot* be done.

If you are inclined to put the questions to several other persons also and to send me their replies, I shall be grateful, but their answers should be *individual* and *independent* ones. And I should like to know *what* the persons are, not necessarily *who*.

I will later let you know what it is all about, and think it will interest you enough to repay you for your trouble. I thank you in advance for your co-operation.

Sincerely yours,
Walter Franklin Prince

[Before going further, what would have been your answers?]

Of the 180 answers received 36 could not be used (including five from magicians who already knew the answer), leaving 144 to be of legitimate use. *All of the 144* answered "no" to query 1, with 128 declaring outright that it was impossible. All 180 answers came from educated men and women including scientists, engineers, philosophers, lawyers, writers, students, housewives, psychic researchers, occultists, and one entomologist. To return to Prince:

> But what does the reader at this moment think? Does anything seem more certain than the appearance of a knot in the handkerchief, all the stated conditions being strictly adhered to, would involve passage of matter through matter, that a portion of the handkerchief would have to pass through another portion of it or through the arm of the person holding it? And, as this would not be a "normal" process, can anything seem more logically consequent than that it must needs be a "supernormal" one?

In his 1933 article, Prince then went on to discuss forty instances of phenomena being declared "impossible" by learned and experienced people, including conjurors, only to have the "impossible" shown to be quite normal by someone else with a different point of view. In one example, No. 40, a committee gave up discovering any trickery involved with a medium, Alfred James. After the committee declared there was no trickery, an experienced magician named Dunton entered the case. After a close, detailed examination and two demonstrations, Dunton, too, declared James' phenomena genuine and offered $500 to anyone who could prove otherwise. This being in 1878, he was putting up real money, which was successfully claimed three weeks later by a non-magician. The magician, preoccupied with the vertical thinking inherent in magicians' methods, missed the simple and "deliciously audacious" gaff that was used.

Returning to Prince's 1928 writing (italics still Prince's):

> As a matter of fact, the knot *can* be made, with every condition assigned rigidly and exactly adhered to. It is the most impossible appearing possible feat of which I have ever heard. It does not require any skill or any practice, but only that one shall be told how to do it. First, lay the handkerchief, stretched out straight by the diagonally opposite corners, on a table and near its edge. Then fold your arms, so that the left hand protrudes over the right arm and the right hand protrudes under the left arm. Stoop and grasp the right extremity of the handkerchief so placed on the table with the thumb and forefinger of the left hand, and, keeping these rigidly in place, then grasp the left extremity of the handkerchief with the thumb and forefinger of the right hand. You are now in position, with the diagonally opposite corners grasped as prescribed. Now, simply unfold your arms and draw them apart, and without lifting or shifting a finger, a knot will be formed in the handkerchief. Not a stipulation has been transgressed.
>
> Did I not expressly say that "the handkerchief may be grasped behind the back *or in any other position*"? Did I not actually give a hint in saying that "it is even allowable to *tie a knot in one's neck and slip it down on the handkerchief*? That sentence might suggest the experiment of tying a knot, not in the neck, but in the arms and to slip the knot down upon the handkerchief. The arms, hands, and handkerchief immovably held practically constitute an endless cord, and, of course, if a knot is loosely made in a cord and the ends of the cord then fastened to make an endless one, it is easy to shift the knot along the cord.

Dr. Prince's forty examples of errant "impossibility," complemented with a direct, simple test of perception, provide a standard against which a declaration of "impossible!" can be measured.

There is no record of the reactions of the 144 respondents after they had learned the answer.

B. Origins of Second Sight

Condensed from Barry H. Wiley, *Revelations of the Impossible Piddingtons: Adventures in Second Sight* (Amazon Kindle, 2010).

> "I rested my head in my hands, and in my excitement laid down the first principles of second sight."
> — Jean Eugene Robert-Houdin, *Memoirs of Robert-Houdin*, 1859

B. Origins of Second Sight

The origin of second sight, or the demonstration of the transfer of unspoken thought without using the natural senses from the mind of one medium or priest to his partner, dates back at least to the publication of Reginald Scot's *The Discoverie of Witchcraft* in 1584, which includes an implication that two-person thought transfer dated even earlier than that. Only twenty-two of the 283 pages of the *Discoverie* are devoted to conjuror's tricks, but one of them is second sight.

Second-sight as a full-formed stage act, however, dates to 1781 when Philip Breslaw, a German magician, advertised "the communication of thoughts of any person to another without the assistance of speech or writing." Three years later, the French performer Chevalier Joseph Pinetti had his attractive wife "seated in one of the front boxes with a handkerchief over her eyes." With her husband in the audience, Madame Pinetti would then "guess at everything imagined and proposed to her by any person in the company." Pinetti claimed their demonstration was an exhibition of genuine preternatural powers.

But it was the brilliant French conjuror and inventor Jean Eugene Robert-Houdin, working with his eleven-year-old son, Émile, as the blindfolded medium, who with his development of the first silent codes created the modern second sight act. The father-son duo first performed second sight publicly in Paris at the Théâtre Robert-Houdin on Thursday, February 12, 1846.

After brief introductory remarks on the mysteries of the human mind, Robert-Houdin seated his blindfolded son on a stool centered on an otherwise empty stage. Émile appeared innocent and helpless, the same role that other mediums, male and female, would assume in the decades ahead as described in Washington Irving Bishop's 1880 booklet, *Houdin and Heller Second Sight Explained*:

> The clairvoyant is usually a young lady, interesting in manner and dejected in appearance, as if distressed by some constant strain on the nervous system. The clairvoyant also presents an appearance of passive submission, as if in fear of some all-powerful controlling influence, and, even when possessed of robust vigor, she assumes an air of having no will of her own, and exceeding timidity.
> The clairvoyant is blindfolded completely.

Suggesting the helpless innocence of the medium on the stage gains the sympathy and thus more effectively engages the belief of the audience.

With the expectations of the audience secured, Robert-Houdin would walk through the spectators, stopping apparently at random to examine a bracelet, a business card, or some other object, that his son would then describe in, at first, faltering phrases; then apparently gathering more confidence, Émile would describe the object in such detail that the only solution had to be that the boy somehow could actually see the object even seated many feet distant, blindfolded and the object held so that he could not see it even without a blindfold. The conclusion being that the boy was seeing with his father's eyes.

At certain times in their routine, when his son seemed to be struggling to "see," Robert-Houdin would ring a small mystic bell as if to aide his son in concentrating — leading reporters, observers, and interested magicians to speculate that the bell conveyed a code of some kind. But the conjuror would ring the bell only once or twice during the performance, or at times Robert-Houdin would not ring the bell at all which left everyone even more perplexed than before.

Even with the extraordinary range of illusions and automata developed by Robert-Houdin throughout his celebrated career, *La Seconde Vue*, second sight, remained one of the magician's signature presentations — and the innovative Frenchman never revealed his methods of creating the second sight illusion.

The basic scenario of the second sight act is that the two individuals, agent and percipient, appear to communicate mentally with each other without using the normal senses; they do not necessarily claim they can read the minds of anyone else in their audiences. On occasion, the percipient, when placed under a deep mesmeric trance, would claim to apparently exercise precognition, to see the future.

Robert-Houdin and his son, Émile, performing *La Seconde Vue,* second sight. 1846.

The use of some sort of clever verbal code to convey information in a second sight act was quickly surmised from the time of Breslaw and confidently explained in books and newspapers — yet the second sight acts continued to mystify as the performers created increasingly subtle codes and signaling techniques to finally achieve, with Robert-Houdin, the performance of portions of the act in complete silence which negated the very idea of codes.

Some innovative second sight performers in the late nineteenth century began to utilize complex coding systems in which subtle movements were coupled with a phonetic system in which sounds, not words, conveyed a broad range of information under even the most demanding conditions.

Almost all second sight systems sold through magic shops in the latter half of the nineteenth century and early twentieth required the use of common words as look, see, what, and others to convey a number that would key an object on a memorized list that could run 300–400 items with additional sub-lists as, e.g., a watch is cued, then a second cue would give the type, then a third would identify the material gold, silver and so on. The cues would be delivered in a casual manner as the performer would move away to select another object. A well drilled performing couple would work two to three spectators ahead so that the audience could not directly identify the agent's words with any specific object. Depending on the talents of the percipient, comedy could be injected, or "corrections" to an earlier description could be included as an aside in the midst of describing a new object. In the late nineteenth century, the techniques of second sight had advanced far beyond the demonstrations of even Robert-Houdin to include phonetic systems in addition or instead of the simply worded questions.

The original phonetic systems of the 1880–1900 period were based on combinations of forty sounds, e.g., th, ing, ish, oi, ou, where the meanings were conveyed by the syllabic sound and from its relative position in a series of sounds.

As the sounds seem to the audience to be only incidental to the performance, the spectators would come away with the impression that the performance had been performed in complete silence. As adaptable and quick as the more complex codes became, to become proficient, to be able to communicate silently, demanded a regimen of daily multi-hour practice by the two performers working together, to the point where the line between the trick and the genuine would become remarkably thin.

But the success of second sight *as entertainment* was not due to just more clever coding or advanced technology, but to the same techniques of showmanship that Breslaw, Pinetti and Robert-Houdin would immediately recognize. Given the mysterious transfer of information, how can the performers, the agent and the percipient, then sell that information effectively in order to amuse, amaze and convince their audiences — or a group of psychical investigators?

One of the principal techniques of presenting second sight is to be productively wrong, i.e., miss, get close to the object, but not precisely. The agent, for example, signs a pocket watch, but then signs that the medium is to miss; so, following the coding, the medium describes the watch in some detail but then calls it a lady's compact. The percipient has clearly seen the object, but not clearly enough, or there has been a disturbance that upsets the percipient's concentration, or any of a number of explanations so readily accepted by scientific psychical researchers.

After all, only tricksters, con-men and politicians claim to be right all the time. Therefore, if the performers occasionally miss, the audiences come to believe that their powers of mental communication, of second sight, must most likely be genuine.

And the audience, the observers, must perceive a process, an effort being made by the performers to communicate that, conceivably, is based not only on possessing a strange talent, but on hard work and sustained study. The suggestion of risk and, perhaps, pushing the human boundaries effectively adds to the tension felt by the audience.

C: The Date of the Coin Is...?

The agent is given a coin by the investigating committee with the barely whispered request that he mentally transmit the date and type of coin to the blindfolded percipient seated twenty or more feet away at the other end of the room with her back to everyone — and, *without the agent speaking,* moving about, or making any noise whatever. A blackboard stands to one side near the investigators where the date and other data are to be written as the medium calls out her mental pictures.

The chief investigator silently signs "Begin"; and steps back to carefully observe along with his colleagues.

Within one to two minutes, always in complete silence, the agent correctly writes the date, the metal and the monetary value of the target coin on the blackboard as data are called out by the blindfolded percipient. The committee is nonplussed.

However, this second sight demonstration is a fake — so, how was it done?

Note: It is not my intent in this book to expose the workings of a modern professional mentalist's routine; my intent is to illustrate various means by which second sight was successfully simulated in the late nineteenth century and early twentieth, even under apparently strict conditions of silence and close observation by experienced psychical investigators. The description of the silent technique and presentation given below is from *Tricks in Magic, Volume 1, Illusions and Mental Phenomena*, compiled by H.J. Burlingame, Clyde Publishing Co., Chicago, 1895.

Beginning with test #37, *Silent Thought Transmission*, Burlingame writes:

> By means of this code all the usual effects generally exhibited at Thought Reading Seances can be reproduced. The medium is completely blindfolded and if necessary can be surrounded by a committee from the audience, to see that the medium is not connected with the performer in any way and that he does not make any queries of the medium or signal to her. Performer need not change his position at all.

The performing conditions outlined by Burlingame generally meet those required by psychical researchers. The blindfold used can be an honest one, i.e., the medium, the percipient cannot see anything.

> The code consists in both medium and performer counting mentally and together. It is a known fact, that the beats for 'common time' are always the same in music, therefore with little practice it is easy for two persons starting on a given signal to count at the same time and rate, and when another signal is given to stop, of course, they will both have arrived at the same number. This then is the actual method employed in this code and from it you will see that any number from 0 to 9 can be transmitted by the performer to the medium; which of course is all that is required. It is best to experiment and find out what rate of counting best suits the two persons employing this code, but the following suggestions are offered: It may perhaps be best to commence counting at a slow rate; then gradually increase; until you find it advisable to go no quicker, and then adhere to one rate and always keep it. Say you have in the room when first practicing, a loud ticking clock, with a fairly slow beat, on the given beat, or signal you both start counting at the same rate as the clock, of course the clock must be removed when the rate has been well learned; or count at the rate of "common time," viz.: 1 and 2 and 3 and 4 and so on, or practice with a "Metronome," such as is used during piano practice for the purpose for setting time and is of course made adjustable. A very good rate to finally adopt is about 70–75 per minute. Whatever rate is found to suit best must be adhered to, you will find at the rate mentioned any number up to 9 can be transmitted with absolute certainty, after an hour or so of practice.

With the rate practiced and established, the agent and percipient positioned by the committee, the psychical researcher hands the agent a coin. Say it is a gold five-dollar piece, dated 1872. As most coins in use at the time were 18xx, then only 7 and 2 need to be coded. However, through prearranged practice an earlier date can be coded — or even an arbitrary date taken as the

C. The Date of the Coin Is...?

test. Use of a researcher's coin helps to eliminate thoughts of trickery while at the same time limiting the coding necessary.

Burlingame continues:

> The performer takes his position with chalk in hand in front of the blackboard, holding coin in his other hand. He does not speak a word but simply looks at coin, after a pause, the medium calls out: "The first figure I picture is a one," or words to that effect, now immediately the lady stops speaking they both commence to count mentally at the rate agreed by practice. In the case the number to be transmitted is 7; as the last word of her sentence is spoken they commence mentally 1-2-3-4-5-6-7; during this short period the performer glances down at the coin as if to verify what the lady has called out, and as soon as they reach the figure "7" the signal "stop" must be transmitted. This is done by the performer putting down on the blackboard sharply the figure called out by the lady, viz.: "One" (1). It will be seen by this method that the signal is quite easy to transmit and it is perfectly natural to put down the figure on the board quickly and sharply. The third figure of the coin is now known to the medium, the last figure "2" is transmitted in the same manner as the previous figure, the lady says the second figure I see is "8," as soon as she ceases speaking they commence the counting again 1-2, on the arrival at the figure "2" the performer puts down the "8," previously called out, sharply on the board, which is the signal for "stop," the lady now knows the full date of the coin. The metal of the coin, gold, silver or copper, must be indicated to the medium previously by the wording of the reply to the owner of the coin after it has been handed to the performer, which can be easily arranged to fancy, the value of the coin or its equivalent number in the same way as the previous figure and between the "7" and "2" that is, after the lady has called out the "7" they commence to count for the value, when an '0' occurs in the date, no pause is made, the performer putting down the figure on the board for the 'stop' signal immediately the lady stops speaking, this if followed carefully will be found quite easy and natural in practice.

Burlingame continues on for another twenty or so more pages giving the basis for several other silent second sight effects.

He continues to describe other second sight effects that utilize other methods, for example, #39, *Second Sight Through Brick Walls*. Each effect that Burlingame describes in his pamphlet incorporates various methods sometimes incorporating silent counting as necessary.

In effect #39, the percipient is sequestered in a room with only a table and chair and with curtains drawn over the windows. Otherwise the room is completely empty. The door is closed with a member of the investigating committee standing guard at the door.

Out the sight or hearing of the medium, the information selected by the committee, e.g., random numbers, playing cards, the time set on a watch, a simple diagram, is chosen and recorded by the committee. The agent listens carefully, all the while writing the information on a pad of cigarette papers in his pocket using abbreviations agreed to by the agent and the percipient. The paper is then squeezed into a small ball and, at a key point of misdirection, the agent drops the ball into the cap of the fountain pen he has been using, refastens the cap to the pen. The agent then gives the pen to a member of the committee to give to the percipient with which to write out her mental pictures.

Asking for privacy for her concentration, behind the closed door of the room in which she has been waiting (her request for isolation is always granted) the medium then reads the information and abbreviations from her partner, and uses the fountain pen to write out the "pictures" she received from the agent. Her results are then passed to the committee member at the door to convey to the committee.

Burlingame's description in #39 reads much like the technique Douglas Blackburn claimed in his 1908 and 1911 articles that he and George A. Smith used to fake their convincing demonstration with Fig. 22 in the SPR telepathy investigations at Dean's Yard in 1883.

At all times, the agent and percipient act in a natural manner acquiescing to whatever conditions the psychical committee requires, as few of the "stringent" conditions actually interfere in their coding. If they do, then the telepathists simply admit the conditions are not right, the lady is tired, etc., and after a few minutes with the conditions relaxed, they try again. After all, *productively failing* only adds to the apparent legitimacy of the whole performance. As most psychical investigators, including scientists like William Crookes, readily agreed, the powers or spirits may not be there all the time. Crookes in writing to William Huggins regarding a spectacular D.D. Home séance, and inviting the astronomer to the next séance, added the warning that sometimes the Home séance will be a blank, and so they try again.

Combining the silent techniques with a complete verbal code that can also signal arbitrary random designs is a major undertaking (the verbal coding charts for some acts cover over forty pages). The end result, however, coupled with solid showmanship and relentless daily practice, can be astonishing — and financially rewarding.

D: Coding of a Random Drawing

Telepathically transmitting a random drawing is usually considered the strongest tests of the abilities of the agent and percipient, and the most fraud-proof. Professor Simon Newcomb considered it the only valid experiment for testing for telepathy. Standard designs such as triangles, tic-tac-toe, hexagon,

D. Coding of a Random Drawing 181

umbrella open, umbrella closed, etc., can be memorized in a list of 102 items, as in *The Radio Vision Mind-Reading Code* first published in 1930, and then later in an orange cover in 1940. Most standard designs, i.e., a house, a triangle inside a circle, etc., with modest variations can then be coded easily using the same code as for other aspects of the two-person act. Such coding of standard designs has been used since at least the time of Robert-Houdin.

In Douglas Blackburn's *John Bull* series of articles, "Confessions of a Famous Medium, Part II, The Inadequacy of Scientific Precautions," December 12, 1908, p. 628, he describes how he and G.A. Smith each memorized a chessboard of 100 squares so that when Blackburn was given the random drawing by Gurney or Myers, he would code the numbers of the squares that the drawing crossed which would allow Smith to draw, using his own memorized image as guide, a close approximation of the designated design, smoothing out the corners in one or two tries. Blackburn observed, "Of course, it was never exact, but sufficiently so to satisfy Gurney and Myers that Smith had been able to visualize what I had in my mind."

In contrast to Blackburn's description, in the *Radio Vision Code*, a memorized sheet of paper is divided into six squares labeled A-I. Each square was then subdivided into six smaller squares, labeled A-I, giving 96 points on the diagram.

In cuing, the first cue given is the large square where the design starts while the next cues are the sequence of small squares within the large. When the agent uses the word "and," the next cue is the next large square and so on.

Given the ready availability of codes for second sight acts in the latter half of the nineteenth century, various codes for random drawings could be found and used, or modified for whatever the specific circumstances might be.

Alice Johnson, in her 1909 "private and confidential" SPR leaflet (see Appendix H), says that Smith described how he, Blackburn, Gurney and Myers would discuss various, even (in Johnson's view) ingenious methods of fraudulently producing the very effects that were the point of the experiments, a circumstance that Johnson found remarkable. However, there have been a number of instances in conjuring history where a performer describes a method to his audience leaving the strong implication that naturally *he* would never stoop to such cheap chicanery.

Alexander, unquestionably the greatest of the stage crystal gazers of his time, roughly 1910–1925, would open his Simla Séance, the crystal-gazing second half of his show, by describing in some detail how his competitors worked their "miracles." He would dismiss such trickery as being beneath contempt — and then proceed to use each of the very methods he had just exposed! His showmanship made the methods essentially irrelevant.

182   E. Techniques of Thought Reading

When a competing escape artist exposed Houdini's coffin escape by showing how the board at the foot of the coffin could be rotated up because of fake screws used, thus allowing Houdini to escape by sliding out the foot of the coffin — which was, in fact, Houdini's method — Houdini responded to the exposure in his show by inviting a committee from the audience to drive several nails into the board at the foot of the coffin to demonstrate that the competitor's description was utterly false. Houdini would then make his escape through a rotating board with fake screws at the *head* of the coffin. What if a couple of spectators wanted to also nail the board at the head of the coffin? Houdini controlled his stage and would simply never allow it.

Again, what the scientists and other investigators never seemed to fully comprehend was the audacity and relentless resourcefulness of the mediums.

E: Techniques of Thought Reading (Contact Mindreading)

> Mind Reading, like any other Art, can only be acquired by faithful and patient practice.
> — C.A. George Newmann, *Elliott's Last Legacy*, 1923

Contact mind reading effectively provides the operator with only two types of information: direction and location. Experience gained in performing and practicing will provide, as Newmann points out above, additional insights that will border on the uncanny — including gradually gaining a non-contact capability that though certainly impressive, still provides no more information than with direct physical contact. Non-contact sensitivity can be developed through using a stiff wire or object as a ruler initially, then transitioning to a handkerchief or a loop of thin wire, then finally to no object intervening between the operator and the subject (the transmitter).

C.A. George Newmann was an acknowledged master of non-contact mind reading in which no tricks or confederates were used. He, in turn, acknowledged only Lucy DeGentry as an accomplished non-contact performer. A more famous woman mind reader, the Englishwoman Maud Lancaster, claimed to be non-contact, but her methods were exposed in 1893 by the celebrated globe-circling investigative reporter of the *New York World*, Nellie Bly. Bly proved that Lancaster relied on secret signals from her sister and her managers, and that the thought reader could not perform unless at least one of her supporters was present. Using Lancaster's own tricks, Bly herself publicly duplicated the most famous of Lancaster's stunts, the murder scenario. Maud Lancaster, however, continued to perform in the U.S. and England successfully for some ten years following the Bly exposure.

John Randall Brown developed all of the effects in the repertoire of a thought reader and muscle reader during the first two years of his career, 1873–4. In all cases, the performer is blindfolded and completely isolated under the watch of a committee, while a member of the committee sets up the stunt. The effects were:

1. Discovery of what the test is without any written or verbal direction from the committee.
2. Finding a small object, usually a pin, that had been hidden somewhere in the theatre, building, or city.
3. Letter delivery, i.e., delivery of an unaddressed letter to a person anywhere within reason.
4. Playing a thought-of melody on a piano.
5. Reuniting a separated couple. A man and woman are selected sitting somewhere in the theatre. The performer determines who they are and brings them together.
6. The Murder Mystery — the favorite of performers and audiences, which can be played for a maximum dramatic effect; particularly if the "victim" selected by the committee or audience is a prominent leader, monarch, or president. The test could then be termed a "mental assassination" with appropriate theatrics. (W. I. Bishop had a poster made specifically with this stunt showing him apparently attacking the Tsar of Russia with a dagger.)
7. The Book Test — the performer goes into a large library and finds the thought-of book, page and word selected by the committee.
8. The Bank Bill Test — the performer writes the thought-of serial number of a banknote on a blackboard. The note had been sealed in an envelope before the show began and the serial number was known to only one person.
9. The Blackboard Test — the performer duplicates an arbitrary design on a blackboard, even to writing in a language as Arabic, Chinese or Russian of which the performer knew nothing. This is one of the most difficult tests for a contact mind reader. Only W. I. Bishop and Stuart Cumberland were consistently successful in duplicating arbitrary designs.
10. The Double Test — inserting a neutral individual between the performer and the transmitter.

To Brown's inventory of wonders, Washington Irving Bishop added the blindfold drive (which is still done today in modified form) in about 1887. This was a potentially dangerous stunt in which Bishop, blindfolded, had one member of the investigating committee seated beside him, with the other members seated in the rear of the carriage. The mind reader standing, holding the reins in one hand, his other hand stretched out toward the adjacent committeeman, drove the team of horses at a gallop through the streets of the city to find a hidden object, with his only sensory input coming from his detecting the nervous tremors of the man seated next to him. The resulting publicity was always extensive.

That inventory of thought reader wonders remained virtually unchanged until 1947 in Detroit. Hypnotist and thought reader Franz J. Polgar, in his 1951 book, *The Story of a Hypnotist,* described why he needed something else beyond the effects listed above:

> When the chairman of the Detroit Town Hall received a telegram claiming that I was possessed by the devil and evil would come out of my performances, I knew I had to give a rather dramatic proof of my theories and demonstrations. I remember the horrified expression of my manager, Ford Hicks, when I told an audience of five thousand: "Hide my check for giving this performance. I'll go outside and you can send as many persons as you wish to watch me. If I can't find the check when I come back, you keep it, tonight will be on me."
>
> My lecture manager and five committee members took me out into the foyer. My manager said, "What about my commission? You can gamble away your money, but not mine."
>
> Even he had not enough faith in me. He thought I was using tricks. In those days a five-hundred-dollar fee was something I could not afford to lose. I think I was the only one who still had confidence in what I could do.

The Detroiters hid Polgar's check under the hat of an elderly lady in the center of the vast throng in the hall.

> When I returned to the hall I asked a volunteer who was known to the audience to give me mental directions without uttering a word. I produced the check from under the lady's hat. It took me four minutes of mental directions, given me by the volunteer's concentrated thought waves, to find this woman in a crowd of five thousand.

Finding-the-check produced so much publicity that it became the regular closing stunt not only for Polgar, but for many other mentalists after that. The hiding places included brassieres, shoe soles, the loaded revolver of a police chief, a room somewhere in the Empire State Building, and the space above the upper plate of a man's dentures. And, almost always, the mentalist found his or her check.

A working list of the principal books detailing the techniques of thought reading or muscle reading, or, as it is called now, contact mind reading is given in the Bibliography. It includes many of the basic works on the subject published over the past several decades.

F: A Thought Reader's Novel*

Oscar Wilde, *Pall Mall Gazette,* June 5, 1889

There is a great deal to be said in favor of reading a novel backwards. The last page is as a rule the most interesting, and when one begins with the catastrophe or the dénouement one feels on pleasant terms of equality with the author. It is alike going behind the scenes of a theatre. One is no longer taken in, and the hair-breadth escapes of the hero and the wild agonies of the heroine leave one absolutely unmoved. One knows the jealously guarded secret, and one can afford to smile at the quite unnecessary anxiety that the puppets of fiction always consider it their duty to display. In the case of Mr. Stuart Cumberland's novel *The Vasty Deep,* as he calls it, the last page is certainly thrilling, and makes us curious to know more about "Brown, the medium."

> Scene, a padded room in a madhouse in the United States.
> A gibbering lunatic discovered dashing wildly about the chamber, as if in the act of chasing invisible forms.
> "This is our worst case," says the doctor opening the cell to one of the visitors in lunacy. "He was a spirit medium, and he is hourly haunted by the creatures of his fancy. We have to carefully watch him, for he has developed suicidal tendencies."
> The lunatic makes a dash at the retreating form of his visitors, and, as the door closes upon him sinks with a yell upon the floor.
> A week later the lifeless body of Brown the medium is found suspended from the gas-bracket in his cell.

How clearly one sees it all! How forcible and direct the style is! And what a thrilling touch of actuality the simple mention of the "gas-bracket" gives us! Certainly *The Vasty Deep* is a book to be read.

And we have read it; read it with great care. Though it is largely autobiographical, it is none the less a work of fiction, and though some of us may think that there is very little use in exposing what is already exposed, and revealing the secrets of Polichinelle, no doubt there are many who will be interested to hear of the tricks and deceptions of crafty mediums, of their gauze masks, telescopic rods, and invisible silk threads, and of the marvelous raps they can produce by simply "displacing the *peroneus longus* muscle." The book opens with a description of the scene by the death-bed of Alderman Parkinson. Dr. Josiah Brown, the eminent medium, is in attendance, and tries to comfort the honest merchant by producing noises on the bed-post. Mr. Parkinson, however, being extremely anxious to revisit Mrs. Parkinson in a materialized form after death, will not be satisfied till he has received from his wife a solemn promise that she will not marry again, such a marriage being, in his eyes, nothing more nor less then bigamy. Having received an assurance to this effect from her, Mr. Parkin-

---

*The Vasty Deep: a Strange Story of To-Day. By Stuart C. Cumberland, two volumes, (Sampson Low and Co.)

son dies, his soul, according to the medium, being escorted to the spheres by "a band of white-robed spirits." This is the prologue. The next chapter is entitled "Five Years After." Violet Parkinson, the Alderman's only child, is in love with Jack Alston, who is "poor, but clever." Mrs. Parkinson, however, will not hear of any marriage, till the deceased Alderman has materialized himself and given his formal consent. A séance is held, at which Jack Alston unmasks the medium, and shows Dr. Josiah Brown to be an impostor, a foolish act on his part, as he is now ordered to leave the house by the infuriated Mrs. Parkinson, whose faith in the Doctor is not in the slightest degree shaken by the unfortunate exposure. The lovers are consequently parted.

Jack sails for Newfoundland, is shipwrecked, and carefully, somewhat too carefully, tended by "La-ki-wa, or the Star that shines," a lovely Indian maiden who belongs to the tribe of the Micmacs. She is a fascinating creature who wears "a necklace composed of thirteen nuggets of pure gold," a blanket of English manufacture, and trousers of tanned leather. In fact, as Mr. Stuart Cumberland remarks, she looks "the embodiment of fresh dewy morn." When Jack, on recovering his senses, sees her, he naturally inquires who she is. She answers, in the simple utterance endeared to us by memories of Fenimore Cooper, "I am La-ki-wa. I am the only child of my father, Tall Pine, chief of the Dildoos." She talks, Mr. Cumberland informs us, "very good English." Jack at once entrusts her with the following telegram, which he writes on the back of a five-pound note:

Miss Violet Parkinson,
Hotel Kronprinz, Franzenbad, Austria.
Safe, Jack.

But La-ki-wa, we regret to say, says to herself, "He belongs to Tall Pine, to the Dildoos, and to me," and never sends the telegram. Subsequently La-ki-wa proposes to Jack, who promptly rejects her, and with the usual callousness of men offers her a brother's love. La-ki-wa naturally regrets the premature disclosure of her passion, and weeps. "My brother," she remarks, "will think I have the timid heart of a deer with the crying voice of a papoose. I, the daughter of Tall Pine — I, a Micmac, to show grief that is in my heart. Oh, my brother, I am ashamed." Jack comforts her with the hollow sophistries of a civilized being, and gives her his photograph. As he is on his way to the steamer he receives from Big Deer a soiled piece of a biscuit bag. On it is written La-ki-wa's confession of her disgraceful behavior about the telegram. "His thoughts," Mr. Cumberland tells us, "were bitter towards La-ki-wa, but they gradually softened when remembered what he owed her."

Everything ends happily. Jack arrives in England just in time to prevent Dr. Josiah Brown from mesmerizing Violet, whom the cunning Doctor is anxious to marry, and he hurls his rival out of the window. The medium is discovered "bruised and bleeding amongst the broken flower-pots" by a comic policeman. Mrs. Parkinson still believes in Spiritualism, but refuses to have anything to do with Brown, as she discovers that the deceased

Alderman's "materialized beard" was only made of "horrid, coarse horsehair." Jack and Violet are married at last, and Jack is heartless enough to send "La-ki-wa" another photograph. The end of Dr. Brown is chronicled above. Had we not known what was in store for him, we could hardly have got through the book. There is a great deal too much padding in it about Dr. Slade, and Dr. Bastian, and other mediums, and the disquisitions on the commercial future of Newfoundland seem endless and are intolerable. However, there are many publics, and Mr. Stuart Cumberland is always sure of an audience. His chief fault is a tendency to low comedy, but some people like low comedy in fiction.

(Wilde did not mention, or notice, as did the reviewer for the *Manchester Guardian*, that the familiar Shakespeare line given on the title page was incorrectly quoted. The *Guardian* also thought the best writing in the book was Cumberland's description of the fog off the coast of Newfoundland.)

G: The Crookes-Fay Galvanometer Test, February 19, 1875

Condensed from Barry H. Wiley, *The Indescribable Phenomenon* (Seattle: Hermetic Press, 2005), Chapter 8.

In 1966, under a grant from the Perrott-Warrick Fund, Christopher J. Stephenson*, a member of the SPR, performed an extensive investigation of the Cromwell Varley-Florence Cook galvanometer séance to determine, if possible after 92 years and from limited data, whether the séance could have been genuine under the conditions established by Varley, and subsequently repeated by Crookes with Cook. A number of investigators, magicians and critics over the years have speculated on how Cook might have beaten the galvanometer, one such controversial speculation included the medium getting detailed secret instruction and training from Crookes. Much was made in criticisms of the then mystery of electricity and that Cook couldn't have beaten the galvanometer circuit unaided — always assuming the whole séance was a fraud.

Stephenson, with a more open mind than many of his predecessors, meticulously reviewed each of the conditions of the séance with the objective to discover what could have caused each of the reported variations in the galvanometer position. His analysis demonstrated how sensitive the galvanometer results were to the tightness of the elastic bands that bound the soldered gold

---

*C.J. Stephenson, "Further Comments on Cromwell Varley's Electrical Test on Florence Cook," *PSPR*, Vol. 54, part 198, (April 1966), pp. 363–417.

coins to the medium's wrists, and even to the point on the gold coin at which the platinum wire had been soldered, i.e., on the edge or on the flat. There is no way of knowing what the detailed conditions actually were, but Stephenson experimented with several variations to separate out and clarify the results. He also organized a complete restaging of the séance with actors speaking the same lines as recorded, and an actress to reenact Florence's probable actions behind the curtain, assuming fraud, to determine if all that was recorded could have been done in the time periods indicated. His conclusions were remarkable.

In the original description given of the phenomena,* it is suggestive that the medium was trying to discover the limits imposed by the galvanometer connection, as Katie King appears at first as a shrouded partial face between the curtains of the cabinet, then after a moment as a full face, then after another few moments an arm appears, and finally the full form — still no reaction from the galvanometer. The shrouded Katie steps out away from the cabinet, the galvanometer connections visible on her wrists — still no reaction from the galvanometer. The spirit form then successfully performs the various tests requested by Varley and returns to the cabinet. The same thing happens when Crookes repeats the experiment with Varley's setup.

First, Stephenson determined that all of the reported phenomena could have been produced fraudulently by Florence *without* her ever leaving the galvanometer circuit, i.e., she needed no instruction on how to beat the circuit, since the circuit was not beaten. Stephenson concluded that Cook, after Varley had explained the experiment to her, relied on her own ingenuity and audacity, and her reading of the sitters and investigators. She continuously pushed the edges of the experiment, anticipating a negative or some reaction from the "galvanometer people" such that she would immediately fall back into the arm chair in a suitable trance before anyone could look behind the curtain. In that mode, she was completely successful.

Second, a subtle and recurring issue that directly reflected Frederick Wickes' observation on scientific men doing unscientific investigations. Varley's, and later Crookes', unscientific assertions regarding the effectiveness of the electrical control misled everyone including Varley regarding the limits of detection of the experiment. Varley had never performed the galvanometer experiment with a human being in the circuit to confirm what the galvanometer response would be to various conditions, including attempted cheating. Instead, he simply assumed his personal understanding was sufficient, and, of course, no one was in a position to refute or challenge him. As one instance

---

*C. D. Broad, "Cromwell Varley's Electrical Tests with Florence Cook," *PSPR*, Vol. 54, part 195 (March 1964), pp. 158–172.

G. The Crookes-Fay Galvanometer Test, 1875

of the unscientific mind-set, he (and later Crookes) stated that the spirit putting its hands into the bucket of brine would throw the galvanometer off-scale if it was actually Cook. *Not so.* So long as the gold contacts themselves did not touch the brine, there would be no change in the galvanometer reading if Florence put her hands into the brine-filled bucket, because body resistance is due largely to the layer of skin just beneath the skin's surface which didn't contact the brine. Stephenson did the experiment that Varley should have done, but didn't.

Further, Varley asserted that the spirit writing on the tablet would cause the galvanometer to oscillate because the vigorous movement of the arms would cause the contacts to shift around on her wrists, if it was Cook and not a phantom. Varley had even asked Katie to wave her arms around without the galvanometer showing any change. But his assertion was just not so. Reproducing the circumstances and with an actress very vigorously moving her arms, Stephenson showed there was no change in the galvanometer's reading. Again Varley's personal assertions amid a lack of rigorous scientific preparation gave the resulting experiment greater authority than it deserved.

Stephenson's final conclusion was that due to Varley's mind-set and his experimental conditions, *nothing* was proven regarding either the reality of Katie King, or the fraud of Florence Cook. Crookes, accepting Varley's prominent authority on electrical circuits, did not challenge his setup, and so repeated the same errors as Varley had in the second Cook séance, drawing the same unjustified conclusions. Edward W. Cox had mockingly suggested the experimenters forget the electricity, just pull the curtain back and look. Either the medium is there or she is not. Case proven. But electricity, as William Crookes confidently stated in public print and even in italics in describing his later séances with Annie Eva Fay, would provide *absolute certainty* regarding the medium's position.

Thus Stephenson proved that one assertion, that Cook trained Fay on how to beat the circuit, fails in that Cook never had to beat the circuit to produce the Katie King manifestation, and therefore there was no information to pass on, if in fact the two competing mediums would have cooperated, which is doubtful. In any case, the Crookes circuit used with Fay was materially different from that used by Varley with Cook. In the Fay situation, the medium had to be completely free of the galvanometer circuit in order to produce the manifestations described.

In considering the circumstances of that chilly evening, February 19, 1875, it is apparent that Annie beat the galvanometer test through the use of the "instant stooge" technique frequently used by magicians and mentalists, in which as a spectator is invited onto the stage to participate in a presentation, the individual is very quietly asked by the performer to "cooperate" in the trick. If done properly and with a friendly air of "let's fool them together," the request is very rarely refused, as the author is personally aware. What if the stooge talks later? If the presentation has been handled well, no one would be motivated to ask, or in Annie's case, the circumstances would prevent it.

The instant stooge would not be Crookes, but his assistant, Charles Henry Gimingham. Working for Crookes since early 1871, Gimingham had free and open access to Crookes' laboratory and frequently worked there unsupervised with Crookes' full trust. Gimingham had also been present at some of the D.D. Home séances, and may have been at other séances but not named.

Of the possibly hundreds of notes and letters sent by Crookes to Gimingham, 51 survive* in the archives of the National Museum of Science & Industry in London. None of Gimingham's letters have survived, since much of Crookes' papers relating to his psychical researches were destroyed by the family upon the scientist's death, and possibly other papers as well. Or perhaps, more simply, Crookes didn't believe retaining his assistant's letters worth the trouble. Addressed always to "My dear Charlie," they demonstrate Crookes' trust and respect for Gimingham's technical opinions and mastery of glassblowing since it was Gimingham who built all of Crookes' ingenious experimental apparatus. Examples of that remarkable mastery are on display in the Science & Industry Museum. As the notes further reveal, Charlie had the keys to the laboratory and most likely to Crookes' desk as well, as Crookes, when traveling, would ask Gimingham to send him materials and notes which Crookes had filed away. But even for all that, there is still in many of the letters condescension on the part of Crookes in his minutely detailed instructions and requests. The requests sometimes were non-scientific, and frequently more the direct peremptory orders that a master gives a servant.

Gimingham was from a lower class, a craftsman who was in a status of permanent subservience to Crookes, with little chance in Victorian society to be anything other than what he was. The approach of a beguiling young American woman so interested in what he was doing would certainly get his full attention, and ultimate cooperation. That Annie would be a guest for dinner or other times at the Crookes house was very much a part of the

---

*One of the 51 surviving Crookes memos, written on August 29, 1874, must be one of the strangest documents written by a rational mind. It clearly confirms Crookes' conviction that Cook was, on occasion, controlled by a non-human presence. After first commenting in the note to Charlie on how remarkably clean he had found the laboratory, Crookes describes performing an exorcism to free Florrie of the presence of a fiend that had been continually annoying her. Crookes goes to assert, "I hope I have now succeeded in consigning it to the bottomless pit whence it came. I don't think it will trouble Florrie again." And he then closes the note by warning Charlie not to smoke too many cigarettes!

Crookes method for putting mediums at their ease, with the assurance that no tricks would be pulled on them. Henry Fay was never included in any of the proceedings.

It wouldn't be much at first, wide-eyed questions to Charlie about galvanometers and how they work. Would the electricity hurt? And so on. In her five years as a professional medium, Annie had learned how to spin a web around almost anyone.

But why would Gimingham be motivated to coach Annie? One, it didn't impact his work so there was no betrayal of his principal duties to his employer; second, Annie was as much outside Victorian society as he was, so there was a common bond of "us against them." Annie only visited society, she was never an accepted participant; third, Gimingham was very much aware of the seriousness of Crookes' commitment to these investigations, and the assistant may well have been put off by the obvious fraud of Florence Cook and others that had impacted Crookes' disposition to such a degree. Annie, in contrast, was only going to play some tricks; fourth, Gimingham was still young and probably enjoyed having fun with his rather stiff boss, especially with a beautiful girl as an accomplice; fifth, Gimingham was not married at the time and the blonde supple "Miss" Fay may have, as in her other casing activities, led him to believe there was more to hope for after the séances; and, sixth, it would give Gimingham a chance to flaunt his own technical knowledge, almost, he would certainly claim as Annie urged him on, as good as his employer's. After all, if it weren't for his skill as a glassblower and his experimental suggestions, where would Crookes be?

If it wasn't Gimingham, then it could only have been Crookes who provided all the detailed information Annie would need. Crookes wouldn't have risked Rayleigh's wraith with a thin imposture in the brief second galvanometer séance, or the possible rejection of the other scientists later. It was Charlie — all the way.

It is very doubtful that Annie would walk into the first galvanometer test on Friday evening, the fifth of February, completely cold and take her chances as Florence Cook was compelled to do with Varley — a séance about which Annie had certainly read in the Spiritualist press. While not concerned with being exposed, after all, if things got awkward all she, like Cook, had to do was fall back in her chair in a faint and let any spiritualists present fill in the blanks for her.

Her chief concern was to ensure that the investigators, Crookes particularly, were not bored. She certainly anticipated that there would be more than one séance with the galvanometer, but how many probably Crookes himself didn't know at the beginning. Consequently, each event had to generate some successes — for both participants.

G. The Crookes-Fay Galvanometer Test, 1875

Only Crookes and others unnamed were present at the first galvanometer test which began at 9:15 P.M. on the fifth of February. Initially, there were large oscillations in the galvanometer, and then the instrument finally stabilized at 9:20. Knockings did not begin until 9:28, becoming at 9:30 steadily more violent thumps, though there was no movement whatever of the galvanometer, which Crookes took to mean that Annie's hands were immobile. At 9:31 the medium was heard to sigh and sob, just as Florence Cook had been recorded as doing in the Varley galvanometer séance. Movements were heard in the library and several articles were thrown into the laboratory through the opening in the curtain. A hand gave Crookes a violin, while there continued to be almost no movement in the galvanometer light. The hand was visible to all others present. At 9:37 a music box was heard being wound up. Still only slight movement in the readings. Then at 9:39, the light swung completely off scale as contact was broken by the medium dropping the handles, with Annie heard to say, "So tired of holding these things." Crookes and the others rushed to the medium finding her entranced, but she recovered in a short time.

Annie had apparently experienced some clumsiness at first in tying the coil of wire* that Charlie had made for her between the handles. If the tying was not done very quickly and tightly within the instrument's response time, the galvanometer would register an abrupt drop in the body resistance of the medium by half, a very large swing on the instrument's scale. As it was, the light swung across almost 70° in the first minute or so before settling at a 237° deflection. With the exception of a sudden later oscillation of 30°, the deflection remained within a 2–3° range for virtually the entire séance.

For Annie's coil of wire to match her body resistance, Gimingham had to have had Annie in the circuit only once to measure her body resistance. He then wound a coil of wire, put it into the circuit to ensure a close match, and adjusted accordingly. Annie did not have to be present during the coil winding or adjustments. A loosening or slipping of the wire which she had wound around the wet brass handles could explain the sudden 30° oscillation, with Annie quickly tightening one end of the wire. If she had tried to tie or tighten both ends of the coil resistance at the same time, she would have put

---

*Copper-nickel alloy high resistance wire was not easily available in England in 1875, but it was on the Continent. A coil wound from that wire would have been relatively small. A coil of fine-gage copper wire as used in the galvanometer construction could have been wound to match Annie's body plus handle resistance, but it would have been relatively large and heavy, but not beyond hiding under Annie's skirts. Given Crookes' frequent Continental trips, it is not unreasonable to assume that the high resistance wire may have been available in the laboratory — but it didn't really matter. Either way, Annie could manage.

G. The Crookes-Fay Galvanometer Test, 1875

her own body resistance back into the circuit, and the oscillation would have plunged instantly even further, at least another 40–50°, a sure giveaway that something odd had happened. It was probably only luck that kept Annie from touching both handles at once.

Satisfied, Crookes hurriedly scheduled another séance for the following evening, the sixth, to accommodate Lord Rayleigh who could not be present on the fifth. Some additional precautions were taken. The library was searched, and the doors and windows sealed shut using the signet ring of an unnamed woman who was present. The séance started at 9:15 P.M. and concluded at 9:30. The rappings and throwing objects into the laboratory was repeated. One new phenomenon that Crookes discovered was his desk unlocked after having locked it with a Bramah lock, just before the séance commenced. There were no large galvanometer oscillations noted during the second séance. There is no evidence that Rayleigh was dissatisfied with the results of the séance, indeed as late as 1891, Rayleigh still considered the séance genuine. There is evidence, however, that he wasn't impressed — he never chose to witness another séance, and may have expressed himself accordingly. Certainly, there was little in the phenomena manifested in the two séances for Crookes to write about.

Annie held two private séances before the scheduled third galvanometer séance on the nineteenth. One, on the evening of the fourteenth, Sunday, which consisted of both her light and dark séance routines was successfully carried off, with a subsequent long write-up in *The Spiritualist*. When Annie was asked by a sitter what she saw behind the curtain when the manifestations were going on, she replied, "Nothing," as her eyes were always closed. Once she opened them, all phenomena stopped. Everyone present immediately embraced that extraordinary logic.

One of the sitters at the second séance held Monday morning, the fifteenth, was Florence Cook with her husband. They had just returned from France over the weekend. Also present was Florence's long-time financial support, Charles Blackburn, who had also brought along two friends from Scotland. Annie could manage only the light séance, as they could not darken the rooms enough for the dark séance. Annie had just moved into 27 Princesstreet, Hanover Square, and the curtains did not cover the windows adequately to keep out the morning sun. This is the only recorded meeting of the two mediums. A brief mention of the séance appeared in *The Spiritualist*. Cook clearly wanted the chance to look over her competition. While the Fay light séance phenomena must have appeared trivial to Cook compared to her Katie King materializations, Annie's personal presence must have piqued some jealousy in the younger medium as Cook actively resumed full-form materializations in the spring once Annie had left England to return to America.

G. The Crookes-Fay Galvanometer Test, 1875

Though Crookes thought Annie knew of only two of the party of men who would be investigating her on the nineteenth, Gimingham clearly had told her who was coming. It was undoubtedly Annie who wanted personal information on each of the men, intelligence that once she knew the identities of the men coming, she could have gained, at least partially, by simply reading the daily London papers. It was something she could do to help her "invisibles" demonstrate specific personal knowledge. Annie had learned from her earliest experiences among the farms and villages of northeastern Ohio that the more personal the revelations of the spirits the more awed the recipient. The quick séances on the 5th and 6th had not allowed for that level of preparation.

In his public report, March 12, 1875, in *The Spiritualist* describing the third galvanometer séance, Crookes made a typical untested assumption regarding William Huggins' book *Spectrum Analysis*, "I have no reason for supposing that Mrs. Fay knew anything about such a book being in existence, or in my library, or that it was written by the particular person present," thus adding further authority to Annie's performance, but without any actual basis.

Charlie had certainly located the books for her, arranging them at her direction, to facilitate her finding them in the dark. (A smoker himself, he also clearly knew where the cigarettes were stashed, a pack of which would be thrown to Ionides.) But it was Crookes who, unknowingly, had added convincing weight to Annie's mysterious knowledge. Francis Galton's travel book was a best seller at the time of the séance, so even without Charlie, Annie would have known about it, once she knew Galton was coming. And so on.

In fact, Francis Galton was one of the more interesting persons at the séance. A polymath of extraordinary accomplishments, Galton had participated with Crookes and Cox in investigating Kate Fox (Jencken) in 1872. Writing to his cousin, Charles Darwin, on March 28, 1872, he said, "I can only say, as yet, that I am utterly confounded with the results, and am very disinclined to discredit them. Crookes is working deliberately and well." He goes on to say, "The whole rubbish of spiritualism seems to me to stand and fall together." He concludes the letter with a description of Fox's automatic writing in the dark on a piece of blank paper that had been specially marked to ensure it could not be switched for another. When the lights came up, there was a long message from Benjamin Franklin, filled with simple clichés and platitudes. Galton wrote, "The absurdity on the one hand and the extraordinary character of the thing on the other, quite staggers me; wondering what I shall yet see and learn I remain at present quite passive with my eyes and ears open."

Darwin responded the next day,* writing, "I hope that Mr. Crookes will

---

*The Darwin letter is 8258 in the Darwin Correspondence Project, University of Cambridge, and is quoted with permission.

G. The Crookes-Fay Galvanometer Test, 1875

stick to this & work it out, & that you will continue to be a witness with, as you say, eyes & ears very open. It is rather dreadful to think what we may have to believe."

Galton wrote Darwin again April 19, 1872, describing a D.D. Home séance. Galton writes, "It is curious to observe the complete absence of excitement or tension about people at a séance. Familiarity has bred contempt of the strange things witnessed."* With Darwin's permission, Galton wrote Home proposing a séance in which the only sitters would be Darwin and himself. Home promptly left for Russia and never responded.

In a further letter to Darwin, May 26, 1872, Galton complimented the manner in which Crookes was conducting his research, concluding by observing, "He is a most industrious taker of notes."

Galton's involvement in séances faded as opportunities for sittings became fewer and as his feelings of imposture grew. With his many other involvements, he finally dropped all regular participation in séances. In January, 1874, Erasmus Darwin, Charles' brother, hired an unnamed medium (thought to be Charles Williams, whom Crookes had endorsed as genuine) to hold a séance in his home with the family, including Galton and Charles, present. Darwin found it "great fun," but left early as the room became uncomfortably hot. The usual manifestations took place, with Galton commenting it had been a good séance, though not a particularly convincing one. After learning of the phenomena displayed, Darwin responded, "The Lord have mercy on us all, if we have to believe in such rubbish." A short time later, a smaller follow-up séance was held with the same medium with T.H. Huxley† present. After which, Huxley wrote a long report detailing all the fraud, concluding that the medium was "a cheat and an impostor." Galton had already reached the same conclusion.

Consequently, Galton came to the Fay séance on February 19, 1875, out of a personal respect for Crookes and his earlier work, but determined not to

---

*A statement echoed by Henry Colles in an article in *The Medium & Daybreak*, March 12, 1875, about a séance given by Annie in Brighton on March 5. Colles closed his strong supportive report by saying, "I cannot help making the reflection that, with all these marvelous manifestations, so many mediums seem to be totally unimpressed by the gravity of their mission."

†Thomas Henry Huxley (1825–1895), renowned British naturalist who became even more famous as 'Darwin's Bulldog,' in aggressively meeting all challenges to Darwin's controversial evolutionary theories described in *Origin of Species* (1859). Huxley coined the word "agnostic" to define his own positions. Asked in 1871 to join an investigation of Spiritualism, whilst saying that he had neither time nor interest, Huxley declined, famously responding, "The only good that I can see in a demonstration of the truth of 'Spiritualism' is to furnish an additional argument against suicide. Better live as a crossing-sweeper than die and be made to twaddle by a medium hired at a guinea a séance." A statement immediately dismissed by Spiritualist supporters as insolent and bigoted.

be put upon. Though already convinced of the futility of investigating such goings on, Galton joined the spirit of the experiment, and with Huggins, surprised their host by tightening the test conditions by unrepentantly nailing down the brass handles.

The séance ran but ten minutes, but the range of happenings during the séance and then discovered afterwards convinced Crookes, *without dissent from the others present*, that an intelligent non-human agency had been at work — or that Annie could exert and control some form of force outside of herself. Anyone could have pulled the curtain back at any time during the séance to look into the library, but even if they had, all that they would have seen in the flickering fingers of the fire dancing their saraband around the dark room would be a shadowy figure resembling the medium. As the host and principal, however, only Crookes would have likely exercised that option, but didn't.

CROOKES - FAY GALVANOMETER TESTS			
Dates	Time to Start of Phenomena	Séance Duration	Body Resistance
Feb. 5–Friday	13 minutes	24 minutes	5,800 BAU
Feb. 6–Saturday	Unknown	15 minutes	Unknown
Feb. 19–Friday	1 minute	10 minutes	6,600 BAU
Feb. 25–Thursday	<1 minute	7-8 minutes	5,636 BAU
			6,012 BAU average ± 10%

Crookes-Fay Galvanometer Data from Barry H. Wiley, *The Indescribable Phenomenon* **(Seattle: Hermetic Press, 2005), page 178.**

All of Annie's phenomena required complete freedom from the galvanometer handles so that she could move quickly about the library, thus any proposed solution that does not account for that freedom cannot be considered even plausibly valid. The chart above clearly shows that Annie's skill in releasing herself from the bounds of the galvanometer circuit quickly improved to becoming effectively instantaneous. Thus it was more than just Gimingham's instruction but Annie's practiced dexterity in addition that created the mystery.

All but one of the recorded manifestations could be attributed to Annie's preparation with Gimingham's support. That one incident was the finding of the old china plate on Crookes' writing desk when the desk had been

G. The Crookes-Fay Galvanometer Test, 1875

confirmed clean before the séance began. How did it get there from its place on a molding in the drawing room upstairs, eight feet off the ground?

Again, there can only be supposition based on Annie's known capabilities and performing strategies. She certainly saw the plates of varying size displayed on the molding in the drawing room during one or more of her visits to the house. The molding was eight feet off the floor. Annie, only five feet tall, standing on a chair and reaching could barely reach that high and it ran too great a risk to try it. Most likely her taking the plate was not premeditated.

Crookes makes the statement in his *Spiritualist* article that, "The plates had been on those moldings for weeks without being moved, for no member of my family had occasion to touch them," which dismisses the fact that the servants undoubtedly periodically took the plates down for cleaning or dusting. Most simply, Annie encountered a maid doing just that, took one of the small plates at an appropriate moment, hiding it in her shawl or elsewhere, and then only later determined what use might be made of the purloined plate. The maid, if any note was made, would probably conclude the plate was mislaid and forget it, since to say anything would put her in an awkward position with the mistress of the house. The family, in any case, routinely paid little attention to the plates, until the evening of the nineteenth of February.

Crookes noted in his article that, "Similar cases of the carriage of solid objects from one place to another by abnormal means are on record in Spiritualistic literature," so the movement of the plate, once noted, was comfortably within precedent. The séance had produced the results he had been looking for.

None of the other participants, except Serjeant Cox, ever wrote of the séance, or publicly dissented from Crookes' report. Given Crookes' normal procedure, he undoubtedly circulated his article among the others for comments prior to submission. The editor of *The Spiritualist* being one of the observers ensured the article would receive ample display. However, as a measure of editor Luther Colby's loathing of Henry Fay and by association, Annie, there is no mention of any kind in the principal American Spiritualist journal, *The Banner of Light*, of the Crookes article endorsing the reality of the phenomena on the 19th. For American readers of the *Banner*, the whole experience never happened.

In an 1885 interview in the *Pall Mall Gazette*,* magician J. N. Maskelyne continued to ridicule the Crookes galvanometer tests as he had at first. First

---

*"A Spiritualistic Exposé—I: A Chat with Mr. Maskelyne," *Pall Mall Gazette,* April 18, 1885, p. 4.

G. The Crookes-Fay Galvanometer Test, 1875

describing Annie as "a fascinating little blonde," he went on, "His [Crookes'] chief 'scientific test' was by means of an electro-magnet. The two handles were placed in Miss Fay's hands, and the other ends of the wires were connected to a galvanometer, the needle of which could be seen by him in the dim half-light and which, if the medium were to loosen her hold, would indicate that fact at once. Could any man be so simple? Why, as soon as she wanted to have her hands free, all she would do would be to transfer one of the handles under her chin, or both, as she was sitting down, under the knees; or she would insert them in the neck of her dress, and all this without breaking contact. The much-vaunted 'scientific test' was absolutely the easiest to circumvent. But it bothered the professor completely." All of which is complete nonsense as Maskelyne* ignores the actual physical conditions of the séances involved, if in fact he ever chose to discover them. Like many magicians or critics, Maskelyne took a superior, even smug, attitude toward the investigators, knowing that most of the public, ignorant of the facts, would be satisfied with any explanation that sounded plausible.

On Thursday, the 25th, another galvanometer séance was scheduled. The report of the earlier galvanometer séances had not yet been published in *The Spiritualist*, thus Crookes invited James Burns, editor of *The Medium & Daybreak*, together with two other prominent Spiritualists, Messrs. Martheze and Bergheim, as well as an unnamed young gentleman to witness Annie's powers.

Burns, in his published report of the séance on the front page of *Medium & Daybreak* which appeared the same day, March 12th, as Crookes' report in *The Spiritualist*, wrote,

> The genuineness of Mrs. Fay's mediumship has been widely questioned — as, indeed, as been the probity of every other medium — more particularly because she permitted herself to be advertised and exhibited in showman fashion. The phenomena occur at her séances with such pre-arranged regularity, that many cannot escape the suspicion that the experiments are a series of tricks, inscrutable to the public, but capable of imitation by

---

*In the 1876 trial of Henry Slade, the slate writing medium, Maskelyne was brought in by the prosecution to demonstrate to the court the methods for producing spirit messages by trickery. The magician took a full half-day for his demonstrations to which the spectators responded enthusiastically. Subsequently, at every opportunity, J. N. took credit for Slade's conviction through his exposure of the medium's deceptions. The truth is that at the conclusion of the trial, the magistrate in his summation dismissed Maskelyne's demonstrations as irrelevant to the question at law, since the conjuror's producing the slate messages by trickery did not prove that Slade, in fact, had done the same. Slade was still convicted but on other grounds. The conviction was reversed on appeal on a technicality which led to Slade swiftly leaving England before he could be served a second time, and he never went back. Inexplicably, after returning to America, he later traveled to Canada which, at that time, placed him again within British law, and he was arrested again.

G. The Crookes-Fay Galvanometer Test, 1875

experts. Others again boast that they can permit themselves to be tied and then perform "all her tricks." At the present moment the showman [Jerome A. Paddock] who worked her séances at Hanover Square is now imitating her manifestations by the reproduction of the old advertisement and the exhibition of a "phenomenon" in the very unspiritual figure of a young lady in tights!

After carefully explaining the galvanometer circuit, Crookes invited the young gentleman to take the role of the medium to demonstrate its actual functioning by gripping then releasing the handles while the rest of the committee traced the movement on the galvanometer scale. After searching and sealing the room, except for the windows which Crookes tried to close, but Burns prevented him, pointing out the room would be uncomfortably hot with the fire going. Overcoming Crookes' insistence, the windows were left partially open. Burns explained in his article that no one could climb into the room without easy discovery by the police outside and the committee inside.

The medium was then called, and the séance commenced at 10:15 P.M. After recording the initial readings of Annie's body resistance, Crookes quickly looked in again at the medium for a moment to assure himself that she was still sitting and still holding the handles (which were not nailed down as in the previous séance). Satisfied, he returned to the galvanometer table. Burns readjusted the curtains, and the phenomena started immediately. The music box was wound up and started playing, then was stopped. A violin was handed through the curtains, the library ladder was slid through the curtains, a small hand put a large book through the curtains and placed it slowly on the floor, the fingers moving for a short time to attract attention. Burns noted that everything was handled with precision, nothing was thrown about.

After seven or eight minutes, the galvanometer flashed to zero. Crookes called to Annie, but there was no response. Crookes and the committee quickly dashed into the library, finding Annie slumped in the chair in a faint, the handles dropped to the floor. When the gas was turned up, the committee discovered that Crookes' writing desk, which had been closely examined prior to the séance as it was a new monocleid (one-key) style with an unpickable Bramah lock, was now opened with several drawers pulled out and small cabinet-doors opened. Burns pointed out that as Crookes had the only key, it was further confirmation of the amazing powers on display. Burns also noted that the committee had the option to peek around the curtain at any time, but chose not to.

In any case, chemist William Crookes was finished with his investigations of the spirit world.

H: SPR Leaflet by Alice Johnson

Private and Confidential

The Statement is being circulated to Members of the Council and a few members.

Mr. Blackburn's "Confession."

One or two enquiries having reached us about the authenticity of a series of articles that appeared in the *John Bull* from December 5th, 1908, to January 9th, 1909, under the heading "Confessions of a Famous Medium," the following statement has been drawn up for the sake of any who may have taken the articles seriously.

Their author, Mr. Douglas Blackburn, the self-styled "medium" in question, was the agent in two series of experiments in thought-transference, with Mr. G.A. Smith as percipient, carried out in 1882 and 1883, under the supervision of Mr. Myers and Mr. Gurney, who gave an account of them in the *Proceedings*, Vol. 1. Mr. Blackburn now publishes a "confession" that the success obtained in these experiments was obtained by means of fraudulent tricks, and describes the tricks which he alleges were used.

Mr. Blackburn is, we think, doing himself an injustice in the charges which he makes against himself. In any case, his so-called confession has little or no relation to the facts. There is a strong reason to believe that several of the incidents he describes never took place at all, for no version of them is to be found in the detailed report in the *Proceedings*. In other cases the circumstances are entirely misrepresented.

To begin with, it would be a mistake to suppose that these experiments were ever regarded, as Mr. Blackburn asserts, as "the bedrock foundation of all the later experiments which are said to prove the existence of Telepathy." On the contrary, the experiments in question were not reprinted (as others were) in *Phantasms of the Living*, nor in any other standard work of the kind. Nor is it true that the conditions were thought ideal. In the first series, contact was allowed; and in the second the experimenters state that "It would, no doubt, be an exaggeration to affirm that the possibility of [auditory] signals was absolutely excluded. We shall endeavor so to vary the conditions of subsequent experiments as to exclude this hypothesis completely."

These are only some among many inaccuracies that will be at once apparent to any one who compares Mr. Blackburn's account with the printed report of the experiments. For instance, he states that some of the experiments were held in his rooms, whereas the whole of the first series were carried out in Mr. Gurney's rooms at Brighton and the whole of the second in the Society's rooms at 14 Dean's Yard. He says also that in some cases Mr. Smith obtained successes when in a different room from himself by means of various tricks which he describes in detail, whereas the report states that the few experiments made with agent and percipient in different rooms all failed. Mr. Blackburn says that a successful result was obtained when Mr. Smith's head was enveloped in a blanket and his ears stopped, only after several attempts; whereas the report shows that this experiment succeeded on the first and only occasion on which it was tried.

Mr. Blackburn also describes a device, which at first sight appears ingenious, for the transmission of diagrams by code from an "agent" to a "percipient." This consists of an imaginary scheme like a chess board of 100 squares, numbered from 1 to 100, on which the "agent" would mentally project a diagram and then signal to the "percipient" the number of the squares crossed by the lines of the diagram. The "percipient" having the same scheme in his head, would be able to reproduce the diagram. Mr. Blackburn says that they were able to produce "absolute replicas"; though in the next paragraph, he asserts that they failed in the long run, because the code was adapted to the production of straight lines rather than of curved lines.

Any one who will try the plan here suggested for reproducing the diagrams actually used in these experiments, as published in the *Proceedings*, will, I think, convince himself that the code is insufficient: either a very much greater number of squares than 100 would be necessary, or many other indications besides the number of the square would have to be conveyed to the "percipient."

Further, an examination of the diagrams shows that while the reproductions are never "absolute replicas," the correspondence between them is not of the kind which the use of such a code would be likely to produce.

Shortly after these articles began to appear, I communicated with Mr. G.A. Smith and then went to see him, to ask for his version of the matter. I was already aware that, for reasons unconnected with experiments, but which Mr. Myers and Mr. Gurney considered sufficient, they had make no more experiments with Mr. Blackburn after the series published in *Proceedings*, Vol. 1. Mr. G.A. Smith, on the other hand, continued to assist them in many hypnotic and other experiments, became Mr. Gurney's private secretary and remained so up to the time of his death, giving help which Mr. Gurney much valued in his psychical work. Mr. Smith has also been long well known to Mrs. Sidgewick and myself in connection with later experiments in telepathy.

I talked to him fully and freely about Mr. Blackburn's articles, which he repudiated entirely. He disclaimed all connection with them and denied the statements made. He assured me that the experiments were all bona fide and that he and Mr. Blackburn never contemplated the possibility of coding until they had learnt of it from Mr. Myers and Mr. Gurney themselves, who were accustomed to discuss with them freely the question of what possibilities had to be guarded against and how the conditions could be improved. Mr. Gurney was especially ingenious and fertile in devising schemes for fraudulent communication, in order to be able to guard against them. Mr. Smith told me, as an instance, that after the successful experiment when his ears had been stopped with putty, his head enveloped in a bolster case, and the whole covered with a blanket, Mr. Gurney had remarked that under those circumstances a diagram might be conveyed to the percipient by concealing it in a hollow pencil or pen-holder. I was amused some time *after* this conversation to see this very method described in one of Mr. Blackburn's articles as having been actually used by him.

Mr. Blackburn as he himself states, did not publish anything about the supposed fraud during the life-time of Mr. Gurney and Mr. Myers, and my discussion with Mr. Smith confirmed me in the view that the "confession" was now made merely in the hope of creating a journalistic sensation.

Alice Johnson

Reprinted with permission. SPR Archive, Cambridge University Library.

Notes

Prologue

1. W.T. Stead (1849–1912) joined the *PMG* in 1880 as an assistant editor. He became editor in 1883 and retained that position until 1889. He boosted the public influence of the *PMG* with such innovations as the interview (first newspaper interview was in 1884 with General Charles Gordon), special issues and challenging positions on social issues. With his interest in psychical investigation, Stead started the journal *Borderland* (1893–1897). He was one of the most prominent passengers lost on the *Titanic* in 1912.

2. *Descent of Man and Selection in Relation to Sex* (London: John Murray, 1871; 2nd ed. 1874).

3. A year later in 1885, with public interest flogged by W.T. Stead's series of articles in the *PMG* on child prostitution, Labouchère proposed an amendment to the Criminal Law Amendment Act. That amendment, which became Section 11 in that act, created a new offense of indecency "between male persons" in public or in private. Indecency in public had always been a crime, but Labouchère added the three words that would, in 1895, entangle Oscar Wilde in three highly publicized trials that eventually resulted in his serving two years in Reading Gaol. Supporting Labouchère, a fellow Member of Parliament proposed increasing the punishment for indecency from twelve to twenty-four months. Both amendments were passed by Parliament without discussion and became law on January 1, 1886. The act was promptly denounced by many social critics as "the Blackmailers' Charter." Labouchère later became the scourge of Washington Irving Bishop and the friend of Stuart C. Cumberland.

4. The public would buy *Truth* each week to see what new lie Labouchère could invent. He once considered calling the journal *The Lyre*. "It is the business of a newspaper to create a sensation," he declared. See Hesketh Pearson, *Labby: The Life of Henry Labouchère* (London: Hamish Hamilton, 1936), p.123.

5. Michael Faraday, "Professor Faraday on Table-Moving," *Athenaeum*, July 2, 1853. Expanded from an earlier letter in the *London Times*, June 30, 1853. In addition to his own experiments, Faraday referred to a lecture given at the Royal Institution in 1852 by W.B. Carpenter on unconscious muscular movement.

6. Edmund Gurney (1847–1888) was a classical scholar and musician but never adopted either as a profession. Co-founder of the SPR and its first honorary secretary, he was the principal writer of the monumental 1,300-page, two-volume SPR study of telepathy, *Phantasms of the Living* (1886). Gurney died in 1888 of an overdose of chloroform under suspicious circumstances, which a coroner's jury later held to be accidental.

7. The Society for Psychical Research was founded in London, February 1882.

8. *Pall Mall Gazette*, May 21, 1884, p. 3.

9. Simon Newcomb, "Psychic Force," *Science*, October 17, 1884. Later republished in condensed form as part of "Professor Simon Newcomb and Mr. Edmund Gurney on Psychical Research" in *JSPR*, February 1885, pp. 268–274.

10. Alan Gauld, *The Founders of Psychical Research* (London: Routledge & Kegan Paul, 1968, p. 209): "Certainly there does not seem to be the slightest reason for supposing that the vast majority of the spectacular physical phenomena reported in the eighteen-seventies and eighteen-eighties were anything other than fraudulent. Whether or not there was, or is, a residue of genuine phenomena is a question."

11. William Alvord, in presenting Simon Newcomb the first Bruce Gold Medal of the Astronomical Society of the Pacific in 1897, said, "The basis of Professor Newcomb's character is intellectual and moral honesty carried to the highest degree. He loves truth and detests shams. He has, as it were, a veritable passion for justice, whether in personal matters or in civil."

12. Barry H. Wiley, *The Georgia Wonder: Lulu Hurst and the Secret That Shook America* (Seattle: Hermetic Press, 2004).

13. Autobiography of Lulu Hurst (Rome and Madison, GA: Psychic Publishing, May 1897). "Who Reads the Book Can Acquire the Power!"

203

The full text of the Hurst book is contained in the Wiley book above, including the Appendix in which the performing details of the act are described.

14. Simon Newcomb, *The Reminiscences of an Astronomer* (Boston: Houghton Mifflin, 1903), pp. 408–416.

15. Simon Newcomb, "The Georgia Wonder-Girl and Her Lessons," *Science*, Vol. 5, No. 105 (February 6, 1885), pp. 106–108. See also Simon Newcomb, "Modern Occultism," *Nineteenth Century*, Vol. 65 (January, 1909), pp. 126–139.

16. In Simon Newcomb's "Presidential Address to the ASPR," *Proceedings of the ASPR*, Vol. 1 (July 1885), after commenting on the earlier SPR telepathy studies of the Creery family, the Blackburn-Smith experiments and others, Newcomb said, "What science concerns itself with is not the mere recurrence of the phenomena, but the nature of the relation between the cause and the effect." Until the causes or conditions that allow for these phenomena to occur are identified, Newcomb insisted, "nothing can be inferred." After using an astronomical example to demonstrate how a unique interesting phenomenon attested to by many observers was eventually, over several years, demonstrated spurious, the scientist concluded, "The most careful collection of facts and observations during three years has failed to show any common feature in the ideas transferred, and has thrown no light on the question of the conditions under which the phenomena can occur. The theory cannot be reconciled on any reasonable hypothesis, even that of thought-transference."

17. Albert E. Moyer, "Simon Newcomb: Astronomer with an Attitude," *Scientific American*, October,1998, pp. 88–93. Moyer suggests that Newcomb was used by Arthur Conan Doyle as the model for Professor James Moriarty, the formidable, implacable foe of Sherlock Holmes.

Chapter 1

1. The story is generally told that all 1,170 copies for sale in the first printing (eighty more copies had been used for copyright purposes and as presentation/review copies) sold out the first day. That, however, is true only for wholesale transactions. The book, at fifteen shillings, did not sell out at retail until some weeks later. Not until the fifth edition in 1869 did Herbert Spencer's expression (dating from 1864), "survival of the fittest," appear — where "fittest" in its Victorian sense simply meant "most suitable," not the idea of the strategic domination of one group or species over another, as it has come to be interpreted over the decades. The Spencer statement has become, over time, the standard four-word summary of all of Darwin's writings.

2. The second edition, with a number of edits and corrections, was published in 1874, with Darwin writing in his preface, "I have endeavored to profit by the fiery ordeal through which the book has passed, and have taken advantage of all the criticisms which seemed to me sound." Darwin's first use of the word "evolution" in print was on page 2 of Volume One of *Descent*. In *Origin of Species*, "evolution" did not appear until the sixth edition.

3. Maria Basheba Trenholm Hayden's husband, William R. Hayden, published the first Spiritualist journal, *The Spirit World*, in May 1853. It survived for one issue. The first successful English Spiritualist paper, *The Yorkshire Spiritualist Telegraph*, was launched in 1855. The most prominent American paper, *The Banner of Light*, started in Boston in 1857. What came to be the most important English papers, *The Spiritualist* and *The Medium & Daybreak*, both started publication in 1869.

4. Electro-Biology was first brought to Great Britain by two Americans in 1850. George W. Stone was the compiler and editor of *Philosophy of Electro-Biology or Electrical Psychology in a Course of Nine Lectures Delivered by John Bovee Dods* (London: H. Baillierie, 1852). The book includes a section of newspaper articles from 1851 on the cures and pain relief achieved by G.W. Stone through Electro-Biology.

Dr. John Elliotson, the respected editor of the *Zoist* and an authority on mesmerism, had publicly put forward his finding that a subject holding a piece of nickel was more readily placed into a mesmeric trance than one holding a piece of lead. Through experiments conducted by Elliotson's colleagues, the result was confirmed that it was the metal that the subject believed he held, coupled with Elliotson's authoritative presence, that had determined how rapidly the trance was induced. Metals, in themselves, were found to have no impact on mesmeric trances.

George Stone was a close friend of W.R. Hayden. When Hayden wrote describing his young wife's newly revealed mediumship, Stone responded enthusiastically. Meeting Maria Hayden in Boston in July 1852 during his lecture tour of eastern America, Stone was impressed with her engaging presence and phenomena. He encouraged the Haydens to accompany him back to England, which they did in October.

G.W. Stone placed advertisements on the front page of the *London Times* in which he begged "leave to inform the nobility and gentry that he has just returned from the United States, accompanied by Mrs. M.B. Hayden for the purpose of Demonstrating the wonderful Phenomena known in that country as Spiritual Manifestations, and which have created the most intense excitement in all classes of society — residence at 26 Upper Seymour Street, Portman Square, at home from Eleven to Two and from Four to Six." The cost was one guinea for one inquirer, and five guineas for ten. Ten was the maximum number of inquirers allowed for a séance. Proceedings held in a gentleman's private lodgings would be five guineas. Five guineas would be the rough equivalent of £100 in 2010. Only the wealthy, therefore, could afford the Hayden spirits.

To help promote the Hayden mediumship, Stone edited and wrote an introduction to a book by a friend, the Rev. Adin Ballou, published in Boston the same year. He announced its publication in the *London Times* on November 25, 1852: *An Exposition of Views Respecting the Principal Facts, Causes & Peculiarities Involved in Spirit Manifestations* (London: H. Baillierie, 1852).

5. The regular presence of Hayden's husband at the table, though rarely mentioned, could allow the medium to be at the other end of the room, or the alphabet card to be hidden behind a book or some other object, with the necessary letters signaled silently by W.R. Hayden to his wife. He could also, if necessary, create the spirit raps himself, while the medium was under close scrutiny or positioned away from the table.

With diligent practice, Mrs. Hayden could follow where the client was on the alphabet card and thus rap the table as needed. She would also snap the joints in her large toes to obtain the necessary sounds. Her suddenly looking at some point in the room at the moment of the rapping would suggest to, and often convince, willing sitters that the raps were coming from different points around the room.

The necessary background information could be obtained by arranging appointments for querents which would allow the Haydens and Stone to research the more prominent people coming in advance of their established time. As she moved her finger around the circle, Mrs. Hayden would only cause raps indicating the choice by the spirits of clients on which she had information. If the spirits didn't contact someone, they were simply asked to return at a later, perhaps more propitious, time.

Some investigators attended séances giving phony names and ask for the spirit of a non-existent dead relative — who usually appeared. The coming of the fraudulent spirits would then be scornfully written up in various public journals. G.H. Lewes in the newspaper *The Leader*, March 12, 1853, wrote perhaps the most stinging exposure of the Hayden séances — but still there were phenomena witnessed by prominent individuals, including mathematician Augustus de Morgan and social reformer Robert Dale Owen, that the Lewes exposure could not explain.

Ultimately, it was the growing enthusiastic interest in spiritual manifestations that erased interest in Electro-Biology from the public's mind.

6. Huxley continued: "Drive it away as I would, however, the suspicion, the offspring, no doubt, of a basely materialistic philosophy, kept coming back — took shape as a theory, and finally, by dint of patience and perseverance, embodied itself into practice. From that time forth, I became the master of two spirits as efficient as those of Mrs. X [Hayden], and I verily believe of the same nature." Huxley produced the raps in the second toe of each foot by bending his toe and then suddenly straightening it, with the result a sharp tap on the sole of his shoe. He recommended thin socks and a roomy, hard-soled boot, being careful to pick out a thin place in the carpet to stand on.

Huxley then described Mrs. Hayden's gentle sense of humor, relating a story from a friend who at a séance held at a country manor had received several messages through Mrs. Hayden from his deceased sister, Mary. At the close of the séance, the company broke up into groups, with Huxley's friend strolling with Mrs. Hayden away from the others to a large bay window.

"Did you ever have a sister Mary?" Hayden asked.

"No," replied the friend.

"I thought not," she said, smiling.

In conclusion, Huxley observed, "Fraud is often genius out of place, and I confess that I have never been able to get over a sneaking admiration for Mrs. Hayden."

A licensed physician since 1865, Maria B. Hayden, M.D., died in New York on February 11, 1883. She was eulogized in the *Boston Herald* the following day in an article that included a listing of her most famous medical patients, including Horace Greeley. Some of Dr. Hayden's prescription forms still exist in the Hayden family archives.

7. Letter of Charles Dickens to Mrs. Fanny Trollope, June 19, 1855, cited by Dickens's son, Sir Henry Fielding Dickens, in *Recollections of Sir Henry Dickens* (London: William Heinemann Co., 1934), p. 63. A further comment fondly recalled by Sir Henry, on page 64, related the time in 1870 when Charles Dickens rented a house at Hyde Park Place, formerly the home of a prominent politician whose wife had been a devoted follower of D.D. Home (see note 8 below). The medium's most celebrated phenomena of the time were his levitations, which were ecstatically described by believers, emphasizing that Home, as proof of his rising, would often leave a mark on the ceiling, usually a cross. Sir Henry wrote: "In the drawing-room (quite a lofty room) we noticed a large stain in the ceiling which my father remarked was obviously the mark of the medium's greasy head as he floated up to the ceiling on one of his manifestations!"

8. Pronounced "Hume" or, as he preferred, "whom." Home (1833–1886) lived on income from his first wife's riches, and thus did not need to ask for payment for his séances. He lived from 1859 to 1871 in London. When his wife died in 1862, Home was forced to return to giving lectures and séances to support himself and his son. Home's most controversial stunt occurred December 13, 1868, when he claimed to have levitated himself out one window of Lord Adare's London house and into another, 30 feet off the ground.

William Crookes investigated Home in 29 sittings, without finding evidence of fraud. Crookes later wrote to Sir Oliver Lodge, "I tried my best to get men of science to look in to it, but all I got for my pains was a suggestion of lunacy for myself and insults for Home."

In 1871, Home married a second time, again to a wealthy Russian. He retired from active mediumship in 1872, having three books ghost-written, one of which, *Lights and Shadows of Spiritualism*, caused Crookes serious embarrassment as it exposed a number of the tricks used by mediums endorsed by Crookes. Home, with his tubercular condition worsening, retired from mediumship at the age of 38. He left London for the Mediterranean coast where he lived until his death of tuberculosis, aged 53, at the Villa Montmorency in Auteil, France, June 22, 1886. He was buried in St. Germain-en-Laye alongside his infant daughter.

Chapter 2

1. Writing in the foreword to *The Life of Sir William Crookes* by E.E. Fournier d'Albe (New York: D. Appleton & Co., 1924), p. v.
2. D'Albe, p. 24.
3. D'Albe, p. 59. The formal announcement of the new element was made in the *Chemical News*, May 18, 1861, "On the Existence of a New Element, probably of the Sulphur Group," in which Crookes proposed the name thallium, after the Latin thallus, a budding twig, as the brilliant green color of the spectral line suggested early vegetation.
4. "Researches on the Atomic Weight of Thallium," *Philosophical Transactions of the Royal Society*, Vol. 163 (1873), p. 279.
5. D'Albe, p. 84.
6. *Quarterly Journal of Science*, vii (July 1870), p. 316.
7. D'Albe, pp.141–142.
8. Described in other notices of the eclipse expedition as a "somewhat elderly ship." Tyndall, for one, had expressed some concern about the ship's seaworthiness.
9. John Tyndall, *Fragments of Science*, 6th ed. (New York: D. Appleton, 1889), p. 314. "Science and the Spirits" originally appeared in *Reader*, 4 (1864), pp. 725–726.
10. Tyndall had granted, in his 1864 paper, "that some physical principle, not evident to the spiritualists themselves, might underlie their manifestations."
11. Michael Faraday, "Lecture on Mental Training," *Royal Institution*, May 6, 1854, p. 65. Also later in *The Athenaeum*, March 28, 1857, p. 397.

Chapter 3

1. D'Albe, p. 190.
2. Eric J. Dingwall, *Some Human Oddities* (London: Home & Van Thal, 1947), p. 96.
3. D.D. Home in his writings about his youthful medial experiences in America usually portrayed his traveling among Spiritualist families, but not spending any time with other mediums, positioning himself as someone who had always stood apart from other sensitives. He does mention that at nineteen he traveled to Springfield, MA, to visit the well-known medium Henry C. Gordon, to participate in one séance at which, he said, nothing happened. From there he went on to live nearby with the Rufus Elmer family, who were ardent Spiritualists.

However, Emma Hardinge in her *Modern American Spiritualism* (1870), p. 103, relates that Home, along with two other young mediums, George Redman and Rollin Square, who were also staying with Gordon, "were all developed for physical manifestations of the most wonderful kind. These young men were frequently lifted up in the air and floated over several feet of ground in the presence of hundreds of witnesses." She also quotes from an article in the *New York Dispatch*, 1853, which appeared under the headline "'Super Mundane' with a Vengeance — Medium Floated in the Air":

Mr. Henry C. Gordon, a well-known medium for spiritual manifestations, being at a circle in this city one evening last week was repeatedly raised from his seat and carried through the room, without any visible power touching him. The room was partially darkened, and the members of the circle could distinctly see him floating with his lower extremities some two to three feet from the floor and some fifteen or twenty feet from the nearest person to him. The idea of any mechanical contrivance in this case is out of the question.... The same event took place with Mr. Gordon in this city some two years ago, of which an account was published.

According to Hardinge, p. 73, in 1851 Henry C. Gordon was the first medium in New York State to perform levitations. Thus Gordon had already been performing various levitations for two years prior to Home's visit, and very likely was Home's mentor in levitations as well as probably other physical demonstrations. Nothing is known of Gordon's later life.

For the best current biography of D.D. Home with full descriptions of Home's many phenomena, see Peter Lamont, *The First Psychic* (New York: Little, Brown, 2005). For the Dumas description, see page 99.

4. As an aside, in my short career as a magician during high school years I was once told by an acquaintance about a conjuror, whose name she didn't know, who had performed some truly amazing tricks a couple weeks back. It sounded like a magician I definitely wanted to see, and meet if possible. When I asked when and where the magician had appeared, it developed that my acquaintance had not actually seen the performer herself; she was only repeating what she had been told, but she gave the place and time of the performance. I was then even more amazed — because

I was the performer she had been describing in such impossible terms! In perhaps only two or three retellings, my fairly basic magic routine for that evening had been embellished to a sequence of stunts not even Houdini could have done. In a very simple way, I had seen one of Home's techniques in play, though I, in this case, had done nothing to promote the magnified performance.

   5. D.D. Home, *Lights and Shadows of Spiritualism* (London: Virtue, 1877), pp. 332–333.
   6. William Crookes, "Experimental Investigation of a New Force," *Quarterly Journal of Science*, July 1, 1871.
   7. R.G. Medhurst and K.M. Goldney, *Crookes and the Spirit World* (New York: Taplinger, 1972), pp. 172–175.
   8. *PSPR*, December 1889. Additional previously unpublished séance notes were included, pp. 143–225.
   9. Elizabeth Barrett Browning to her sister, August 17, 1855, from Laura Huxley, ed., *Elizabeth Barrett Browning: Letters to Her Sister, 1846–59* (London: John Murray, 1929).
   10. Letter from Robert Browning to Mrs. Elizabeth Kinney, quoted in its entirety in William Lyon Phelps, "Robert Browning on Spiritualism," *Yale Review*, 23 (1933), pp. 125–138. See also Browning's letter in the *London Times*, November 28, 1902, in which he said after witnessing one Home performance, "that the whole display of hands, spirit utterances, etc., was a cheat and an imposture." Robert Browning's dislike of Home took on the characteristics of a mania, with Home described as "a dung ball," "bestiality incarnate" and "that spirit-rapping scoundrel," among other epithets. The basis of Browning's intense disgust has been attributed by various writers to Home's apparent homosexuality.
   11. Angelo Lewis (Professor Hoffmann), *JSPR*, July 1889, p. 120.
   12. Harry Kellar, *A Magician's Tour* (Chicago: Donohue, Henneberry, 1891), pp. 168–172.
   13. Alfred R. Wallace, "Mr. Crookes and Eva Fay," *Nature*, December 6, 1877, p. 101.
   14. William B. Carpenter, "Mr. Crookes and Eva Fay," *Nature*, December 13, 1877, p. 122.
   15. Frank Podmore, *The Newer Spiritualism* (London: T. Fisher Unwin, 1910), p. 51.
   16. Gordon Stein, *The Sorcerer of Kings: The Case of Daniel Dunglas Home and William Crookes* (Buffalo: Prometheus Books, 1993), p. 83. Novelist and Houdini biographer William Lindsay Gresham, in the midst of researching a book on Home that he did not complete before his suicide in 1962, claimed he had found a small one-octave harmonica in the Home Collection at the SPR London headquarters, which clearly could explain the accordion effect. However, no such harmonica was included in the original inventory of the collection done by Eric J. Dingwall. Gresham also suggested that a hook on the end of a black string could be used to catch the lower edge of the accordion which with a slight motion of the wrist could cause the bellows to inflate and deflate as reported by some observers.
   17. The D.D. Home Collection came to the SPR in February 1927, via a gift from a nephew of Alexander N. Aksakoff, a former Czarist councilor and a supporter of Home. It included seven hundred letters written to Home by William Crookes, Allan Kardec, Mrs. Jane Lyon, and others; manuscripts of the two books published by Home's widow; a partial manuscript of a book by Home on Spiritualism to be called *Modern Spiritual Manifestations*; a number of photographs of Home and prominent men and women of his time; unpublished records of sittings with Home; a bronze bust of Home; an accordion used by Home; and a plaster cast of his left hand — but no small harmonicas.

Chapter 4

   1. Approximately $500 annually.
   2. "Spiritualism Outdone," *New York Times*, July 4, 1874.
   J. Randall Brown's personal scrapbook of the first two years of his career is in the McManus-Young Collection of the Library of Congress. The Call Number is BF1171.S46 1890. It makes for a fascinating afternoon of reading. Brown did not collect the clippings from just one newspaper in a town, but from all the newspapers that had covered his performance. Together they provide a multifaceted appraisal of Brown's early thought reading performances, giving an impression of Brown himself as well as suggesting the strongest points of his presentation.
   3. Dariel Fitzkee, *Contact Mindreading — Expanded, with an introduction by C.A. George Newmann*, 3rd ed. (Oakland, CA: Magic Limited, 1945).

Chapter 5

   1. Polymath Francis Galton, F.R.G.S., F.R.S. (1822–1911), criminologist who invented scientific finger printing, psychologist who created differential psychology, anthropologist, statistician, meteorologist, explorer of Africa and cousin of Charles Darwin. In 1872 he had participated in séances with Crookes that he deemed inexplicable at the time, but after numerous other séances, Galton had, by 1875, become a confirmed skeptic regarding the reality of spirit communication.
   2. As mentioned in Chapter 1, Huggins (1824–1910), who founded the field of stellar spectroscopy, was always a skeptic but acknowledged experiencing phenomena he could not explained.
   3. Edward William Cox (1809–1880) was a prominent legal authority who received his law degree from the Middle Temple in London in 1843 and was raised to the degree of Serjeant-at-Law twenty-five years later. He wrote numerous legal works as well as books on psychology: *What Am I?* and *The Mechanism of Man*. Cox was founder of the Psychological Society, which voted

to disband upon his death. Even after many séances with prominent mediums over the years, Cox never accepted the spirit hypothesis, though he had experienced phenomena for which he could not discover an explanation.

4. The Royal Society was founded in 1660 under the patronage of Charles II, making it the oldest independent scientific academy in the world. Its fellows, elected by their peers, were the most eminent scientists of the day. Membership of the Royal Society has included Sir Isaac Newton (president 1703–1727), Charles Darwin, and Albert Einstein. William Crookes was president from 1913 to 1915.

5. William Crookes, "A Scientific Examination of Mrs. Fay's Mediumship," *The Spiritualist*, March 12, 1875, pp. 126–128.

6. Edward W Cox, *The Mechanism of Man* (1879), Vol. ii, Experiment XII, pp. 446–450.

7. Carl Murchison, *The Case For and Against Psychical Belief* (Worcester, MA: Clark University, 1927).

8. D'Albe, p. 179.

9. R.G. Medhurst. *Crookes and the Spirit World*, New York: Taplinger, 1972, p. 237. The letter was first published in *Light*, May 12, 1900.

10. Crookes joined the Theosophical Society in 1883, and remained a member to his death. In contrast, Luther Colby, writing in the *Banner of Light*, said, "We don't want the cream of Spiritualism adulterated with the skim-milk of Theosophy."

11. R.G. Medhurst and K.M. Goldney, "William Crookes and the Physical Phenomena of Mediumship," *PSPR*, Vol. 54, Part 195 (March 1964), pp. 25–157. Crookes' letter is on p. 114.

12. Mme. Dunglas Home, *D.D. Home, His Life and Mission* (London: Trubner & C., 1888), p. 396.

13. Medhurst and Goldney, "William Crookes and the Physical Phenomena of Mediumship."

Chapter 6

1. George M. Beard, as a result of his experimentation, became a competent thought reader himself.

2. George Miller Beard, "The Physiology of Mind-Reading," *Popular Science Monthly*, Vol. 10 (February 1877), pp. 459–473. The term muscle reader, however, was first used by a Philadelphia journalist in 1875 in reporting on amateur thought-reading experiments by a Mr. Whitehouse, none of whose demonstrations included Brown's copper wire experiments. The writer dismissed the wire demonstrations as simply tricks that Mr. Whitehouse had not yet learned, and he closed his article with the observation that "all fools are not dead yet." Dr. Beard's later use of the term muscle reader in his 1877 article established the expression in popular vocabulary. Beard later claimed in his 1882 pamphlet on the study of trance that he had coined the term in 1874.

Beard followed up his February 1877 article with a letter titled "Mind-Reading by the Ear," *Popular Science Monthly*, Vol. 11 (1878), p. 362, in which he quotes in turn, in its entirety, an anonymous letter from someone he describes as "an expert in the art of mind-reading by the eye or by the touch." Beard's point is that a mind-reader can also detect the thoughts of a subject through listening to his or her footsteps, and he quotes the experiences of the unnamed writer as his proof. The writer claims to have been involved in the subject "in an amateur way for the past ten years," which would have pre-dated J.R. Brown by six years. Such a timeline seems very unlikely as Beard himself had been astonished when first experiencing Brown's demonstrations in New York, having never seen anything like the thought reader's skills in all of the scientist's experimentation on trance and nervous conditions.

As Beard wrote in his 1877 article:

The general fact that mind may so act on body as to produce involuntary and unconscious muscular motion was by no means unrecognized by physiologists, and yet not until the "mind-reading" excitement of two years ago was it demonstrated that this principle could be utilized for the finding of any object or limited locality on which a subject, with whom an operator is in physical connection, concentrates his mind.

3. Privately printed in 1882, the 40-page pamphlet is a miscellaneous collection of writings by Beard and others. It includes in full the article by George J. Romanes, "Thought Reading," *Nature*, June 23, 1881, which will be examined in detail later in regard to the thought reading exploits of Washington Irving Bishop.

4. In his respected tract *Contact Mind Reading—Expanded* (Oakland, CA: Magic Limited, 3rd ed., 1970), p. 38, Dariel Fitzkee wrote regarding J. Randall Brown's double test:

Before closing this work I want to point out an interesting line of speculation with contact mind reading, even though it may cause some of the more skeptical of my confreres to shout, "Fake."

At various times I have experimented with the placing of a third person between myself and the transmitter, each of us holding a different hand. The third person was as ignorant as I of the test to be done. We used the same method of contact for all.

Now please don't insist that I explain why it is possible, and do not insist that it can't be done if I can't explain it. BUT IN THE MAJORITY OF THESE TESTS THE DIRECTIONAL IMPULSES AND THE NECESSARY CLUES HAVE BEEN RENDERED TO ME BY THE THIRD PERSON, EVEN THOUGH IGNORANT HIMSELF AS TO THE TEST TO BE PERFORMED.

This has actually happened. Not once, but many times. At this moment, although I have never attempted it in public, I should have no more hesitation in attempting some of the more simple tests with a third person between myself and the transmitter, then I would attempt any form of contact mind reading.

I repeat, I don't know why, I can't explain why; and I should be very much interested in any information which may clarify this for me. But it happens! Try it with confidence, in the same frame of mind as the direct contact method. I think you will find it will work. (See Appendix F for a more complete discussion of the techniques of muscle reading or contact mind reading.)

5. Persifor Frazer, Jr., "Mind Reading," a paper read before the Social Science Association of Philadelphia on May 12, 1875.

6. "Brown, the Mind Reader," *BoL*, October 23, 1875.

Chapter 7

1. "Mind-Reading," *New York Times*, February 2, 1877.

2. The Bishop letter is listed in the online Lincoln Archives (www.lincolnarchives.us). It reads:

New York June 21, 1864

Dear Sir:

It is with pleasure that I present to you (the bearer) Capt. D (David). Cate of the U.S.N. knowing him to be one of our bravest men (he has captured many rebel steamers). Will you give me the honor of accepting the enclosed photograph of my son, whom God has endowed with great military talents; he was only eight years old on the fourth of March, 1864 & he is pronounced to be prepared in the gun, sword & artillery drills, by many of our Generals. He was made first lieutenant, at the age of seven years, and is now Capt. of the New York Cadets, his whole heart is on military matters & he regrets he is not old enough to go and "help take Richmond," he is determined to be a soldier, notwithstanding he has had beloved uncles and cousins killed in the frightful war.

As I am willing to give up my only child to defend this country, will you inform me, which is the best military school where I could place him through your selfless influence. A mother's love must be sufficient apology for my presumption in my speaking to you of this matter. We think he is worthy of his name, which is Washington Irving Wellington Bishop. The gentleman with my son is Peter Clark, Esq., the hero of Fort Sumpter [*sic*], he is holding a piece of the real Sumpter flag & and relating its history to my son.

As my husband says you are the only man on this continent capable of filling the Presidential chair, believe me, if we had it in our power you would never vacate it, until God called you to another and better world.

With kindest regards to yourself & family, I remain your loyal friend,

Eleanor Fletcher Bishop
New York

To:
Hon. A. Lincoln
President of the United States
P.S. Please address all letters to my husband's office, Nathanial C. Bishop, No. 1, Broadway, New York.

The underlining is in the original. The author is indebted to writer-historian Jerry Kuntz for locating the letter.

3. "The Greatest Humbug Yet: How Professor Crook's 'Gifted and Wonderful' Medium, Annie Eva Fay, Performs Her Tricks," *New York Daily Graphic*, Wednesday, April 12, 1876.

4. "How Bishop Fooled the 'Solid Men of Boston,'" *BoL*, February 3, 1877. Bishop charged $400 for his unnamed male assistant and himself at the Parker House. Other incidentals, rides, dinners, and so forth, added up to another $380. Of the $320 remaining after "personal expenses," Bishop received the agreed 75 percent of the balance, leaving $80 for the preservation of Old South. "Only a pennyworth of bread for all that sack," as one reporter commented.

5. "Visiting the Mediums. Wonderful Revelations About Business and Pleasures. W.I. Bishop in the Role of Inquiring Female. Startling Results from Foundationless Causes." *Boston Herald*, November 12, 1876. After the photograph of Bishop dressed as a woman was discovered by Luther Colby, editor of the *Banner of Light*, the Spiritualist press referred to Bishop as "Petticoat" Bishop. After a long preface, the reporter wrote:

We now come to another phase of the interviewing business in which Mr. Bishop appears as the distressed female, anxiously looking to the spirits for counsel and advice. Mr. Bishop (let us call him Miss Bishop, for convenience).... Miss Bishop went to a well-known theatrical costumer's on Hayward Place, and doffing her coat, vest and shoes, and turning up her pants, she was soon invested in female attire, and looked "charming indeed." A smooth shave, regular features, and an art to imitate the female step and manner, and the skill of the costumer, made Miss Bishop irresistible. Thus equipped in company with the writer, to whom the spirits have given her such a strange affinity, Miss Bishop sallied forth into the darkness. Let it be here recorded for shortness that several mediums, etc., were visited, but only two cases are cited to give an idea of how the thing worked. Down and up and around, over dirty crossings and along wet sidewalks with umbrella erect to keep off the rain went the loving pair, exciting little remark save some admiring glances of passers-by under the gaslight directed at Miss B, which made her escort feel furiously jealous.

The reporter offers long descriptions of encounters with an astrologer and a medium. The astrologer suspected something even to running her fingers over the nape of Miss Bishop's neck. Her "wiggery," as the writer called it, held up to inspection.

The reporter continues:

A later car brought the couple of investigators back again to the vicinity of Parker's where the writer and Miss Bishop enjoyed an oyster lunch without the sex of the latter being even suspected. But it is needless to tell how Miss B. was ogled by the gay old fellows in the horse cars; how she passed under the most searching glances of friends and acquaintances, and how finally, she became known and was the cynosure of all eyes of Parker's, where the last her "affinity" saw of her she was calmly smoking a cigar in the public hall of the hotel, much to the enjoyment of the porters and surprise of belated guests. That night Miss Bishop ceased to be, and now it is Mr. W. Irving Bishop, the exposer of mediums and Spiritualist humbugs. And so ends this chapter, the reader left to do his own moralizing and draw his own conclusions.

6. "The Body of Nathaniel C. Bishop Exhumed," *New York Times*, April 12, 1874.

7. W.F. Barrett, "On Some Phenomena Associated with Abnormal Conditions of Mind," *Spiritualist Newspaper* 9 (September 22, 1876), pp. 87–88. And later revised, *PSPR*, Vol. 1 (1882–83), April 24, 1883, pp. 238–244.

8. Carpenter to Barrett, November 2, 1876, WFB-CUL, SPR.MS3, A2/12.

9. Barrett would later claim the dates were 1862–1867.

10. S. Forgan, "Tyndall at the Royal Institution," in R.C. Mollan, ed., *John Tyndall: Essays on a Natural Philosopher* (Dublin: Royal Dublin Society, 1981), pp. 49–60.

11. John Tyndall, *Fragments of Science*, Vol. 1, *Inorganic Nature*, 6th ed. (London: Longman, Green and Co., 1879), XXII, "Science and the 'Spirits,'" pp. 496–504. Tyndall's essay ridiculed Spiritualism: "Surely no baser delusion ever obtained dominance over the weak mind of man."

12. William Fletcher Barrett, "Some Reminiscences of Fifty Years Psychical Research," *PSPR*, Vol. 34 (December 1924), pp. 281–282.

13. Fraser Nichol, "The Founders of the S.P.R.," *PSPR*, Vol. 55 (March 1972), pp. 341–367.

14. "To the Editor of the Times," *London Times*, September 22, 1876, p. 10.

Chapter 8

1. Carpenter's letter, "Re W.I. Bishop," which describes the card trick, appeared in *Nature*, June 30, 1881, p.188. Thomson Whyte of Edinburgh wrote in *Nature*, July 7, 1881, in "Re W.I. Bishop," p. 211, to describe two methods for accomplishing the trick. The first, the use of two decks with the same back-pattern, in one of which "fifty-two cards are all alike." The second, Bishop tells the subject to "drop your left hand down" on rows and cards without first telling the subject what that action will designate, whether to pick up the row or card, or to leave it. By using the identical undefined words at each point, Whyte explains, the operator can subtly force the subject to the one card he wants the subject to finally land on, assuming that the operator knows the placement of the correct card.

If the operator declares in advance what is to happen when the subject drops his hand, and the correct card is arrived at, then Whyte admits, the result would be beyond normal probabilities. Even better, if neither the operator nor the subject knows the location of the card selected, and the correct card is selected, then a special phenomenon has truly been demonstrated.

Whyte complained that Carpenter granted W.I. Bishop the power of "will-compelling," a power that even Bishop himself hadn't claimed. Whyte had seen Bishop perform some card tricks at Edinburgh in 1879. This is the earliest explicit description of magician's equivoque that I have encountered.

2. "Bishop's Spiritual Experience," *BoL*, December 21, 1878.

3. "Mr. Bishop and the Western Infirmary," *BoL*, April 26, 1879. Quoted from the *Glasgow Evening News*.

4. "J. Page Hopps in re W.I. Bishop," *BoL*, April 12, 1879.

5. One of the mediumistic feats most closely identified with Annie Eva Fay that was regularly exposed by W.I. Bishop was the spirit cabinet, an effect in which the medium is tied by members of a committee at the neck, hands and feet with calico strips to iron staples driven into a large wooden post within a black curtained cabinet. The knots are sealed with wax. But then, once the curtains are closed, loud noises start almost immediately, pie tins are thrown over the top of the cabinet, music instruments are played—yet, when the curtains are thrown open again, the medium is found to be in a trance state and tied exactly as before, leaving the audience to believe that all the manifestations were by the spirits. A member of the committee volunteers to join the medium and the spirits in the cabinet. When the curtains are thrown back, the volunteer is found to have his tie and coat removed, and whatever other "spiritual" manifestations the medium chooses to inflict. This effect was originally called the "Cotton Bandage Test." Annie Fay called the spirit cabinet "The Light Séance" as all the lights on the stage or in the room were kept on, with only the medium in darkness.

When I interviewed Eric J. Dingwall, the last person to have actually known Annie Fay, he told me about the time he was the volunteer to go into the cabinet with her. He whispered to her that he felt she should know that he was a member of the Magic Circle. To which Fay laughed and the "spirits" had their fun with Dingwall, he said, so fast that he could not catch what was happening.

I had an experience similar to Dingwall's. I went into the cabinet with its greatest contemporary exponent, Frances Falkenstein. Though the medium was apparently entranced, and tied securely to the post (I helped tie her), the "spirits" arrived quickly, putting a bucket over my head, and had their fun. An amazing experience.

The spirit cabinet was created by a Springfield, Massachusetts, carpenter, Marshall M. Ellis, and first publicly used in 1864 by his daughter, twelve-year-old Laura V. Ellis. Some 150 years later, the spirit cabinet is still presented by performers around the world.

6. The original letter, nine pages long, is in the Houghton Library at Harvard University, call number bMs Thr 467, Bishop, W.I.

Chapter 9

1. The Rev. A.M. Creery, "Note on Thought-Reading," *PSPR*, Vol. 1 (1882–1883), pp. 43–46.

2. In contrast to Rev. Creery's assertion that his daughters were at their thought-reading best when in a playful mood, Douglas Blackburn's counter observation is appropriate:

And here we would remark en passant that in conducting experiments involving strange and delicate conditions, it is essential, if good results are desired, that a spirit of sober, painstaking inquiry should characterize the proceedings. Very little that is satisfactory can reasonably be expected if the subject be placed on a level with a round card game or other "party" pastime, for which it is too often regarded as a substitute.
— From Douglas Blackburn, *Thought-Reading, or Modern Mysteries Explained* (London: Simpkin, Marshall & Co., 1884), p. 21. Blackburn's comments on the subject will be shown later to be of special interest.

3. W.F. Barrett, "Mind-Reading versus Muscle Reading," *Nature*, July 7, 1881, p. 212. See also W.F. Barrett, "Mind and Muscle-Reading," *Nature*, July 14, 1881, p. 236, where Barrett corrects a typo; and see the commentary "Professor Barrett's Experiments in Thought-Reading," *Light*, July 16, 1881, p. 222.

Chapter 10

1. "Thought Reading," *Lancet*, May 14, 1881, p. 795.

2. "Thought Reading," *British Medical Journal*, May 13, 1881, p. 710.

3. George J. Romanes, "Thought Reading," *Nature*, June 23, 1881, pp. 171–172.

4. The letter Dr. Carpenter wrote to W.I. Bishop appeared in the *London Daily Telegraph*, May 14, 1881:

Dear Sir:
The experiments you were good enough to show me at my own home some time ago, Professor Huxley also being present, satisfied us, as I know they previously satisfied a number of the professors of the Edinburgh and Glasgow universities of your remarkable power of "thought reading" which you derive from your careful study of the indications unconsciously given by subjects of your experiments, and from your particular aptness in the interpretations of those indications. With Mr. Bishop's art extended we should all have windows in our breasts, and spies could peep into our open hearts.

In reprinting the Carpenter letter in his programs and handbills, Bishop deleted the portion beginning with "which you derive..." and ending with "...indications."

The letter continued for a few more paragraphs and concluded, "It is clear to me that all your work in this direction is done upon strictly scientific principles, and tends to enlarge our knowledge of the automatic interactions of mind and body." That even scientists could not recognize unscientific behavior is not surprising, as scientists can be conned as easily as anyone else.

In the *London Daily News* of May 11, 1881, a reporter observed: "Dr. Carpenter and Professor Huxley, not the men to be readily deceived by plausible charlatans, are convinced that Mr. Bishop's attempts to advance knowledge are honest and sincere." This supportive line Bishop also eagerly utilized in his publicity.

5. Bishop later developed a quick response to such situations: "If I fail a hundred times and succeed once, you must explain that one success, or acknowledge yourself beaten."

6. "The Bishop and the Duke," *BoL*, July 16, 1881.

7. "Thought Reading," *British Medical Journal*, May 13, 1881, p. 710.

8. Robert Lund, "Mother Fletcher," *M.U.M.*, July 1958, pp. 63–64, 67. Some later thought readers mimicked Bishop's technique of frenetic gyrations and fainting at the end of a hard test. One performer, Theo Pull, would chew a small piece of soap so that he could foam at the mouth, appearing to be "on the verge of a fit of nervous exhaustion."

9. Henri Labouchère had also become known for a system for playing roulette at Monte Carlo. The system, known as the Labby, became one of the most popular utilized by the sporting crowd at the famous casino. Critics like Victor Bethell noted, however, that the Labby could actually accelerate the player's losses under the wrong circumstances and, as a result, required substantial capital and time to properly execute — which was true of most Monte Carlo systems. The Reverse Labby soon rose in popularity as it moderated the rate of loss. It isn't known if Labouchère himself developed the system, or if he only published it

in *Truth*. For more on Labouchère, see Prologue, notes 3 and 4. For a complete discussion of the Labby systems, see V.B. (Victor Bethell), *Monte Carlo Anecdotes and Systems of Play* (London: William Heinemann, 1910). Bethell wrote an earlier book, *Ten Days at Monte Carlo at the Bank's Expense* (London: William Heinemann, 1898), in which he and a friend used a roulette system to pay their expenses. The system worked and is described in detail. See also Barry Wiley, "Monte Carlo Systems: Myths and Promises," *History Magazine*, December/January 2010.

10. John Nevil Maskelyne (1839–1917) was the founder of the Maskelyne family of conjurors which continued to perform in London until 1935. First with George Cooke and later with David Devant as partners, he presented the greatest and longest running magic show in English history. Maskeylne started his career in 1865 by exposing and apparently duplicating the spirit cabinet routine of the famous Davenport Brothers, after accidentally discovering their rope-tying secrets. He continued his anti–Spiritualistic exposures through much of his long career. Chasing the spirits always paid well, even when J. Nevil Maskelyne actually did not know how the mediums achieved their phenomena.

Chapter 11

1. Balfour Stewart, "Note on Thought Reading," *PSPR*, Vol. 1 (1882–1883), pp. 35–38.

2. W.F. Barrett, F.W.H. Myers, and E. Gurney, "Thought Reading," *Nineteenth Century*, Vol. 11 (1882), pp. 890–900.

3. Horatio Donkin, "A Note on Thought-reading," *Nineteenth Century*, Vol. 12 (1882), pp. 131–133.

4. Romanes to Barrett, October 28, 1882, SPR Archive Barrett Papers (Box 2, A4, No. 109). Earlier letters (Nos. 104–107) demonstrate that Romanes had been following the Creery experiments since at least June 1881.

5. The morning after Brown's appearance at the Bijou, it was discovered that the box office had been robbed of $275 and all of the stage jewelry used in the play *Midnight Belle*, a performance that went on after Randall Brown's demonstrations. The Bijou management had advertised only *Midnight Belle* in newspapers; Brown's act was publicized solely through distribution of handbills.

6. "Mr. Brown Hits the Number," *New York Times*, June 10, 1889.

Chapter 12

1. Quoted on page 3 in Stuart Cumberland's program for his Steinway Hall performances on October 4 and 5, 1880, courtesy of Peter Lane.

2. S.C. Hall, "Mr. Charles Stuart Cumberland," *Light*, December 31, 1881, pp. 414–415. Writing a year after the Charing Cross performance, Hall claimed in his letter to the editor that he had been the only Spiritualist present in the group that night. He demanded to know what mediums Cumberland had sat with, and whose "tricks" he was exposing. Cumberland ignored Hall and continued with his routine. In fact, at that point, Cumberland had for the most part only seen Bishop's performances of exposures; he had actually sat with only one medium, Harry Bastian, whom Cumberland successfully exposed. Cumberland was simply lucky enough to have one medium's scalp to hang up on his promotional materials. Hall complained in his long letter, "I could only protest against a fraud that assumed to expose a fraud."

3. "A Few Antecedents of 'Stuart Cumberland,'" *BoL*, May 5, 1883.

4. Stuart C. Cumberland, "Illusionary and Fraudulent Aspects of Spiritualism," *Journal of Mental Science*, July 1881, pp. 280–287; January 1882, pp. 628–635.

5. Spiritualists everywhere dismissed Stuart Cumberland's exposure of Bastian by applying the "Transfer Law" first espoused by the editor, Mr. Hall, of the *Portland* (Maine) *Evening Courier* in 1865. This law was that any marks made on a spirit form would obviously, under appropriate conditions, be transferred to the medium in the identical locations as those on the spirit form. There-fore, finding India ink, lamp black or red cochlea on a medium when it has been thrown or squirted onto a spirit form would be normal and is to be expected.

Harry Bastian was ultimately exposed without excuses a few months later by Crown Prince Rudolf in Vienna when, once the "spirit form" appeared, Rudolf caused a secret door to suddenly drop down behind the spirit form to block access back to the cabinet. Then the lights were turned up, revealing Bastian in spirit costume running frantically around the room looking for an escape. When a door was opened, Bastian ran out into the night without his boots, and without his reputation.

6. "Thought-Reading," *The British Medical Journal*, May 13, 1882, p. 710.

7. James B. Pond, unlike some other "majors" who appeared after the Civil War, had actually been a major in the Union Army and had earned a Medal of Honor for his heroism.

8. "Mr. Cumberland's Wonderful Feats," *New York Daily Tribune*, November 29, 1882.

9. "Thought Reading Powers: A Very Successful Exhibition by Mr. Stuart Cumberland," *New York Times*, November 29, 1882.

10. "To the Editor of *Light*," *Light*, August 26, 1882, p. 392.

11. "Sittings with Spirits: A Mind-reader and a Medium Brought Together," *New York Times*, December 3, 1882.

12. "A Queer Séance — Mr. Stuart Cumberland Undertakes to Explain a 'Spirit Manifestation,' and Succeeds to His Own Satisfaction," *New York Herald*, December 3, 1882.

13. Phillips is the subject of "Writing on Closed Slates," *Light*, July 9, 1881, a letter describing a successful séance with A.J. Phillips in New York. According to the letter, Phillips, who the writer noted was not talkative, made messages appear on cleaned, closed slates, along with other tests with pieces of paper. The writer could not discern any evidence of fraud.
14. "Mr. Cumberland's Mind Reading," *New York Evening Post*, December 8, 1882.
15. "Exposing the Spirits: Stuart Cumberland's Feats," *New York Tribune*, December 10, 1882.
16. "Cumberland on Spiritualism: His Power Exhibited Before a Large Audience," *New York Times*, December 12, 1882.
17. "After Stuart Cumberland," *New York Times*, December 26, 1882.
18. "The Rival Mind-Readers," *New York Times*, December 27, 1882.
19. Quoted in "Cumberland," *BoL*, January 6, 1883.
20. Quoted in "Cumberland Exhibits to 'Empty Seats and a Bleak Gallery,'" *BoL*, March 10, 1883.

Chapter 13

1. Blackburn stood 5'9", with waxed black mustache, brown eyes, thinning black hair, and stocky build. He always wore dark suits, wing collar, and bow-tie, and usually a dusting of ash down both lapels from the cheroots he loved to smoke.
2. Douglas Blackburn, "Confessions of a Famous Medium — 1, Story of the Great 'Scientific Hoax,'" *John Bull*, December 5, 1908, p. 599.
3. Blackburn, "Confessions." Blackburn wrote: "The SPR had just been formed, but Smith and I had never heard of it. We only saw in these two gentle, courteous men [Gurney and Myers] a couple of credulous spiritualists, and we resolved that we should be doing the world a service by fooling them to the top of their bent, and then showing how easy a matter it was to 'take in' scientific observers."
4. *The Brightonian*, December 3, 1881, p. 2.
5. *The Brightonian*, December 3, 1881, p. 7.
6. In addition to complex random drawings, the most difficult information to code for a second sight act is proper names from any ethnic background with the correct pronunciation.
7. Blackburn, "Confessions." Blackburn wrote: "As editor of a widely-read paper I was able to boom Smith very effectively, I remaining in the background as the impartial journalist investigator who occasionally assisted at an experiment."
8. William F. Barrett, "Appendix to the First Report on Thought-Reading," *PSPR*, Vol. 1 (1882–1883), pp. 47–64.
9. "Second Report of the Committee on Thought-Transference," *PSPR*, Vol. 1 (1882–1883), pp. 70–97. Thought Transference was considered to be a more accurate term to describe the phenomena recorded than Thought-Reading, thus the change from the First Report.
10. Blackburn included an item on the Gurney-Myers investigation in *The Brightonian*, Saturday, December 16, 1882:

At a general meeting of the Society held at Chandos Place, London, [Saturday, December 9] and presided over by Professor Sidgewick, Messrs. F.W.H. Myers and Edmund Gurney presented an interesting report on a series of experiments in thought-reading conducted by them on Mr. G.A. Smith, the Brighton mesmerist, and Mr. Douglas Blackburn. These experiments, with those reported by another Committee of investigation, were regarded as having satisfactorily established the existence of Thought Reading. The London Daily News and the Echo have called special attention to the proceedings.

11. W.F. Barrett, "Psychical Research," *Light*, December 30, 1882, p. 592.
12. The Committee did not include the actual dates in January and April in their report. The April dates were written on the diagrams used. The dates were probably omitted for both sessions to avoid the appearance of hastiness in preparing the committee report for the General Meeting.
13. H.B. Donkin, "Occultism and Common Sense," *The Westminster Gazette*, November 26, 1907; and Sir James Chrichton-Browne, "Occultism and Telepathic Experiments," *The Westminster Gazette*, January 29, 1908.
14. This became known as the "faggot theory," i.e., if the cumulative results, both weak and strong, were all bound together like twigs into a faggot, the end result would then be strong enough to stand on its own — a position not uniformly shared within the SPR.

Chapter 14

1. The only complete copy of "Thought Reading on the Brain" with its colorful cover, is at the Bodleian Library, Oxford University. A full-color reproduction is in Barry Wiley, "The Thought Reader Craze," *Gibeciere*, Winter 2008.
2. Bishop, explaining that he wanted to be considered more than just a thought reader, once or twice a year would publish a song. (Bishop's cousin, T. Brigham Bishop, was a popular songwriter of the time.) He would buy lyrics from a songwriter and then buy music to match the lyrics from another composer. The suppliers of the compositions, unknown to each other, agreed that their names need not appear. According to British novelist Henry Byatt, who wrote lyrics at an early stage of his career, Bishop had paid him double what he could have earned selling the lyric to a music publisher and had no problem with Bishop putting his own name on Byatt's words. On occasion, Bishop would have his songs published in local newspapers as part of his publicity.
3. Augustus Thomas, "The Print of My Re-

membrance," *The Saturday Evening Post*, April 1, 1922, and Augustus Thomas, *The Print of My Remembrance* (New York: Charles Scribner's Sons, 1922).

Chapter 15

1. Stuart Cumberland, "To Mr. Gurney and Mr. Labouchère," *Pall Mall Gazette*, May 26, 1884, p. 2.
2. Grant Allen, "Mr. Stuart Cumberland's Muscle-Reading," *Pall Mall Gazette*, May 28, 1884, p. 2.
3. "Mr. Stuart Cumberland and His Critics," *Pall Mall Gazette*, May 29, 1884, p. 2.
4. H.B. Donkin, "Mr. Stuart Cumberland's Muscle-Reading," *Pall Mall Gazette*, May 30, 1884, p. 2.
5. The Lewis notebooks are in the archives of the Magic Circle in London. The Cumberland entry is through the courtesy of Peter Lane. Writing as Professor Hoffmann, Lewis was author of many prominent books on conjuring.
6. *Pall Mall Gazette*, November 24, 1884, p. 4.
7. Stuart Cumberland, *The Queen's Highway: From Ocean to Ocean* (London: Sampson Low, Marston, Searle and Rivington, 1887).
8. Stuart Cumberland, *What I Think of South Africa: Its Peoples and Its Policies* (London: Chapman & Hall, 1896). By agreement, the publishers could reject anything in Cumberland's 1897 South African manuscript that they felt might be libelous. They agreed to publish the manuscript, but when the proofs were revised, the publishers discovered a possible libel lurking in a chapter on a certain eminent personage. The offending chapter was sent to legal counsel, who split on their decision; some believed the passage libelous, and others did not. Whereupon the publishers struck the chapter out. The curious point is that the libelous chapter was partially made up of blank pages. The absence of any printed matter in the eyes of some counsel constituted libel by suggesting something about the personage was unprintable.
9. Stuart Cumberland, "The Khedive of Egypt," *The Strand Magazine*, Vol. 8 (July 1894), pp. 92–96.
10. Stuart Cumberland, *The Rabbi's Spell, A Russo-Jewish Romance* (London: Frederick Warne & Co., 1886). A review appeared in *The Guardian*, February 3, 1886, p. 181. The reviewer praised the book, then noted that reading the book would be a new experience as the book was printed in blue ink on greenish-blue paper in response to a recent statement by a noted German doctor that reading black on white could harm the reader's eyesight.
11. Stuart Cumberland, *The Vasty Deep: A Strange Story of To-day* (London: Sampson Low and Co., 1889), 2 volumes. Oscar Wilde wrote a review, which appeared in the *Pall Mall Gazette*, June 5, 1889, as "A Thought Reader's Novel." Please see Appendix D. Another review appeared in the *Manchester Guardian*, May 29, 1889, commenting that "as a story *The Vasty Deep* does not rank high."
12. Stuart Cumberland, *A Fatal Affinity: A Weird Story* (London: Blackett's Shilling Novels, 1889). Also published in the United States as *Marked for a Victim: A Tale of Modern Black Art* (New York: J.S. Olgivie, 1889; New York: Street & Smith, 1902). The American edition was bound with H. Rider Haggard's *Maiwa's Revenge*.
13. "Thought Reading and the Detection of Crime: Mr. Stuart Cumberland's Experiments," *London Evening News*, November 19, 1888.
14. Stuart Cumberland, "My Vision of Jack the Ripper," *Stuart Cumberland's Mirror*, July 29, 1889; and "Jack the Ripper Again — Another Dream," August 26, 1889. (*Stuart Cumberland's Mirror*, Ltd., was closed and liquidated on May 18, 1892; see *Commercial Gazette*, March 30, 1892, p. 308 under "Voluntary Windings-Up." Cumberland started another paper, *The Empire*, which ran through 1898.)
15. *The Times*, September 12, 1889.
16. "The Thought-Reader and the White Chapel Murders," *Local Government Gazette*, September 19, 1889.
17. Stuart Cumberland, *Spiritualism—The Inside Truth* (London: Oldhams, 1919). Reviewed in *The Occult Review*, Vol. 29 (October 1919), p. 240, by H.S. Redgrove, who considered the book "valueless" in its "lack of precision and scientific sense." Redgrove ended his review with a question: "Could the student have a better example of the fact that what men so often seek in lieu of knowledge is the confirmation of their own prejudices?"
18. Johnstone ended his performing career in prison, having been convicted of a palmistry fraud in partnership with a doctor who was also jailed. Following his release, Johnstone successfully pursued a medical career.
19. Lancaster, who claimed she did not need to touch her subjects in order to read their minds, was exposed by the famous reporter for the New York World, Nellie Bly, even to the point of Bly's duplicating Lancaster's most famous stunt, the murder scenario. See Barry H. Wiley, "Nellie Bly on Magnets, Mind Readers & Fakirs! Fakirs! Fakirs!" *Gibeciere*, Summer 2010.

Chapter 16

1. A. Taylor Innes, "Where Are the Letters? A Cross-examination of Certain Phantasms," *The Nineteenth Century*, August 1887, pp. 174–194; and "Where the Letters Are Not," *The Saturday Review*, October 8, 1887, p. 483.
2. Dr. G. Stanley Hall, "Review of *Phantasms of the Living*," *American Journal of Psychology*, Vol. 1 (1888), p. 128ff. Hall raised the issue that the Creery sisters' capacity for thought transference

seemed to decline as test conditions became more stringent, even though it was an observation already denied by Gurney in *Phantasms*. On pp. 133–134, Dr. Hall, however, after urging some tolerance for the young girls' simply becoming bored with the extended experiments, observed: "But it is strange that this decline should coincide step by step with closer study of them, and still more so that all the girls should lose this marvelous power simultaneously." An observation that even Gurney, had he been alive, would have had difficulty in answering rationally.

3. SPR Archive, Cambridge University Library, SPR.MS3/A3/3.
4. Edmund Gurney, "Note Relating to Some of the Published Experiments in Thought Transference," *PSPR*, Vol. 5 (1888), pp. 269–270.
5. To inform the percipient of the type of telepathic information being considered, e.g., a playing card, a name, a location, or a random figure, in Simon Newcomb's opinion would render the experiment scientifically useless.
6. SPR Archive, Cambridge University Library, SPR.MS3/A3/6.
7. A.M. Creery, Letter, *JSPR*, Vol. 3, no. 44 (November 1887), pp. 269–270.
8. Editor, *JSPR*, Vol. 3, no. 43, p. 164.
9. John Edgar Coover, *Experiments in Psychical Research at Leland Stanford Junior University* (Palo Alto, CA: Stanford University, 1917). Coover's Appendix C, "The Creery Experiments," pp. 463–476, offers a careful analysis of the results of the experiments with the girls. Coover concludes that codes and intelligent guessing were used throughout, even in tests where the investigators were confident that the Creerys did not know the object or thing used in the experiment.
10. W.F. Barrett, *Psychical Research* (London: Williams and Norgate; New York: Henry Holt and Company, 1911), p. 53. Note also on page 107, Barrett's comment, "How telepathy is propagated we have not the remotest idea."

Chapter 17

1. From the first report of the Literary Committee in *PSPR*, Vol.1 (1882), p.147: "we venture to introduce the words Telaesthesia and Telepathy to cover all cases of impression received at a distance." The term telepathy, which had been constructed by Frederic W.H. Myers in 1882 from the Greek words for "distance" and "intimate feeling," quickly became the preferred term. He first revealed the word to Henry Sidgwick in a letter November 2, 1882 (courtesy of Trevor Hamilton). William F. Barrett had proposed and begun using "ideoscopy," a term that quickly fell into disuse.
2. *Dickens Dictionary of London* (1879) gives St. George's Hall 800–900 seats, or 1,500 seats when including the galleries.
3. Born David Wighton, February 22, 1868, in Holloway, England. He, with J. Nevil Maskelyne, published in 1911 one of the definitive books on the conjuring arts, *Our Magic*.
4. Translucidation was not explained in Devant's *Our Magic*. Translucidation and its associated illusion, Mental Magnetism, were both fully described in Chapter XVI of Devant's later book, *Secrets of My Magic* (1936).
5. The Maskelyne letter is in the Lodge Papers in the SPR Archive at Cambridge University Library, SPR.MS35/1241, and was located for the author by Tom Ruffles and Anne Davenport.]
Maskelyne wrote, "I have been much interested in your letter concerning the 'envelope trick.'" Of course, as a rule, we refuse to say whether or not a suggested explanation of any trick is correct." The fact that Maskelyne did respond to Lodge's proposed explanations indicates that they were very wide of the mark.
"Mental Magnetism" was a two-person mindreading routine performed by Devant and Dora in which Dora on the stage carried out actions only whispered by spectators to her brother. The method for "Mental Magnetism" was entirely independent of the second portion. The cards and envelopes later used in Translucidation were distributed at the beginning of the two-part routine to ensure a quick transition from one part to the next. Maskelyne in his response to Lodge emphatically denounced the use of confederates or accomplices as a "fraudulent deceit." Maskelyne concluded his letter:

> The method employed by Devant in signaling to his sister [in "Mental Magnetism"] the requisite information is unknown to any other persons among us. Candidly, I have not the least idea of how it is done. If I wanted to know, he would tell me at once. Or, failing that, I could set to work to find out the secret for myself. But the performance is no concern of mine. I have only seen it once or twice, & without finding any desire to learn the precise means adopted. It is evidently a very ingenious conception, & I am quite content to have the benefit of it, without feeling inquisitive about it. You may, perhaps, think this rather strange; but, the fact is, we are always so busy in producing new effects that we never think about those already produced.

Chapter 18

1. Smith told Dr. Eric J. Dingwall in 1954 that he had run into Blackburn two or three times at the British Museum while Smith was still employed in SPR business. Other than those brief encounters, the two men never saw each other again.
2. Stephen Bottomore, "Smith versus Melbourne Cooper: An End to the Dispute," *Film History*, Vol. 14, no. 1 (2002), pp. 57–73; and Frank Gray, "George Albert Smith's Vision and Transformations: The Films of 1898," in Simon Popple and Vanessa Toulmin (eds.), *Visual De-*

lights: Essays on the Popular and Projected Image in the 19th Century (Trowbridge, England: Flick Books, 2000), pp. 170–180. Note also that in 1896 Professor Henry Sidgewick still considered the Blackburn-Smith telepathy experiments as genuine: Sidgewick, Henry, "Involuntary Whispering Considered in Relation to Experiments in Thought Transference," *PSPR*, Vol. 12 (1896), p. 311.

3. Where it was reviewed under the headline, "A South African Satirist," *The Spectator*, August 26, 1899, pp. 288–290. The reviewer observed, "A new satirist has arisen, and, appropriately enough, from Africa the land of surprises." After two and a half pages discussing Blackburn's book, the reviewer concluded that he would "commend the book to the reading public as a first-rate work of art, which deserves a permanent place amid the literature of social and political satire."

4. Stephen Gray, "Douglas Blackburn: Journalist into Novelist (1857–1929)," *English in Africa*, Vol. 5, no. 1 (March 1978), pp. 1–48. Contains a number of the articles written by Blackburn during his South African years, including, on page 11, a delightful brief article, "The Foolishness of H. Rider Haggard" in which Blackburn dismisses the famous novelist as only a "manufacturer of fiction." Blackburn's 1904 novel, *Richard Harley, Prospector*, was a parody of Haggard's African fiction.

5. Crichton-Browne retells the story in "Telepathy," in *The Doctor's Second Thoughts* (London: Ernest Benn, 1931), pp. 58–64. Though repeating many of the same recollections as the 1908 article, Crichton-Browne in 1931 recalled 12–15 observers, not 20, and says that Blackburn urged the assembled critics "to put them to the test." He also added, "I tried to keep an open and an even mind, but I admit that at the first glance I was not prepossessed in favor of the performers. They did not seem to me to be the sort of persons from whom we might expect scientific accuracy or any new revelation." He concluded:

I know that many men of light and leading and discernment now regard telepathy as an established fact, and in these days of wireless it would be rash to deny the possibility of it. I can only say that having diligently sought after it for many years I have never come upon any really trustworthy evidence of its existence.

6. Alice Johnson, "Mr. Blackburn's 'Confession,'" privately printed, 1909. See Appendix H for the complete text, printed with permission of the Cambridge University Library.

7. "First Report of the 'Reichenbach' Committee," *PSPR*, April 24, 1883, pp. 230–237. Barrett, Gurney and Myers were part of the ten-man committee.

8. S.J. Davey, "The Possibilities of Mal-Observation, etc., from a Practical Point of View," *JSPR*, January 1887, pp. 8–44; Richard Hodgson, "The Possibilities of Mal-Observation and Lapse of Memory from a Practical Point of View," *PSPR*, Vol. 4 (1887), pp. 381–404; S.J. Davey, "Experimental Investigation," *PSPR*, Vol. 4 (1887), pp. 405–495; and Richard Hodgson, "Mr. Davey's Imitations by Conjuring of Phenomena Sometimes Attributed to Spirit Agency," *PSPR*, Vol. 8 (1892), pp. 253–310.

9. Douglas Blackburn, "Sir Oliver Lodge's Innocence," *Sunday Times* [London], September 16, 1917.

10. Cambridge University Library, Lodge Papers, SPR Archive, SPR.MS35/145.

11. W.F. Barrett, "Transference of Thought: Sir W. Barrett's Conclusions," *Times* [London], December 20, 1924, p. 8.

12. Eric J. Dingwall, ed., *Abnormal Hypnotic Phenomena: A Survey of Nineteenth-Century Cases*, 4 volumes (New York: Barnes & Noble, 1968). See Appendix, pp. 153–58, for comments on Blackburn-Smith.

Chapter 19

1. "First Report on Thought-Reading," *PSPR*, Vol. 1, part I, July 17, 1882, p. 20.

2. Douglas Blackburn, "Confessions of a Famous Medium — IV, Private versus Professional Humbug," *John Bull*, December 26, 1908, p. 706.

Bibliography

At the end of this general bibliography the reader will find a section of references specific to the SPR/Blackburn-Smith telepathy investigations, and a section specific to the techniques of contact and non-contact mindreading.

Journal abbreviations used:
BoL *The Banner of Light*
JSPR *Journal of the Society for Psychical Research*
PASPR *Proceedings of the American Society for Psychical Research*
PSPR *Proceedings of the Society for Psychical Research*

"Additional Revelations. Mr. Bishop Explains More in Detail. The Ring, Goblet, Shot and Holding Tests. Spiritualism and Juggggery— Its Past and Future." *Boston Herald*, November 6, 1876, p. 1.

Advertisement for W.I. Bishop's appearance at the Music Hall, Jan. 4, 1887, *Boston Globe*, December 28, 1886.

Advertisements of Annie Eva Fay showing W.I. Bishop as manager: *New York Herald*, January 16, 20; February 10, 17, 1876. Also *New York Times*, January 16, 20; February 10, 17, 1876.

"After Bishop: Charles Howard Montague of the Globe." *Boston Globe*, December 24, 1886.

"After Stuart Cumberland." *New York Times*, December 26, 1882. W.I. Bishop's circular denouncing Cumberland.

Alfredson, James B. *Newmann: The Pioneer Mentalist*. Glenwood, IL: David Meyer Magic Books, 1989.

"All Who Saw J. Randall Brown...." *Cedar Rapids Evening Gazette*, March 10, 1893, p. 8. Exposure of Brown's "wire test" discussing impression pad.

"Amateur Thought Reading." *Illustrated London News*, October 19, 1889, p. 505.

Baggally, W.W. *Telepathy: Genuine and Fradulent*. London: Methuen, 1917.

Balmer, Edwin, and William MacHarg. "A Matter of Mind Reading." *Hampton's Magazine*, October 1910, pp. 477–488. A Luther Trant detective exploit. Fiction.

Barrett, W.F. "Mind-Reading versus Muscle Reading." *Nature*, July 7, 1881, p. 212.

_____. *Psychical Research*. New York: Henry Holt, 1911.

Barrett, W.F., Edmund Gurney, and Fredric H.W. Myers. "First Report on Thought-Reading." *PSPR*, Vol. 1 (July 17, 1882), p. 13.

_____, _____, and _____. "Thought-Reading." *Eclectic*, August 1882, pp. 180–188.

_____, _____, and _____. "Thought Reading." *Nineteenth Century*, June 1882, pp. 890–901.

Barrett, William. "Pseudo-Thought-Reading." *JSPR*, 1 (February 1884), p. 10.

Beard, George M[iller]. "The Physiology of Mind-Reading." *Popular Science Monthly*, 10 (February 1877). "I had established conclusively to my own mind that the so-called mind reading was really muscle-reading." p. 462.

_____. "Mind Reading by the Ear" [letter to the editor]. *Popular Science Monthly*, 11 (1878), pp. 362–363.

_____. "The Delusions of Clairvoyance." *Scribners Monthly*, Vol. 18, no. 3 (1879), pp. 433–40.

_____. *The Study of Trance, Muscle Reading and Allied Nervous Phenomena in Europe and America with a Letter on the Moral Character of Trance Subjects, and a Defence of Dr. Charcot*. [40pp.] New York: 1882.

Bell, Robert. "Stranger Than Fiction." *Cornhill Magazine*, August 1860, pp. 211–224.

Bishop, Eleanor Fletcher. *Human Vivisection of Sir Washington Irving Bishop, the First and*

World Eminent Mind Reader. Philadelphia: Seldon & Marion, 1889.

Bishop, W.I. "Bishop to Montague." *Boston Globe*, January 4, 1887.

———. "Bishop's Nerve: The Secret of His Wondrous Power." *Boston Globe*, January 2, 1887.

———. "W. Irving Bishop: Replies to the Statements of Mrs. Annie Eva Fay." *Boston Globe*, December 25, 1886.

Bishop, Washington Irving. "Spiritualism." *The Leisure Hour Magazine*. Pt. 1, January 1881, p. 45; Pt. 2, February 1881, p. 122; Pt. 3, April 1881, p. 240.

"Bishop and His Pretended 'Exposure'(?)." *BoL*, September 21, 1878.

"The Bishop and the Duke." *BoL*, July 16, 1881.

"The Bishop Case." *BoL*, June 8, 1889.

"The Bishop Expose." *BoL*, December 8, 1877.

"Bishop Owns Up at the Harvard Rooms." *BoL*, August 18, 1877.

"Bishop Reads: Not Minds But the Globe's Expose." *Boston Globe*, December 21, 1886.

"Bishop vs. Bishop." *New York Times*, June 3, 1869. The divorce suit between Eleanor Bishop and Nathaniel Bishop — again.

"Bishop's Challenge to Mediums Accepted." *BoL*, July 29, 1876.

"Bishop's Spiritual Experience." *BoL*, December 21, 1878.

Blackwood, William. "Spiritual Manifestations." *Blackwood's Edinburgh Magazine*, Vol. 73, no. 451 (May 1853), pp. 629–646.

"The Body of Nathaniel C. Bishop Exhumed." *New York Times*, April 12, 1874.

"Brooklyn Academy of Music, Thursday, June 15, 1876." Amusements Notices, *New York Herald*, June 13, 1876.

"Brooklyn Academy of Music, Thursday, June 15, 1876." Amusements Notices, *New York Herald*, June 14, 1876.

"Brown, the Mind Reader, Meets with Defeat and Exposure at Davenport, Iowa." *The Fort Wayne Sentinel*, January 20, 1897. "Wire test" fails.

"Brown, the Mind-Reader." *BoL*, October 23, 1875.

Burns, James. "About Scientific Spiritualism." *The Medium & Daybreak*, September 30, 1870, pp. 201–202.

Byatt, Henry. "How I First Met Irving Bishop." *The Magician Monthly*, April 20, 1910, p. 74, and May 20, 1910, p. 86.

———. "More About Irving Bishop." *The Magician Monthly*, June 20, 1910, p. 103.

Capper, Alfred. "Confessions of a Thought Reader." *Universal Magazine*, Christmas Number, 1901, pp. 105–111.

Capper, Alfred O[ctavius]. "We Nod and Glance and Bustle By." *A Rambler's Recollections & Reflections*. London: George Allen & Unwin, 1915.

Carlyle, E. Raymond. "Medium's Grip." *Séance*, Fall 1988. The details of how a medium can free one hand in a dark séance while the sitters are confident they are controlling both the medium's wrists.

Carpenter, William B. "Re W.I. Bishop." *Nature*, June 30, 1881, pp. 188–189.

Carrington, Hereward. *The Physical Phenomena of Spiritualism*. Boston: Herbert B. Turner, 1907.

"Charles H. Foster vs. W. Irving Bishop." *BoL*, February 17, 1877. Confrontation at Harvard Rooms in NYC between Foster and Bishop, in which Foster challenged Bishop to duplicate his billet reading as Bishop had been claiming. Bishop ran from the stage.

"A Chat with Mr. Stuart Cumberland." *Pall Mall Gazette*, June 4, 1884, p. 11.

"Chickering Hall. By General Request...." Amusements Notices, *New York Herald*, May 28, 1876.

"Chickering Hall. By General Request...." Amusements Notices, *New York Herald*, May 31, 1876.

"Chickering Hall. By Special Request, Startling Exposure!" Amusements Notices, *New York Herald*, June 7, 1876.

"Chickering Hall. Startling Exposure!" Amusements Notices, *New York Herald*, June 6, 1876.

"Chickering Hall — This (Thursday) Evening...." Amusements Notices, *New York Herald*, June 8, 1876.

"Chickering Hall — Thursday Evening." Amusements Notices, *New York Herald*, June 8, 1876.

Christopher, Milbourne. *ESP, Seers & Psychics*. New York: Thomas Y. Crowell, 1970.

———. "The Man Who Died Twice." *True Magazine*, June 1946.

"Clairvoyance." *The Leisure Hour Magazine*, June 1879, p. 412.

Clarke, James W. "Mind Reading: What It May Do for Us By and By." *Boston Globe*, January 9, 1887.

Coates, James. *How to Thought Read*. Chicago: Secular Science, 1900.

Crockett, Art. "The Strange Death of Washington Irving Bishop." *Fate*, October 1958.

"Crumbs of Comfort for Orthodoxy." *BoL*, July 8, 1876.

Cumberland, Stuart C. *People I Have Read*. London: C. Arthur Pearson, 1905.

_____. "Pin-finding and Thought-Reading at Charing Cross." *Pall Mall Gazette*, 39 (1884), 10.

_____. *Spiritualism—The Inside Truth.* London: Odhams, 1919.

_____. *That Other World: Personal Experiences of Mystics and Their Mysticism.* London: Grant Richards, 1918.

_____. "A Thought-Reader's Experience." *Nineteenth Century*, 20 (1886), pp. 867–885.

_____. *A Thought-Reader's Thoughts.* London: Sampson Low, Marston, Searle & Rivington, 1888. First serialized in *The Echo* beginning July 7, 1888.

"Cumberland Exhibits to 'Empty Seats and a Bleak Gallery.'" *BoL*, March 10, 1883.

"Cumberland in Australia." *BoL*, June 26, 1886.

"Cumberland on Spiritualism: His Power Exhibited Before a Large Audience." *New York Times*, December 10, 1882.

D.C. [De Morgan, Sophia]. *From Matter to Spirit: The Results of Ten Years' Experience in Spirit Manifestations.* London: Longman, Green, Longman, Roberts and Green, 1863. Preface by Augustus de Morgan.

"Dallying with Spirits: Mr. Cumberland's Mind Reading and Mrs. Fox's Ghosts." *New York Times*, December 2, 1882.

Devant, David. "Illusion and Disillusion." *Windsor Magazine*, December 1935.

Dickens, Charles. "Thought Reading." *All the Year Around*, July 17, 1886. Reprinted in *M.U.M.*, February 1954, p. 371.

Dingwall, Eric J. *Some Human Oddities: Studies in the Queer, the Uncanny and the Fanatical.* London: Home & Van Thal, 1947.

"The *Doctors*, Too, Pronounced...." *BoL*, June 8, 1889.

Donkin, Horatio. "Miracles and Medium-Craft." *Fortnightly Review*, Vol. 34 (1883), pp. 263–277.

_____. "Note on Thought-Reading." *Nineteenth Century*, July 1882, pp. 131–133.

Downey, Edmund. "Washington Irving Bishop." Chapter VII in *Twenty Years Ago*. London: Horst and Blackett, 1905. Pp. 171–190.

"Eglinton and Cumberland." *BoL*, February 14, 1885.

Elliotson, Dr. John. "The Departed Spirits." *The Zoist*, July 1853, pp. 191–201.

"An English Challenge to Stuart Cumberland." *BoL*, February 3, 1883.

"English Notes." *BoL*, September 21, 1878.

"Entertainment Extraordinary!" Amusements Notices, *New York Herald*, June 4, 1876.

"Entre Nous." *Truth*, August 2, 1883.

"Exposing the Mediums: Spiritualistic Tricks Shown Up by Mr. Cumberland." *New York Times*, December 12, 1882.

"Exposing the Spirits: Stuart Cumberland's Feats." *New York Tribune*, December 10, 1882.

"A Few Antecedents of 'Stuart Cumberland.'" *BoL*, May 5, 1883.

"The Fowler-Cumberland Challenge...." *BoL*, January 2, 1882.

Frazer, Persifor, Jr. "Mind Reading." Paper read before the Social Science Association of Philadelphia, May 12, 1875.

Froude, J.A. "A Cagliostro of the Second Century." *Nineteenth Century*, September 1879, pp. 551–570.

Gauld, Alan. *Founders of Psychical Research.* London: Routledge & Kegan Paul, 1968.

Gibson, Walter B. "The Strange Case of Washington Irving Bishop." *Mystery Digest*, May 1957.

Gow, David. "Amongst the Thought Readers." *Occult Review*, Vol. 46 (November 1927), pp. 318–320.

Gresham, William Lindsay. "King of the Spook Workers." In Alexander Klein, ed., *The Double Dealers: Adventures in Grand Deception.* New York: J.B. Lippincott, 1958. An entertaining portrayal of D.D. Home.

"He Was Mind Reader Bishop's Tutor." *Trenton Times*, April 21, 1890.

Hemingway, Mollie Ziegler. "Look Who's Irrational Now." *Wall Street Journal*, September 19, 2008.

"Hide and Seek at Westminster—'Thought Reading' by Mr. Irving Bishop." *The Graphic*, June 28, 1884.

Hodgson, Richard. "Telepathy." *Chautauquan*, January 1893, pp. 409–413. Dismisses Bishop and Cumberland performances as just the "willing game" and goes on to discuss "real" telepathy.

Houdini, Harry. "Washington Irving Bishop: A Master Mind Reader." *The Conjurers' Monthly Magazine*, Vol. 2, nos. 11 and 12 (July 15, 1908, and August 15, 1908).

"How Bishop Fooled the 'Solid Men of Boston.'" *BoL*, February 3, 1877.

Huxley, T.H. "Spiritualism Unmasked." *Pall Mall Gazette*, January 1, 1889. Reprinted in *Linking Ring*, September 1954.

"Impostors on the Wing." *BoL*, April 15, 1882. (J.R. Brown.)

"The Invisible World." *The Boston Banner*, October 12, 1853, p. 719.

"It Seems That Young Bishop, the Scamp...." *BoL*, August 9, 1879.

"J. Page Hopps in re W.I. Bishop." *BoL*, April 12, 1879.

"J. Randall Brown, Appearing as a Mind Reader." *The Oshkosh Daily Northwestern*, June 15, 1891.

"J. Randall Brown, The Celebrated Mind-Reader and Botch Sleight-of-Hand Performer." *Decatur Daily Republican*, February 27, 1882. A scathing review of Brown's performance. "Not worth the 25¢."

Jay, Ricky. *Learned Pigs and Fireproof Women*. New York: Villard Books, 1986.

Jenkins, Elizabeth. *The Shadow and the Light: A Defence of Daniel Dunglas Home, the Medium*. London: Hamish Hamilton, 1982.

"Johnstone, the Mind Reader." *Religio-Philosophical Journal*, September 27, 1890.

"Johnstone the Mind Reader." *Religio-Philosophical Journal*, October 11, 1890.

Koval [Briggs], Frank. *Washington Irving Bishop: The Man Who Died Twice*. Privately printed, 1992.

Lamont, Peter. *The First Psychic*. New York: Little, Brown, 2005.

"The Latest English 'Medium Exposer.'" *BoL*, December 16, 1882, quoting *New York Herald*, December 8, 1882.

Leavitt, M[ichael]. B[ennett]. *50 Years of Theatrical Management, 1859–1909*. New York: Broadway Publishing, 1912.

"Let Us Preserve Old South...." *BoL*, January 13, 1877.

Lodge, Oliver. "Thought Transference." *The Forum*, 41 (1909), pp. 56–62.

Luckhurst, Roger. *The Invention of Telepathy*. Oxford: Oxford University Press, 2002.

———. "Passages in the Invention of the Psyche: Mind-reading in London, 1881–1884." In *Transactions and Encounters: Science and Culture in the Nineteenth Century*. Manchester: Manchester University Press, 2002.

Lund, Robert. "Lore of the Mystics: Mother Fletcher." *M.U.M.*, July 1958. C.A. George Newmann's comments on Bishop.

"A Marvelous Feat." *Davenport Daily Leader*, July 14, 1896. Brown's "wire test."

McGrath, D.J. "Brain Waves: Are They Floating Around Through Space?" *Boston Globe*, December 19, 1886.

Medhurst, R.G. *Crookes and the Spirit World*, New York: Taplinger, 1972, p. 237. The letter was first published in the *Light*, May 12, 1900.

"A Medium Turned Exposer." *BoL*, September 23, 1876.

"Mediums as Pretended Exposers of Spiritualism." *BoL*, August 5, 1876.

Minch, Stephen. *From Witchcraft to Card Tricks*. Seattle: Hermetic Press, 1991.

"Mind Reading." *St. Joseph Herald*, June 19, 1880. A public invitation to J.R. Brown to demonstrate his powers.

"Mind Reading." *The Waukesha Freeman*, January 8, 1880. J.R. Brown performance.

"Mind-Reading, or Psychometry." *BoL*, March 3, 1877. (J.R. Brown.)

"Mindreader Brown in Washington." *Hornellsville Weekly Tribune*, April 25, 1890.

"Mindreading." *BoL*, October 31, 1874.

"Mindreading." *The Swiss Cross*, Vol. 1, no. 1 (January 1887), p. 13. Magazine of the Agassiz Society.

"Misrepresentations of J. Randall Brown." *BoL*, February 25, 1882.

"Mr. Bishop and the Western Infirmary." *BoL*, April 26, 1879.

"Mr. Bishop's Promised Exposure." *BoL*, November 18, 1876.

"Mr. Brown Hits the Number." *New York Times*, June 10, 1889.

"Mr. Brown, the Mind-Reader, and the Eddys." *BoL*, November 21, 1874.

"Mr. Cumberland's Challenge." *New York Times*, December 3, 1882.

"Mr. Cumberland's Mind Reading." *[New York] Evening Post*, December 8, 1882, p. 1.

"Mr. Cumberland's Wonderful Feats." *New York Daily Tribune*, November 29, 1882.

"Mr. Curtis' Rejoinder." *BoL*, September 23, 1876.

"Mr. Geo. Wm. Curtis in *Harper's Magazine* on Spiritualism." *BoL*, July 29, 1876.

"Mr. Irving Bishop, 'Thought Reader.'" *The Illustrated London News*, June 23, 1883, p. 622.

"Mr. Irving Bishop's 'Thought-Reading' Experiments." *Pall Mall Gazette*, June 4, 1884, p. 10.

"Mr. J. Randall Brown, the World-Famed Mind Reader and Exposer of Modern Spiritualism." *New Philadelphia Democrat*, December 13, 1877.

"Mr. Maskelyne and Mr. Irving Bishop." *Sussex Daily News*, December 3, 1885.

Mr. P.A. Johnstone...." *BoL*, September 27, 1890. Description of Johnstone reading the mind of a Chicago hotel manager and opening the hotel safe, after having all five of his senses neutralized with blindfolds, gloves, ear and nose plugs, and while smoking a cigar. Johnstone did not touch anyone.

"Mr. W.I. Bishop." *BoL*, November 11, 1876.

"Mr. W.I. Bishop...." Religious Notices, *New York Herald*, May 28, 1876.

"Mr. W.I. Bishop in Boston." *BoL*, November 4, 1876.

"Mr. W.I. Bishop's Career in Glasgow." *BoL*, May 31, 1879.

"Mr. W.I. Bishop's Exposure of Spiritualism." *BoL*, November 11, 1876.

"Mr. Washington Irving Bishop." *BoL*, July 1, 1876.

"Mr. Washington Irving Bishop." *The Illustrated Sporting and Dramatic News*, June 25, 1881. Courtesy Peter Lane.

Montague, Charles H. "Bishop Is a Success: His Feats in Music Hall Last Evening." *Boston Globe*, January 5, 1887.

_____. "Bishop's Defense: Mr. Montague Has Something to Say About It." *Boston Globe*, January 3, 1887. Front page, center.

_____. "Mind Readers: Bishop Seems to Think There Are Two Roads." *Boston Globe*, December 26, 1886.

Moore, R. Laurence. *In Search for White Crows: Spiritualism, Parapsychology, and American Culture*. New York: Oxford University Press, 1977.

Morley, Henry, and W.H. Wills. "The Ghost of the Cock Lane Ghost." *Household Words*, 6 (1853), pp. 217–223.

"Muscle Reading: Death of Mr. Stuart Cumberland." *The London Times*, March 3, 1922, p. 14 (also a brief notice on page 1).

"Muscle-Reading by Mr. Stuart Cumberland: A Reception at the 'Pall Mall Gazette Office,'" *Pall Mall Gazette*, May 24, 1884, pp. 1–2.

N.E.E.N. "Spirit Rapping." *The Zoist*, April 1853, pp. 86–96.

Nardis, Fred. *Wonder Shows: Performing Science, Magic and Religion in America*. New Brunswick, NJ: Rutgers University Press, 2005.

"A New 'Mind-Reader.'" *BoL*, September 20, 1890. Paul Alexander Johnstone, twenty-six. In Chicago, he duplicated Bishop's last presentation at the Player's, then fainted, recovered, finished the test, and fainted again. The *Boston Globe* commented on the risk Johnstone took in fainting with doctors present.

Noakes, Richard. "The 'Bridge Which Is Between Physical and Psychical Research': William Fletcher Barrett, Sensitive Flames, and Spiritualism." *The British Journal for the History of Science*, 42 (2004), pp. 419–464.

_____. "Spiritualism, Science and the Supernatural in mid–Victorian Britain." In Nicola Brown, Carolyn Burdett and Pamela Thurschwell, eds. *The Victorian Supernatural*. Cambridge: Cambridge University Press, 2004.

_____. "Telegraphy Is an Occult Art: Cromwell Fleetwood Varley and the Diffusion of Electricity to the Other World." *The British Journal for the History of Science*, 32 (1999), pp. 421–459.

O'Donnell, Bernard. "The Masked Medium Spoof." In Alexander Klein, ed. *Grand Deception*. New York: J.B. Lippincott, 1955.

Palfreman, Jon. "William Crookes: Spiritualism and Science." *Ethics in Science & Medicine*, Vol. 3 (1976), pp. 211–227.

"'Petticoat' Bishop." *BoL*, November 17, 1888.

"Petticoat Bishop in Glasgow." *BoL*, April 5, 1879.

"Petticoat Bishop (W.I.) is now kicking...." *BoL*, February 8, 1879.

Podmore, Frank. *The Newer Spiritualism*. London: T. Fisher Unwin, 1910.

"Politicians at Play: 'Thought-Reading' at the House of Commons." *Illustrated London News*, June 28, 1884. Sketches of Cumberland performing with members of Parliament including Prime Minister William Gladstone.

Prince, Walter Franklin. *The Enchanted Boundary: Being a Survey of Negative Reactions to Claims of Psychic Phenomena, 1820–1930*. Boston: Boston Society for Psychical Research, 1930.

"Professor Huxley Discovers an Honest Man — Mr. W.I. Bishop Is the Fortunate Individual — Dr. Carpenter Is Made Happy." *BoL*, September 27, 1879.

"The Rival-Mind Readers." *New York Times*, December 27, 1882. Cumberland's and Pond's response to Bishop's attack.

"Rivaling Stuart Cumberland." *New York Times*, December 13, 1882. George M. Beard's duplication of many of Cumberland's thought reading demonstrations.

Robertson, George Croom. "The Physiology of Mind-Reading." *Nature*, July 14, 1881, p. 236.

Romanes, George. "Dr. W.B. Carpenter and Mr. W.I. Bishop." *Nature*, July 7, 1881, p. 211.

_____. "Thought Reading." *Nature*, June 23, 1881, pp. 171–172.

"Save Old South." *BoL*, February 10, 1877.

"The Scope of Psychometry. Further Observations by Prof. J.R. Buchanan upon the Science of Mind Reading — A Remarkable Instance in His Own Experience." *BoL*, April 3, 1875. Details of J. Randall Brown's performance at New Haven, Connecticut.

"'Scrutator,' 'Sleight of Touch.'" *Truth*, June 26, 1884, p. 954.

"Searching for a Soul." *BoL*, June 29, 1889.

"A Sensational Second Sight Act." *Goldston's Magician Annual, 1909–10*. London: A.W. Gamage. David Devant's Translucidation illusion appears on p. 75.

A Serious Inquirer. "Spirit Manifestations." *The Patriot*, September 19, 1853, p. 618.

"Sittings with Spirits: A Mind-reader and a Medium Brought Together." *New York Times*, December 3, 1882.

"Something for Massachusetts Lawmakers to Think About." *BoL*, May 25, 1889.

"Something That Bishop Don't Do." *BoL*, November 18, 1876.

"The Soul and the Scalpel." *BoL*, June 29, 1889.

"Spirit Rapping." *The National Miscellany: A Magazine of General Literature*, May 5, 1853, pp. 124–133.

"Spirits and Mediums." *BoL*, July 8, 1876.

"Spiritualism a Pestilent Superstition." *BoL*, August 12, 1876.

"Spiritualism and Its Agencies on Trial." Amusements Notices, *New York Herald*, May 18, 1876.

"Spiritualism and Its Agencies on Trial." Religious Notices, *New York Herald*, May 14, 1876.

"Spiritualism and Its Agencies on Trial." Religious Notices, *New York Herald*, June 4, 1876.

"Spiritualism Outdone." *New York Times*, July 4, 1874. J.R. Brown's first appearance in New York.

"Spiritualism Unveiled. Mr. Bishop's Exposures in Music Hall. 'Spooks' and 'Spirits' Sadly Demoralized. The Humbug Hardy's a Hard Act." *Boston Herald*, November 5, 1876, p. 1.

"Spiritualism Versus Jugglery." *New York Times*, June 2, 1876.

"Startling Exposure. W. Irving Bishop." Amusements Notices, *New York Herald*, June 3, 1876.

Stein, Gordon. *The Sorcerer of Kings: The Case of Daniel Dunglas Home and William Crookes.* Buffalo: Prometheus Books, 1993.

"Stop Making Sense: Why Do People Believe in Magic?" *The Economist*, October 30, 1992, p. 99.

Stuart-Glennie, John S. "Thought Reading as a Class of Mutual Influence." *Leisure Hour*, Vol. 31 (1882), pp. 688–691.

Sugden, Rev. E.H. "Note on Muscle Reading." *PSPR*, Vol. 1 (December 1883), p. 291.

"The Sunday *Herald* on Bishop." *BoL*, November 11, 1876.

Tabori, Paul. *Companions of the Unseen*, New York: University Books, 1968.

Teale, Oscar. "The Mystery of Spiritualism—Magic Versus Spiritualism." *The Sphinx*, no. 5 (August 1925), p. 183, and no. 6 (September 1925), p. 207.

"That 'Exposure.'" *BoL*, November 25, 1876.

Thomas, Augustus. "The Print of My Remembrance." *The Saturday Evening Post*, April 1, 1922. Thomas was Bishop's last advance man, who after Bishop's death went on to write seventy plays.

_____. *The Print of My Remembrance*. New York: Charles Scribner's Sons, 1922.

_____. *The Witching Hour*. New York: Harper & Brothers, 1908. Novel drawn from Thomas' play of the same name that premiered in New York in 1907. (The witching hour was 2 A.M.) The 1907 play was based, in turn, on his one-act play of 1890, *A Constitutional Point*, which became Act 2 of *The Witching Hour*. Both plays were based on Thomas' experiences with W.I. Bishop.

Thomas, Frank W. "Odd Adventures in Queer Callings II—Confessions of a Mind Reader." *The Saturday Evening Post*, November 10, 1900, p. 23.

"A Thought Reader on His Travels." *Pall Mall Gazette*, December 30, 1884, p. 11.

"Thought Reading." *British Medical Journal*, May 13, 1881, p. 710.

"Thought Reading." *British Medical Journal*, May 21, 1881, p. 814.

"Thought Reading." *Lancet*, May 14, 1881, p. 795.

"Thought Reading." *Saturday Review*, May 21, 1881, pp. 652–653.

"Thought Reading." *Standard*, May 10, 1881, p. 5.

"Thought Reading Demonstrations." *British Medical Journal*, February 23, 1881, p. 383.

"Thought Reading or Telepathy: An Open Letter to Mr. Stuart Cumberland, by A Student of Spiritual Science." Melbourne, Australia, 1886.

"Thought-Reading Powers: A Very Successful Exhibition by Mr. Stuart Cumberland." *New York Times*, November 29, 1882.

"Thought Reading Tricks for Amateurs." *Strand Magazine*, December 1919.

Thurschwell, Pamela. "George Eliot's Prophecies: Coercive Second Sight and Everyday Thought Reading." In Nicola Brown, Carolyn Burdett and Pamela Thurschwell, eds. *The Victorian Supernatural.* Cambridge: Cambridge University Press, 2004.

Truesdell, John. *The Bottom Facts Concerning the Science of Spiritualism.* New York: G.W. Carleton & Co., 1883.

The Truth. July 26, 1883. A faked version of *Truth* by W.I. Bishop.

Tuckett, Ivor L. *The Evidence for the Supernatural.* London: Kegan Paul, Trench, Truebner & Co., 1911.

Van Loan, Charles E. "Tales of the Midnight Club." *Los Angeles Examiner*, September 18, 1904. A comic mind-reading short story.

"Visiting the Mediums: Wonderful Revelations About Business and Pleasure. Mr. W.I. Bishop in the Role of an Inquiring Female. Startling

Results from Foundationless Causes." *Boston Sunday Herald*, November 12, 1876.

"W. Irving Bishop — Who Whilom Gulled...." *BoL*, July 27, 1878.

"W. Irving Bishop in London." *BoL*, December 21, 1878. Describes the photograph of Bishop in female dress.

"W. Irving Bishop, the Alleged Mind-reader...." *BoL*, January 16, 1886.

"The War Between Mr. Labouchère and...." *BoL*, June 21, 1884.

"Washington Irving Bishop." *BoL*, April 5, 1879.

"Washington Irving Bishop." *BoL*, May 18, 1889.

"We Learn from the *Cornubian and Redruth Times*...." *BoL*, July 25, 1885.

Wells, H.G. "Peculiarities of Psychical Research." *Nature*, December 6, 1894, pp. 121–122. A coldly critical, even contemptuous review of Frank Podmore, *Peculiarities of Psychical Research* (London: Walter Scott, 1894). The Wells review prompted pro and con responses under the same title from Karl Pearson, *Nature*, December 13, 1894, p. 153; from Edward T. Dixon, and a second letter from Karl Pearson, December 27, 1894, p. 200; and from Oliver Lodge, *Nature*, January 10, 1895, p. 247.

"Whistle for Bishop. He Is Wanted to Come In and Explain." *Boston Globe*, December 28, 1886.

Whyte, Thomson. "Re W.I. Bishop." *Nature*, pp. 211–212, July 7, 1881. Proposes two methods for the Bishop card trick that so impressed Dr. W.B. Carpenter, which includes a basic description of equivoque, which Whyte refers to as a children's trick.

Wiley, Barry H. *The Indescribable Phenomenon: The Life and Mysteries of Anna Eva Fay*. Seattle: Hermetic Press, 2005.

_____. "Nellie Bly on Magnets, Mind Readers & Fakirs! Fakirs! Fakirs!" *Gibecière*, Summer 2010.

_____. "The Thought Reader Craze." *Gibecière*, Winter 2008.

Winter, Alison. *Mesmerized: Powers of Mind in Victorian Britain*. Chicago: University of Chicago Press, 1998.

"The Youthful Mr. Bishop...." *BoL*, November 1, 1879.

Zolotow, Maurice. "The Mind Reader and the Autopsy." *Detective, the Magazine of True Crime*, Summer 1951, front cover, pp. 1–2, 75–90, and back cover.

The SPR Blackburn-Smith Telepathy Investigations

Barrett, W.F., Edmund Gurney, and F.W.H. Myers. "First Report on Thought Transference." *PSPR*, Vol. 1, part 1, 1882, pp. 13–64.

Blackburn, Douglas. "Animal Superstitions." *Man*, December 1904, pp. 181–183. Omens and beliefs of various South African tribes related to animals and birds.

_____. "Confessions of a Famous Medium." *John Bull*, December 5, 1908, p. 590; December 12, 1908, p. 628; December 19, 1908, p. 671; December 26, 1908, pp. 706–708; January 2, 1909, p. 7; January 9, 1909, p. 39.

_____. "Ghosts and Mediums I Have Known." *Tonbridge Free Press*, February 13–April 30, 1920. A series of five articles.

_____. "Kaffir Telepathy." *The Spectator*, December 13, 1902, pp. 938–939. Written from Natal. He concludes with, "That news is sometimes transmitted under conditions unknown to Europeans is, I am satisfied, a fact; but the explanation lies neither in the legs of a horse nor the lungs of a Kaffir."

_____. "A Sense of Humor." *Boston Globe*, September 12, 1920, p. 13. A short story.

_____. "Sir Oliver Lodge's Innocence." *London Sunday Times*, September 16, 1917.

_____. "Thought Reading Extraordinary." *Light*, August 26, 1882.

_____. *Thought Reading or Modern Mysteries Explained: Being Chapters on Thought-Reading, Occultism, Mesmerism, &c. Forming a Key to the Psychological Puzzles of the Day*. London: Field and Tuer, 1884. One hundred pages.

Blackburn, Douglas, and Captain Waithman Caddell. *The Detection of Forgery: A Practical Handbook*. London: Charles & Edwin Layton, 1909.

Blackburn, Douglas, with Captain W. Waithman Caddell. *Secret Service in South Africa*. London: Cassell & Co., 1911. See pp. 88–89 for H. Rider Haggard's letter regarding Kaffir telepathy in response to Blackburn's letter in *The Spectator*, December 13, 1902.

Blackburn, Douglas, et al. "Confessions of a 'Telepathist.'" *JSPR*, October 1911, pp. 115–132.

Chrichton-Browne, James. "Occultism and Telepathic Experiments." *The Westminster Gazette*, January 29, 1908, p. 3.

"Confessions of a 'Telepathist.' Mr. Douglas Blackburn & the Scientists. 30-Year Hoax Exposed. How the Deception was Planned and Worked." *London Daily News*, September 1, 1911.

Croft-Cooke, Rupert. *The Altar in the Loft*. London: Putnam, 1960. Note Chapter VIII, "Douglas Blackburn," and later Blackburn references, pp. 208–211, pp. 218–221.

_____. *The Glittering Pastures*. London: Putnam, 1962. Note Chapter Nine, "The Vickybird," and Chapter Ten, "Bateman's," on Douglas Blackburn; note also comments on Aleister Crowley and Rudyard Kipling.

"Death of Mr. Douglas Blackburn: The Looker-On." *Tonbridge Free Press*, April 5, 1929, p. 3.

Dingwall, E.J. "Dr. Gauld and Mr. Hall." *JSPR*, 43 (1965), pp. 218–220.

Dingwall, Eric J., ed. *Abnormal Hypnotic Phenomena: A Survey of Nineteenth-Century Cases*. 4 volumes. New York: Barnes & Noble, 1968. See Appendix, pp. 153–158, for comments on Blackburn-Smith.

Donkin, H.B. "Occultism and Common-Sense." *The Westminster Gazette*, November 26, 1907, p. 3.

Epperson, Gordon. *The Mind of Edmund Gurney*. Madison, NJ: Fairleigh Dickinson University Press, 1997.

Gauld, Alan. "Mr. Hall and the S.P.R." *JSPR*, 43 (1965), pp. 53–62.

_____. "Rejoinder." *JSPR*, 43 (1965), pp. 220–224.

Gilbert, Mostyn. "J. Fraser Nicol: An Appreciation of His Dedication to Psychical Research." *JSPR*, 56 (1990), pp. 113–124.

Gray, Stephen. *Douglas Blackburn*. Boston: Twayne, 1984.

_____. "Douglas Blackburn: Journalist into Novelist (1857–1929)." *English in Africa*, Vol. 5, no. 1 (1978), pp. 1–48. In preparing this article along with other sources, Gray purchased all of the Blackburn materials collected by Trevor H. Hall for his book on Edmund Gurney.

_____. *Free-Lancers and Literary Biography in South Africa*. Amsterdam: Editions Rodopi B.B., 1999.

Gurney, Edmund, F.W.H. Myers, and W.F. Barrett. "Second Report on Thought Transference." *PSPR*, Vol. 1, part 2 (1882), pp. 70–97.

H.B.L. "Douglas Blackburn: An Appreciation." *Tonbridge Free Press*, April 5, 1929.

Hall, Trevor H. "Some Comments on Mr. Fraser Nicol's Review of *The Strange Case of Edmund Gurney*." *International Journal of Parapsychology*, Summer 1968, pp. 149–164.

_____. *The Strange Case of Edmund Gurney*. London: Gerald Duckworth, 1964. BBC2 produced a show for the *Theater 625* series based on the Hall book. Titled *The Magicians:*

Edmund Gurney and the Brighton Mesmerist, the show aired on October 29, 1967. Script by Ken Taylor, with Richard Todd appearing as Douglas Blackburn. It should be noted that any conclusions drawn by Trevor H. Hall in this book are suspect, as Hall's research technique relied on introducing a surmise in one chapter that becomes a fact in a later chapter, a serious research issue pointed out in several reviews of the book.

Johnson, Alice. *Mr. Blackburn's Confession*. Privately printed for members of the SPR, London, 1909. Four pages. SPR Archives, Cambridge University Library. See Appendix H for complete text.

Lambert, G.W. "*The Strange Case of Edmund Gurney* by Trevor H. Hall." *JSPR*, 60 (1966), pp. 78–84.

Nicol, J. Fraser. "A Rejoinder—And Some New Facts." Unpublished manuscript, 26 pages, 1968. J. Fraser Nichol Papers, SPR Archive, Cambridge University Library. Article was intended to be published in the *International Journal of Parapsychology* as a response to Trevor Hall's "Some Comments," but was withheld when pending libel action was settled out of court.

_____. "The Silences of Mr. Trevor Hall." *International Journal of Parapsychology*, Winter 1966. A highly critical review of the Hall book on Edmund Gurney that drew an initial threat of a libel action.

R.M. "Thought Reading." *Light*, June 11, 1881, p. 181.

Techniques of Contact and Non-contact Mindreading

(Books and articles devoted to explaining or performing contact and non-contact mindreading.)

"All About 'Thought Reading,' a Complete Exposure of Modern Methods of Fooling the Public." *Illustrated Police Budget*, January 5, 1907. Courtesy Peter Lane.

Atkinson, William Walker. *Practical Mind Reading*. Philadelphia: Lyal Book Company, 1907.

Banachek. *Pschophysiological Thought Reading, or Muscle Reading and the Ideomotor Response Revealed*. Houston: Magic Inspirations, 2002.

Beard, George M. *The Study of Trance, Muscle-Reading and Allied Nervous Phenomena in Europe and America*. Privately printed, 40 pages, 1882.

Bishop, W.I. *Houdin and Heller's Second Sight Explained*. Edinburgh: John Menzies & Co.,

78 pages, one shilling, 1880. Booklet written by Frederick Wickes, who used Bishop's name "by arrangement." Wickes wrote an expanded version in 1907, claiming to have developed several stunts for Bishop's act: Wickes, Frederick, *Thought Reading Explained, Second Sight and "Spiritual" Manifestations*. London: Simpkin, Marshall, Hamilton, Kent, 104 pages, one shilling, 1907.

Burlingame, H.J. *How to Read People's Minds or, The Mystery of Mind Reading Revealed.* Chicago: 1905.

Carleton, Henry Guy. "W. Irving Bishop's Tricks." *New York World*, March 6, 1887. A detailed and humorous exposure.

Corinda, Tony. *13 Steps to Mentalism.* New York: Louis Tannen, 1968. Step Two: Pencil, Lip, Sound, Touch and Muscle Reading.

Dexter, S. Edward. *Entertaining with Contact Mindreading.* London: George Armstrong, 1952.

Dumont, Theron Q. "Higher Phases of Mind-Reading." *Advanced Thought*, May 1917, pp. 113–16. Experiments to include finding a card in a deck, working out a trip on a map, word in a book, duplicating figures.

———. "Mind-Reading Experiments." *Advanced Thought*, March 1917. Contact thought reading exercises.

———. "More About Mind-Reading." *Advanced Thought*, April 1917, pp. 63–65. A continuation of the March article with more experiments.

Fitzkee, Dariel. *Contact Mind Reading Expanded.* 3rd ed. Oakland, CA: Magic Limited, 1970. (1st ed., 1935; 2nd ed., 1945.)

Gatchell, Charles. "The Methods of Mind Readers." *Forum*, 11, April 25, 1891, pp. 192–204.

Hanussen-Steinschneider, Erik Jan. *Mind Reading and Telepathy.* Jimmy+Anita Bix, 2008. A translated new edition of the work originally published by Waldheim-Eberle Verlag, A.G., Vienna, 1920.

Larsen, William W., Jr., ed. *The Mental Mysteries and Other Writings of William W. Larsen, Sr.* Los Angeles: The Genii Publishing Co., 1977. Chapter 5: Contact and Non-Contact Mindreading.

Macaire, Sid. *Mind Reading or Muscle Reading as Exhibited by Washington Irving Bishop and Others.* London: Simpkin, Marshall, 1889.

Maskelyne, J.N. "The Art and Craft of Thought-Reading." *Pall Mall Gazette*, March 1907.

McGrath, D.J., and Charles Howard Montague. "The SECRET: How the Minds of Many Men are Read." *Boston Globe*, December 19, 1886.

Nelson, Robert. *Hellstromism*. Columbus, OH: Nelson Enterprises, 1935.

Newmann, C.A. George. "Experimental Telepathy with Playing Cards." In Harry Houdini, ed., *Elliott's Last Legacy.* Adams, 1923; reprint, Toronto: Coles, 1980. p. 274.

Roberts, Edmund Wilson. "Successful Attempts in Scientific Mind-Reading." *Cosmopolitan*, March 1899, pp. 561–564. Contact mindreading experiments beginning with pin-finding.

Satori. *Making Contact, The Real Secrets of Contact Mindreading.* Humble, TX: H&R Magic Books, 1998.

Taylor, Walford. "Contact Mindreading — A Chronological Bibliography Review — Part 1." *The Magic Circular*, June 2011.

———. "Contact Mindreading — A Chronological Bibliography Review — Part 2." *The Magic Circular*, August 2011.

———. "Contact Mindreading — An Introduction." *The Magic Circular*, December 2010.

———. "Getting to Grips with CMR." *The Magic Circular*, April 2011.

———. "Thirteen Steps to Contact Mentalism." *The Magic Circular*, February 2011.

Index

Numbers in **_bold italics_** indicate pages with photographs.

Alexander (stage mindreader) 181
Allen, Grant 132–133

Barrett, Prof. William Fletcher 63, 70–74, 113, 116, 142, 144, 162–164; see also Creery Children
Beard, Dr. George Miller 38, 44, 58–59, 105
Beecher, Rev. Henry Ward 104–105
Bentley, Phyllis 137
Bishop, Eleanor Fletcher 65, 130
Bishop, Washington Irving (Wellington) 2, 65, _**66**_, _**67**_, _**68**_, _**69**_, 75–76, 144; autopsy 129; British National Spiritualist Association Investigation 78; card trick **77**–78, 79–81, 85–91, 102, 108, 110, _**112**_, 123–126, _**127**_, 128; death 130
Blackburn, Douglas 85, 105–106, 110–113; Brighton tests 114–116; Dean's Yard test 116–117, _**118**_, _**119**_; John Bull articles 157–161; London Daily News article 161–163, 181; withdraws from SPR testing 120–121, 152, 153, 155
Breslaw, Philip 174
Brown, J. (John) Randall 3, 38, _**39**_, 40, _**41**_, 58–62, 63–_**64**_, 94, _**95**_, 183; death 97; telegraph test 60–61; Wire Test 96–97
Burlingame, H.J. 178–180
Burns, James 198–199

Carpenter, Dr. William B. 70, 76–78
Cicero 47
Coding of a Random Drawing 180–181
Colles, Henry 195
Contact mindreading (muscle reading) 182–184
Cox, Edward W. 28, 48, 54–55; coins the term _psychic_ 11
Creery, Rev. Andrew Macreight 74, 82–84, 92, 142–143
Creery children 86–87, 92–93, 141–142
Crichton-Browne, Sir James 154–156

Crookes, Mrs. Ellen 48
Crookes, William 17; discovery of Thallium 18, _**19**_, 20–23, 45–46, _**51**_, 52, _**53**_, 56–57, 78; see also Crookes-Fay galvanometer tests; Home, Daniel Dunglas; Fay, Annie Eva
Crookes-Fay galvanometer tests, February 19, 1875 187–199
Cumberland, Stuart Charles Francis 1–3, 9, 99–100, _**101**_, 131–134, _**135**_; A.J. Philips challenge 106–109; death _**137**_–138; FRGS 134; Harry Bastian exposure _**103**_, 104–105; Jack the Ripper _**136**_; Shilling Shockers 135; Violet Houghton case 100, 102; see also Garner, Charles

Darwin, Charles 1, 11, 138, 194–195
Davenport, Anne 151
Davey, S.J. 162
De Morgan, Augustus 14–15
Devant, David 144, 146–149, 151
Devant, Dora 146–149
Dickens, Charles 15–16
Dingwall, Dr. Eric John 48, 164
The Discoverie of Witchcraft 174
Donkin, Dr. Horatio 2, 93, 133, 154

Einstein, Albert 8

Faraday, Michael 11
Fay, Annie Eva 46, 47–49, _**50**_, 65, 189–194, 196–199
Foster, Charles H. 97

Galton, Sir Francis 48, 155, 194–196
Garner, Charles 80, 98; see also Cumberland, Stuart Charles Francis
Gimingham, Charles Henry 190–192, 194, 196
Glasgow appearance of W.I. Bishop 78–79
Goldston, Will 148

228 Index

grass, green 168–169
Gurney, Edmund 2, 92, 114, 132, 139–141, 144

Harrison, William H. 48
Hayden, Maria Basheba Trenholm 11–12, *13*, *14*–15
Hodgson, Richard 162
Home, Daniel Dunglas 16, 24–28, *29*, 30–31, *32*, 33–37
Hopkinson, Professor Alfred 92
Houdini, Harry 46, 182
Household Words 12
Huggins, Sir William 10, 21, 28, 48
Hurst, Lula (Lulu) 5–7
Huxley, Prof. Thomas Henry 75, 195

Ionides, C.A. 48

Johnson, Alice 156, 200–202

Labouchère, Henri du Pré 2, 88–91, 133
Lewis, Angelo (Prof. Hoffman) 134
Lodge, Sir Oliver 144–149, 151, 163

Maskelyne, John Nevil 2, 46, 90–91, 197
Maskelyne, Nevil 148–149, 151
Montague, Charles Howard 125, 126
Myers, Frederic W.H. 93, 106, 114, 140, 144

Newcomb, Prof. Simon 4–5; *see also* Hurst, Lula (Lulu)
Newmann, C.A. George 182

Pall Mall Gazette (*PMG*) 1, 3, 123–124, 131, 133
Peters, Mrs. Bleik 61–62
Phantasms of the Living 139–141, 143, 152
phonetic systems of second sight 176

Pinetti, Chevalier Joseph 174
Podmore, Frank 139–140, 161
Polgar, Franz J. 184
Pond, Maj. James B. 104, 108
Prince, Dr. Walter Franklin 55–56, 171–172
Punch, or the London Charivari 12

Robert-Houdin, Jean Eugene 173–174, *175*
Rogers, E. Dawson 105
Romanes, George John 93–94, 154–155

St. George's Hall 146, 149
Sensors Magazine 167
Sidgewick, Eleanor 152, 162
Sidgewick, Henry 139–141, 155
silent coding for second sight 177–179
Smith, George Albert 105, 110, *114*, 115–116, 152–153, 156, 164
Society for Psychical Research (SPR) 4, 120–121, 152, 156–157
Stead, William Thomas 1, 124, 131, 134
Stephenson, Christopher J. 187–189
Stewart, Prof. Balfour 92
Stone, George W. 11
Superhero powers 167

Thomas, Augustus 126–128; *The Witching Hour* 129
Thought Reading on the Brain song 122
Translucidation 146, 148–149, *150*, 151
Tyndall, Prof. John 2, 16, 21, 71–72

Whewell, William 10
Whitehall Review 99, 137
Wickes, Frederick 9, 81
Wilde, Oscar 1, 131–132; *A Thought Reader's Novel* 185–186
The Witching Hour 129